Traditions of
The Classical Guitar

16·99

Frontispiece. The Classical Guitar: a guitar made by Gerald Scott, an English luthier. This instrument is unusual in having twenty frets. Courtesy of David Marsden.

Traditions of
The Classical Guitar

by

Graham Wade

JOHN CALDER ·
LONDON

OVERTURE PUBLISHING

Overture Publishing is an imprint of

ONEWORLD CLASSICS LTD
London House
243-253 Lower Mortlake Road
Richmond
Surrey TW9 2LL
United Kingdom
www.oneworldclassics.com

Traditions of the Classical Guitar first published in Great Britain by
John Calder (Publishers) Ltd in 1980
This new edition published by Oneworld Classics in 2012
© Graham Wade, 1980, 2012

Printed and bound by CPI Group (UK) Ltd, Croydon, CR0 4YY

ISBN: 978-0-7145-4379-6

Contents

LIST OF ILLUSTRATIONS

for Beth

Yet if the only form of tradition, of handing down, consisted in following the ways of the immediate generation before us in a blind or timid adherence to its successes, 'tradition' should positively be discouraged. We have seen many such simple currents soon lost in the sand; and novelty is better than repetition. Tradition is a matter of much wider significance. It cannot be inherited, and if you want it you must obtain it by great labour.

T.S. Eliot
Tradition and the Individual Talent

The tradition is a beauty which we preserve and not a set of fetters to bind us.

Ezra Pound

Foreword

I am extremely grateful to Alessandro Gallenzi for reprinting *Traditions of the Classical Guitar*, originally published by John Calder in 1980.

This was the first book I wrote about the history of the guitar, and it appeared at a fascinating phase in the instrument's development. In the late 1970s many great pioneers of the guitar's twentieth-century renaissance were still flourishing. These included Andrés Segovia (1893–1987), Emilio Pujol (1886–1980), Federico Moreno Torroba (1891–1982), Federico Mompou (1893–1987), Regino Sáinz de la Maza (1896–1981), Alexandre Tansman (1897–1986), Joaquín Rodrigo (1901–99), Eduardo Sáinz de la Maza (1903–82), Luise Walker (1910–98), Laurindo Almeida (1917–95), Rey de la Torre (1917–94), John W. Duarte (1919–2004), and so on.

Moreover, in that decade the concert careers of Alirio Díaz (b. 1923), Narciso Yepes (1927–97), Julian Bream (b. 1933) and John Williams (b. 1941) were at their height, while a host of brilliant younger aspirants were garnering an international reputation.

In the 1970s we anticipated the vital prospect of receiving more and more new works from leading composers in addition to the possibility of discovering quantities of unknown repertoire from the past.

By our present stage in the twenty-first century the guitar's journey has indeed reached extraordinary levels of fulfilment. Just about every area of the instrument's history has now been researched in detail from the sixteenth century to the present day. The full lives and works of artists such as Milán, Narváez, Dowland, de Visée, Santiago de Murcia, Weiss, Sor, Giuliani, Tárrega, Torres, Mertz, Coste, Regondi, Barrios, Llobet, Villa-Lobos, Segovia, Bream, Brouwer and so on, have been laid before us in copious editions, biographies and documentary films. The classical guitar is now taught in almost every conservatoire in the world and technical standards among young performers have never been higher.

Also, since the 1970s the Early Music movement, with its thrust towards greater scholarship and authentic performance styles, has reached unprecedented heights of popularity and esteem. At the same time luthiers have practically revolutionized traditional concepts of guitar construction to exploit the instrument's full sonorities, as well as making available replicas of vihuelas, renaissance lutes, baroque guitars, theorbos, early-nineteenth-century guitars, etc.

In particular, the steady output of works inspired by Julian Bream from composers such as Walton (1902–83), Berkeley (1903–89), Rawsthorne (1905–71), Tippett (1905–98), Britten (1913–76), Searle (1915–82), Arnold (1921–2006), Henze (b. 1926), Takemitsu (1930–96), Maxwell Davies (b. 1934), Bennett (b. 1936) and Brouwer

(b. 1939) now represents another monumental tradition within the repertoire's evolution.

In *Traditions of the Classical Guitar* I attempted to interpret the history of the various types of guitar since the sixteenth century. The developing thread of increasing expressiveness and technical resourcefulness culminated in a new epoch for the concert guitar essentially founded by Segovia but propelled towards a truly contemporary approach by Bream, Williams, Díaz and Yepes.

But, for all that, *Traditions of the Classical Guitar* upset certain individuals who disliked the close focus on the achievements of Andrés Segovia. Fortunately Maestro Segovia himself gave his blessing to the publication (although this was by no means a foregone conclusion). Having read the book, he invited me to the Westbury Hotel, London, to discuss the work in detail. From this encounter several trips to Madrid and a variety of other books would emerge including *Segovia – a Celebration of the man and his music* (1983), and *Maestro Segovia* (1986).

Traditions of the Classical Guitar was written under difficult circumstances at a time when my wife Elizabeth, the dedicatee, was battling serious illness. Thus some of the rough edges and inadvertent errors of fact or quotation were not always smoothed out (much to the glee of certain critics). However, the reprint presents the work in its original version, and those who wish to sample a more objective approach to guitar history are invited to compare this publication with my *Concise History of the Classic Guitar* (Mel Bay, 2001).

Since those halcyon days of the late 1970s over three decades have passed, years which I spent playing, teaching, lecturing or writing about the guitar and its personalities. Looking at things from the quite different historical, social and musical perspectives of today, I find (with elements of nostalgia for what now seems a kind of golden age) that I still stand by the essential message of the book, recognising within it my youthful but abiding passion for the classical guitar and all that the nylon strung box represents as an expressive force of beauty and logic, emotion and intellect, sweetness and light. My personal credo about the instrument, as formulated in the original preface, has not changed:

In a noisy and raucous age the simple voice of the classical guitar takes the listener back to an intimate, personal musical environment. The guitar's natural sound, being unamplified, corresponds to the dynamics of the speaking human voice; its simple directness appeals immensely in the somewhat dehumanized context of industrial society.

Graham Wade
April, 2011

Preface

The classical guitar in the twentieth century owes its popularity and esteem primarily to the work of Andrés Segovia. He drew together the divergent strands of the traditions of the guitar, established a repertoire and by the force and sweetness of his personality inspired disciples and audiences with the necessary fervour for an intense pursuit of the instrument's secrets.

Segovia's work was two-fold. First and foremost he possessed an instinctive awareness of the musical potential within the guitar, and worked throughout his career towards the transformation of his inner vision into musical reality. This aspect of his task points forward to the continuing and hopeful development of the guitar as up and coming young concert artists inherit the maestro's legacy and in their turn provide a worthwhile expressive medium to which composers can turn.

Secondly Segovia uncovered and explored the music for fretted instruments of previous centuries. This in its turn was developed in unprecedented fullness as musicologists and scholars researched the sources of this historic repertoire and often transferred the music back to the authentic instruments. In this way Segovia's gift has not only been to the guitar but he has opened our ears to areas of music that might otherwise have remained obscure.

The last twenty years or so have been crucial in establishing the guitar as an instrument worthy of serious and sustained musical attention. During these two decades the classical guitar has evolved from being a rarity in the concert hall to become a familiar instrument in all the major recital centres of the world.

These years have seen not only a massive consolidation of Segovia's international esteem, but also the establishment (in circles well beyond just that of guitarists) of the reputation of several great players of the instrument; in particular such eminent musicians as Alirio Diaz (b. 1923), Ida Presti (1924-1967), Narciso Yepes (b. 1927), Julian Bream (b. 1933) and John Williams (b. 1941) have by their superb playing revolutionised the guitar's status wherever they have played in the world.

Inspired by their example, composers of many nationalities have enthusiastically created worthwhile music for the guitar, thousands of amateurs have taken lessons, many dedicated and gifted teachers have emerged, carrying the battle for the guitar's survival into schools, colleges, universities and conservatoires. The music publishing trade has poured a tide of guitar publications onto the market and more guitar records have been issued in these twenty years than would once have been considered possible or desirable.

My own involvement with the classical guitar began in 1954. Since then, in teaching the guitar and in giving recitals, I have frequently observed the profound effect that the expressive voice of the guitar has on people's sensibilities. In a noisy and raucous age the simple voice of the classical guitar takes the listener back to an intimate, personal, musical environment. The guitar's natural sound, being unamplified, corresponds to the dynamics of the speaking human voice; its simple directness appeals immensely in the somewhat dehumanised context of industrial society. For this reason the instrument has become popular in a great many countries, often cutting across traditional cultural boundaries. What began as an essentially Spanish instrument has now developed into a truly international experience.

The purpose of this book is not to give a straightforward historical account of the classical guitar and its origins. This has already been accomplished in Harvey Turnbull's book *The Guitar from the Renaissance to the Present Day*. Since our time together at university (and even before that in the Cambridge Classical Guitar Society), Harvey Turnbull's scrupulous and scholarly thinking has been an immense, formative influence on my own approach to the guitar. His remarkable book puts the history of the instrument in most of the necessary perspectives. The aim of my book is rather to develop and deepen certain trends of thought about the guitar which it seems needful to examine in detail at this stage in the guitar's rapid evolution.

All musical instruments, through their history and contemporary existence, offer a complex web of traditions, attitudes, developments, concepts and limitations. The guitar's traditions are explored here in its role as a solo instrument. The classical guitar is primarily considered as a medium for solo performance despite its own persistence in all ages as an accompanying medium. The riches of its repertoire are represented by solo works and the finest guitar music of any age is that written for the individual to perform.

This could not be applied to most other instruments, though it might be true for keyboard instruments, the lute and possibly the harp. The violin, 'cello, viola, flute, oboe, etc. (though possessing a solo repertoire of the highest musical significance) resound through musical history most of all as instruments within an ensemble of two or more in close partnership. The guitar, like the piano, has for some considerable time been admired by serious composers for its capabilities as a self-sufficient solo instrument; this is its central tradition.

Such a complex history deserves an extensive and admiring exploration. The guitar has frequently been the victim of ignorance, cynicism and incredulity on the part of its detractors. Segovia's work was to raise the guitar to a level where the full richness of its multiple traditions could be developed in all their substance and charm. The purpose of this book is then, to examine the basis of these traditions and to look at the contemporary relevance of the guitar as a musical force.

I am grateful to many people who have helped in the preparation of this book. In particular I am indebted beyond words to the patience, musical understanding and wisdom of my wife, Elizabeth.

I would also like to thank Robin Pearson of the Spanish Guitar Centre, Nottingham, for assistance and encouragement; Peter Burke, artist and luthier, for help and advice with diagrams and for providing the art work for the musical examples; Nicholas Reed, Librarian of the City of Leeds College of Music, for his unstinting efforts on my behalf; Frederick Boaden, musician and photographer, for his generous aid with photos; Bill Swainson, for indispensable editorial advice, and John Calder for providing the original stimulus for the work.

G.W.
July, 1979

PART ONE
THE EARLY GUITAR

1. The Evolution of the Guitar

In Flaundres whilom was a compaignye
Of yonge folk that haunteden folye,
As riot, hasard, stywes, and tavernes,
Where as with harpes, lutes, and gyternes,
They daunce and pleyen at dees bothe day and nyght.

Chaucer: *The Pardoner's Tale*

The evolution of a musical instrument is a mysterious and powerful creative force, stretching over centuries and in some instances prolonged through the entire devious history of humanity. The violin represents a marvellous example of how the corporate authority of generations can shape wood strung with gut towards a kind of perfection. Rising to its ideal proportions and qualities of sound in the late sixteenth and seventeenth centuries, the violin was in time to catch the tide of remarkable composers in the Baroque and classical periods of musical development in Europe.

During this time, after centuries of the predominance of the lute and plucked instruments in general, a great psychological and emotional change overcame western music. Plucked sound was replaced in the mainstream of instrumental composition by the dominance of bowed strings. The violin, developing under the influence of its great families of makers, Amati, Guarneri, Stradivari, Stainer, etc., evolved from the comparative mediocrity of earlier prototypes into the magnificently voiced instrument known to Mozart and Beethoven, Tchaikovsky and Brahms. Once those perfections of quality had been attained the violin did not evolve further in its fundamental shape, size and voice.

Yet bowed instruments comprise one of the oldest groups of artifacts used in music, and the violin's relatives, near or distant, are to be found in many geographical and social contexts; the Arabian rabab, the Chinese hwuchyn, the Mongolian marinhur, the Bulgarian gadulka, etc., all exist as contemporary musical instruments possessed of time-honoured traditions.

Centuries of expertise of one kind or another in the art of bowed music preceded the creation during the Italian Renaissance of the superb instrument which became the central expressive medium of western Europe. The golden age of violin making was a comparatively brief, explosive burst of activity. Between Nicolo Amati (1596-1684), his pupil, Antonio Stradivari (d. 1737) and Giuseppe Guarneri del Gesù (1698-1744), the accepted principles of ideal violin structure and pedigree were established; the dates of these luthiers' lives and the traditions which they inherited and fulfilled were crucial in the evolution of European music.

Similarly the development of various kinds of keyboard instrument, from the smaller species of spinet, virginal, clavichord and harpsichord to the massive structure of the grand piano, corresponds to profound metamorphoses in the musical textures, philosophies and ideals of western composers. From the gentle tinklings of Elizabethan keyboards to the elaborate ornamentation of Rameau, and from the equal temperament of Bach's harpsichords to the vast thunder of Beethoven's piano sonatas, represents in a little over two centuries an enormously varied and fully-developed range of keyboard instruments, each one perfectly appropriate to the creative sensibility of its respective era.

The genius and disposition of instrument-makers wield immeasurable power over the subsequent efforts of composers. To imagine Beethoven born one hundred years earlier or Mozart unleashed on a modern Steinway is to speculate on a new world of musical endeavour. Bach, Scarlatti, Mozart, Beethoven, Chopin and Liszt were among the greatest performing virtuosi of their time, each name being associated of course with the specific type of keyboard instrument available to them and, in several instances, changing compositional direction when a keyboard with different expressive powers came under their hands.

But as the keyboard and bowed instruments gained ground between 1550 and 1800, the great favourite of previous centuries encountered nemesis. The lute, popular since the early Middle Ages and perhaps even beyond that, achieved its zenith in the matchless compositions of John Dowland and the other Elizabethan lutanists, and (before its total decline) was touched in a final magnificent flourish by the resplendence of Bach's lute works.

The lute contours changed very little and in the sixteenth century the six or eight course instrument achieved both expressiveness and practicality. But by the time it had acquired about twenty-four strings in the middle of the eighteenth century, it had become an instrument for the specialist virtuoso, leaving the struggling amateur with the overwhelming task of taming a monster. Like that doomed species the dinosaur, the lute collapsed under the weight of its own body, to be replaced musically by the greater contrapuntal facility of the keyboard.

The final indignity for the lute was the invention of the lute-harpsichord (one of these was found among the possessions of J.S. Bach); this sounded similar to a lute but was easier to play being in the form of a small keyboard. The actual printed literature of the lute extends from Petrucci's first printed lute books in Venice (1507-8) to the work of Bach, Weiss, Baron and Kapsberger, etc. in the eighteenth century. The demise of the lute's plaintive voice was a sad event in European music.

It remains axiomatic that each type of musical instrument can be taken to a particular level of development. After this point has been reached by the combined activites of makers, performers and composers (the latter two frequently being one and the same) further modification actually becomes counter-productive. Once a reasonable perfection of expressiveness and performance has been attained other instruments tend to usurp the position previously maintained by the developed instrument. In this way, slowly but definitely, the piano drives out the harpsichord, the violin removes the need for the viol, the Baroque largeness of the lute replaces its Renaissance predecessor. Approximate dates can be established concerning this rather melancholy process, usually by cross-reference to the dates of both makers and composers. The reign of some instruments (for example the violin) can be very long lived; in some instances, as with the arpeggione, a fretted 'cello type of instrument played with the bow (and possessing six strings tuned like the guitar), the life of the creation remains breathlessly short. (Only Schubert's 'Arpeggione' Sonata remains extant for the instrument). Central to the significance of each developing instrument is the use that composers within a given society will make of it and how its expressive potential can be released for the musical purposes of its time.

In this process of development the classical guitar missed its vocation until the middle of the nineteenth century. Then began what could be termed the equivalent of the violin's Cremona era; the guitar's golden age in terms of its construction and performers, as well as in terms of its repertoire, exists between approximately 1840 (when the first of the modern guitar makers of greatness, Antonio de Torres Jurado was in his twenties) and the present day, full as it is of fine luthiers and great players. (It should be noted that as in the time of Stradivari, so in the mid-nineteenth century, fine instruments were constructed when the prevailing music of the period was not really commensurate with the musical potential of those instruments. Just as the Stradivarius violins had to wait some time for Bach, Mozart and Beethoven, so the guitar of Torres would have to wait for the more finely expressive music of the twentieth century; perhaps in some respects the guitar is still waiting for its ultimate musicality to be fulfilled.)

Guitars before 1840 had not attracted the serious attention of great composers and for many good reasons. The guitar, despite antecedents of its species that were of great antiquity going back to early civilisations of 1400-1350 B.C., remained somewhat inferior to its main competitors. From 1500 to 1800 it was too often a delightful toy, a poor relative of the lute, a coterie instrument, a folk instrument and an expressive medium only in the obscure backwaters of musical ingenuity. The guitar during this time was too small, too heavy, and lacked sufficient strings for a plucked instrument.

Guitar makers produced highly ornamented works of craftsmanship, and their instruments were greatly valued as *objets d'art*. However their love of ornate filigree made these guitars more like decorated cabinets than true musical instruments and they were fit for little more than accompaniments to the voice or elementary solo music.

Confronted by its heavier, more cumbersome rival, the lute could do nothing but reign supreme. The lute was lighter and thus more strident (even if gently so) and it possessed more strings and therefore, implicitly, more musical possibilities. It possessed an elegant family tree with many talented and distinguished players supporting its traditions throughout the European courts. Its plaintive resonances penetrated amiably through banquet hall and tavern, dance floor and palace, with a specific clarity and carrying power the guitar could not emulate.

Here and there on the broad canvas of musical history a school of 'guitarists' would spring up, often spearheaded by one or two individuals whose tenacity and talent, or inventive eccentricity (coupled, perhaps, with a certain skill at the lute as well), won them a place at court or manor-house. In those quires and places where lutes were played there would always be some sort of opportunity for a slightly different variety of plucked sound; no doubt a few interludes on the guitar provided a welcome relief to the incessant chatter of the lutes.

Moreover women liked the guitar. It was always easier to play than the lute and easier to look after. Mary Queen of Scots gave her favourite, Riccio, one of the most exquisitely made guitars of the Renaissance. But it is a useful rule of thumb that the more ornamented an instrument, the less effective a contribution it is to the musical life around it. The more immaculate the trimmings, the more a guitar is designed to be looked at rather than played. If the lute ultimately expired from a surfeit of strings, then the courtly guitar of the Renaissance suffered most from an excess of decoration. Layers of protective inlay, ivory, carved wood and even jewels, could suffocate its tiny voice before the song began. These guitars told a story of countless hours of dedication as craftsmen laboured with fine wood and expert designs to produce a sample of elaborately inlaid furniture. But the narrative was absorbed by the eye not the ear, and the instrument's progress, like an overswaddled baby, stifled beneath its heavy trappings. The very existence of all this embroidery denoted the attitudes to the instrument that were prevalent.

Even the great Stradivari, creating guitars (unornamented) from a labour of love, could not coax the instrument forward into a golden age. Its day had not yet come, and the darkest hour was to fall during the eighteenth century when prejudice against the guitar and a sublime unawareness reached their highest point.

In Spain the guitar maintained its existence, carried forward by the love of the people for their native instrument. The Moorish conquest of southern Spain inflicted huge wounds on Spanish pride, and when in 1492 the hated Arabs were expelled, it is said that the Spanish preferred 'la guitarra' to 'el-oud' (still loved in Arabic countries) because the Arabic lute reminded them still of oppression. This romantic story, part of the myth of the guitar, is not entirely true as lutes could usually be found in the Spanish courts.

But the sixteenth century in Spain saw the rise and fall of a relatively small but intense tradition of guitar playing with its concomitant written literature of tutors and compositions. This was the era of the vihuela, a mysterious kind of guitar more akin to the lute than most guitars could claim to be, and yet remaining essentially a guitar-shaped instrument. Then the vihuela disappeared from the courts and was never heard again. Its peculiar fragmented history is an ideal example of the guitar's characteristic bursts of activity, surfacing perhaps for one generation before sinking back into silence.

For the history of the guitar lacks real coherence or continuity. Little traditions were pursued in various areas of Europe and then came to nothing, being in T.S. Eliot's words, 'simple currents soon lost in the sand', and lacking the personalities stimulated to revive them. In our own century scholars, musicologists, composers and guitarists have worked industriously to uncover these slender outcrops of the guitar's periods of energy. Frequently, the outcome of these researches has been to provide material that concert players could make use of in their recitals or amateurs could play at home. At the same time much of the music recovered in this way, though of considerable historical significance, has proved too insubstantial to allow claims that any major composer of genius worked through the guitar.

In the end we are left with the spectacle of a disunified patchwork created by patterns of unrelated groups of players working with the instrument to produce unambitious but agreeable examples of their art. Often these traditions, miniature and remote as they may seem to those who are not guitarists, and lasting perhaps thirty or forty years, achieved a high standard of instrumental competence and even virtuosity. But this music does not approach the sublimity of the lute compositions of Dowland or Bach.

Guitarists have perhaps tended not to be too anxious about the quality of the music written for their instrument. What has always appealed to them is the guitar's actual sound, its timbres and resonance, its tone-colours and associations. Even in the twentieth century the intimate solo nature of the guitar survives the comparative lack of weight of much of its repertoire.

Certainly audiences that attend guitar recitals or haunt those places where guitarists gather and perform in less formal circumstances expect brilliance and dexterity, qualities not necessarily synonymous with musical depth. In any event, great music cannot be written for an instrument without the participation of great composers; such personalities have not been drawn to that strange limbo in which the guitar found its characteristic milieu.

The guitar's main attractiveness since the sixteenth century has been within informal musical contexts, intimate music making, private and amateur endeavours at self-fulfilment. To some extent this condition applies even to the twentieth century which has seen the flourishing of hundreds of Classical Guitar Societies, Guitar Circles, etc., coteries where the guitar can be studied and adored away from the gaze of a hostile or indifferent environment.

In the social life of the Renaissance and Baroque eras the guitar, where it appears, existed in the complementary habitats of court and folk traditions. The courts tended to be personal, insular and provincial, or cosmopolitan, sophisticated and sensitive, depending on the temperament of the monarch or prince; a court by its very nature encouraged the development of talent attractive and flattering to the central figure.

As fashions and rulers changed so musical taste, likes and dislikes, fluctuated. Whim and desire on the part of the man in charge could especially affect crucial matters such as the availability of printing presses for the publishing of instrumental methods (as in the case of Henri II of France), and who obtained permission, whether musician or writer, for work to be presented to a wider public. Thus a tradition of instrumental music strong in one decade could wither and expire quite rapidly; the guitar has perhaps suffered by changes in musical fashions more than most instruments.

The folk traditions are even more elusive than the comings and goings of fashionable society, being hardly dependent at all on a printed or licensed literature. Also whereas the courtly instruments are later preserved in palaces and museums, the folk instruments vanish from sight. In Spain the national love of the guitar was a permanent aspect of the country's cultural identity, and this created the dissemination of guitar-like instruments throughout South America during the Spanish conquests as well as preserving the guitar in Europe through those eras when the rest of the continent momentarily lost interest in it. In the twentieth century the spread of interest in flamenco and ethnic South American guitar music, and the influence of both of these on composers, are the visible and aural legacies of the people's abiding affection for the guitar in Spanish, Portuguese and Latin-American countries.

For the researcher who wishes to chart the tributaries of the guitar's fragmentary traditions, two possibilities exist of establishing the facts. Measurement of instruments in museums offers one indisputable line of enquiry, though no guarantee that the guitars that remain extant represent characteristics common to all such guitars of its period. Study of published music, including printed methods and the manuscript tablature kept in private anthologies by players, provide the other familiar route to knowledge.

With traditions of vocal, keyboard and bowed strings, both of these musicological activities are more rewarding as there are more sources to explore. The guitar offers a less rich assortment of buried treasures, yielding only a small enduring repertoire and often raising questions that are not easily answered.

The guitar existed frequently in the undergrowth of musical life, not impinging on the central traditions of choral or instrumental ensembles, and was not considered as a viable means of creative expression. The guitarist is thus a spectacle of isolation and detachment from the mainstream of music. His activities, unlike those of the lutanist, were held in low esteem by those not dazzled by the guitar's allure, such as it was, a state of affairs that still obtains to some extent even today.

Guitar publications throughout the ages are often significant for what they cannot tell us. Naturally it would be impossible in the twentieth century to imagine the high standards of virtuosity in guitar playing by reading a method on how to play the guitar; on the other hand the compositions written for Segovia would tell us a little more about what he achieved, though without gramophone records even this guide to his mastery would be incomplete.

Publications about music, taken from any period of musical history, tell us something (and often a great deal) about the prevailing moods centred round a particular instrument. But most published works since the sixteenth century are more concerned with the general public of beginners, amateurs and competent performers aspiring to better things than with the tiny proportion of professional players. Dowland's music in *Varietie of Lute Lessons* tells us far more about the standard of Renaissance lute playing than Burwell's Lute Book because it brings us closer to the actuality of a great player's work. But even Dowland's tablature cannot unlock for us what must have been the fine magnificence of his playing in its fullest flowering. A gap invariably exists between sounds from the instrument and notes on the page, and this is bridged only by the player's presence.

Moreover the greatest players seldom stoop to the menial task of writing methods and tutors, and what they do write leaves much to the imagination. So the glory or poverty of a guitar tradition cannot be precisely estimated by the publications we possess. All we can say is that certain extant works have proved of some musical value and are suitable for recitals in our century. Assessing the wealth of a tradition from published sources is never a simple matter, even without taking into account improvisation in the Renaissance and Baroque periods. Notes on the page bear frequent witness to rich and active traditions slightly obscured by the horizon of history.

The efforts of musicologists over the last few decades have brought about a novel awareness of the musical life of previous periods that had been lost for centuries in a total haze. Researches now go back to the Middle Ages, allowing early music to be performed on replicas of medieval instruments to enthusiastic audiences. Over the last few years it has become fashionable to give music back to the original instruments wherever possible; it has become unfashionable to play Bach on the grand piano (let alone Scarlatti) and Mozart is now performed quite often on a keyboard appropriate to the music of the eighteenth century.

This drive towards scholarly authenticity in the presentation of music has affected the structure of the guitar recital as well. Replicas of vihuelas, four string guitars, Renaissance and Baroque lutes, citterns, five string guitars, and even early nineteenth century guitars, are entering the concert halls. The guitarist cannot play the lute music of the sixteenth century or the compositions for Baroque guitar with the same carefree disdain for historical truth that existed only two decades ago.

However modern guitar history has by instinct put the cart before the horse; first the Renaissance and Baroque music had to be played on the guitar before sufficient interest in the origins of lute and vihuela transcriptions and compositions for other varieties of guitars prompted the activity of researchers. The creative impulse of the players preceded the historical concern of musicologists.

Criticism levelled at concert guitarists (and particularly Segovia) for their lack of authenticity in presenting Renaissance and Baroque music on the guitar has no more validity than blaming the Wright brothers for not using a jet engine to power man's first flight. It was, indeed, Segovia's love of the guitar that enabled scholars fifty years after his professional debut to explore the mysteries of the early guitar repertoire. Conversely it must be emphasised that modern classical guitarists need urgently to evaluate whatever researches are undertaken in order that too violently anachronistic playing of a totally unhistorical nature should never be perpetrated in a state of blissful ignorance.

It is intended here to examine in some detail how guitarists of the present age have dealt with the legacy of compositions for fretted instruments before tracing back the historical roots of these works. For this purpose the guitar's history between about 1530 and 1840 can be considered as follows:

> 1536-1576 The tradition of the vihuela
> 1549-1570 The four-course guitar
> The five-course guitar:– 1596-1680 The Spanish tradition
> 1640-1690 The Italian tradition
> 1620-1690 The French tradition
> 1780-1840 The six string guitar.

(All these dates are approximate but convenient. The various strands of activity are not necessarily related as extensions of an abiding fundamental tradition. Any coherent line of development is contained only within the shape and sound of the guitar itself, and even that may represent highly diverse factors.)

2. Guitarists and their Repertoire: The Heritage of the Renaissance.

Whoever has approved this idea of order . . . will not find it preposterous that the past should be altered by the present as much as the present is directed by the past.

T.S. Eliot: *Tradition and the Individual Talent*

Throughout his concert career Segovia often began his recitals with a performance of various compositions from the sixteenth century literature for fretted instruments. The number of pieces he selected were few and provided a kind of hors d'oeuvres before the more substantial part of the programme.

These sixteenth century items were an opportunity for the guitarist to accustom his audience (and perhaps himself) to the sounds of the guitar within that particular recital hall, and to explore the acoustics in subdued, delicate compositions. Sometimes, by deliberately playing the pieces even more sotto voce than was necessary, a degree of attentiveness from the audience was exacted as their curiosity was aroused — curiosity not about the sixteenth century but about the guitar's tonal and dynamic range. From the great soloist's guitar emanated a tiny aura of tone colours, hypnotically attractive perhaps because of their very elusiveness.

The effect was indeed magical, like the primeval stirrings of the first bird-song, wafted to the ear as enchanted fragments from a distant island. For thousands of the public this was their introduction to the guitar's sonorities. Segovia used these antique relics of golden civilisations most tellingly for his own purposes — that of enticing his audience into the web of sound, delicate but intense, which for him characterised the guitar.

From the whole gamut of Renaissance music available and suitable for transcription Segovia chose remarkably little. His selection of pieces did not increase much at any time in his career and he continued to play and record his favourite sixteenth century vihuela and lute transcriptions without ever widening his horizons too far.

These consisted of Pavanas by Luys Milán, a Fantasia No. XVI by the same composer, Romanesca and Gallarda by Alonso Mudarra, and Canción del Emperador (on 'Mille Regretz' by Josquin), often combined with a set of Variations on Guárdame las Vacas by Luys de Narváez. This was, as it were, the first line of attack, Segovia's central Renaissance offering. In any one recital only one or two of these would be performed.

Frequently six lute pieces arranged from the tablature by the Italian musicologist Oscar Chilesotti were played as if forming a suite, though the origins of these items is obscure. The 'Suite' became immensely popular as an opening group for guitar recitals as dozens of lesser players imitated the master's example.

Segovia did not explore Dowland's music very much. Melancholy Galliard, My Lady Hunsdon's Puffe, Song and Galliard, were exhumed from the great mass of available tablature but the larger works were left to one side for a later generation to explore.

Of the other composers for vihuela only Pisador and Valderrábano were included occasionally represented by rather insubstantial gallardas or sonetos. The lutanists of the Elizabethan age and earlier (apart from the few Dowland items mentioned) were not included in Segovia's recitals.

Up to about 1960 few of the concert-going public expressed much interest in the origins of these pieces or in the civilisations which had created them. Not many of the audience appreciated that this limited group represented the key to a remarkable musical culture which deserved attention in its own right. The items were considered as traditional gambits for opening a recital, and as delightful appetisers. Amateur guitarists found they could obtain the printed music for the pieces and technically the compositions were accessible to a comparative novice. Professional recitalists followed the maestro by beginning a concert with a rendering of one or more of Milán's Pavanas or Narváez's Guárdame las Vacas.

Meanwhile Segovia interpreted these compositions with an aristocratic exquisiteness, much as he would the pieces of any other period, setting his personal stamp on the material with a style that was later to cause scandalised dismay to Renaissance and Early Music enthusiasts. His aim was to exploit the tonal richness of the guitar. Thus, say, in a group of Milán's Pavanas, the tempo would be elliptically displaced to allow a sensuous vibrato on particularly inviting notes; a haughty rubato would eliminate the listener's awareness of the dance pulse and the precise placing of strong and weak beats. The maestro's cavalier disregard of the composer's apparent specifications for the actual time value of each note was never, of course, arbitrary. Quite the opposite; the style was the product of years of careful exploration of each item as expressed through the medium of his guitar. Tonal sensuousness was the ultimate objective, and all the music Segovia played was thus regarded as a vehicle for the enrichment of the instrument. The fruit was plucked from the tree and admired more for its flavour than its structure.

Between 1909 and the late fifties the enthusiastic guitar public had little opportunity to compare performances of Renaissance music for fretted instruments. To most of the aficionados Segovia's playing established an umbilical connection between the contemporary guitar in the concert hall and the 'early' guitar, whatever that might be. The general opinion was that this was how the composers of the sixteenth century might have preferred their music to sound if only they could have met Segovia; moreover these compositions were regarded as trivia heralding greater feasts to follow. The context gave no hint of the immense wealth of instrumental music printed and performed in the sixteenth century. But the music at that time did seem in Segovia's hands to be directly appropriate to the spirit of the music — courtly, aloof, aristocratic, and yet personal and poignant.

A basis for comparison was eventually forthcoming. Alirio Diaz and Narciso Yepes, two of the world's greatest players, incorporated more pieces from the vihuela into their programmes. At his debut in Britain in 1961 Yepes opened his recital with Mudarra's Fantasia que contrahaze la harpa en la manera de Ludovico, causing one of the most informed guitar critics on the English scene to comment,

> The recital began soberly with an interesting and, to us, new Fantasia by Mudarra, alternating between sparse counterpoint (and even monody) and arpeggiated passages of surprising dissonance for their period. A certain waywardness in the soloist's rhythmic pulse was disturbing.
>
> (John W. Duarte, *B.M.G.*, April, 1961)

Perhaps the most potent influence on recitalists at that time in their efforts to come to terms with Renaissance music was the work of Emilio Pujol. Ever since the 1920's Pujol, a pupil of the great Spanish player and teacher Francisco Tárrega, had been performing in public a wide variety of vihuela music. In 1936 Pujol, using a reproduction vihuela (made for him by the luthier Miguel Simplici), played a full recital of sixteenth century compositions including Milán's Pavanas, Narvaéz's Guárdame las Vacas, Mudarra's Fantasia, and songs by Fuenllana, Pisador, Valderrábano, Mudarra and Milán. This concert took place in Barcelona at the second 'Congreso de la Sociedad Internacional de Musicologia', and performed before a specialist

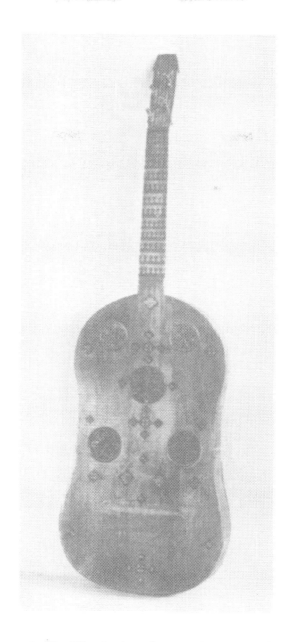

1. *The Vihuela:* the only extant instrument of its
kind. Courtesy of the Musée Jacquemart-André,
Paris.

2. *A modern copy of the Vihuela:* a concert vihuela
made by David Rubio. Courtesy of David Rubio.

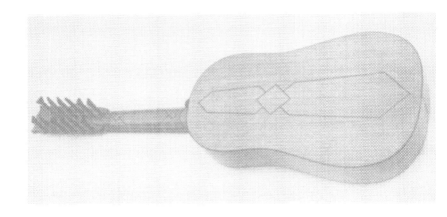

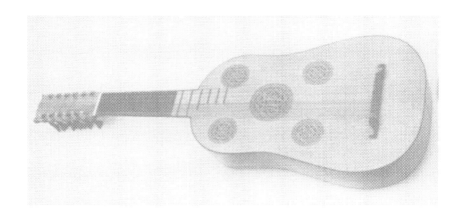

audience it represented a serious attempt to recapture the vihuela traditions.

In 1938 at the Salle Erard, Paris, a similar recital took place, again with villancicos and romances (sung by Conchita Badia). As well as the familiar solos mentioned above, Pujol included Narváez's Baxa de Contrapunto, and Milán's Fantasia del Quarto Tono.

Emilio Pujol published many of the works of the vihuelistas including the Pavanas of Milán and assorted items by Mudarra, Fuenllana, Pisador and Valderrábano in his own series *Bibliothéque de Musique Ancienne et Moderne pour Guitare* (Edition Max Eschig, Paris). A crucial text in the wider dissemination of awareness of vihuela music was his *Hispanae Citharae Ars Viva* (Schott, London 1955). In his Preface, Pujol refers to the pioneering efforts of earlier musicologists such as Conde de Morphy, Oscar Chilesotti and Felipe Pedrell, whose studies initiated the slow recovery of the vihuela repertoire from the oblivion of centuries.

Pujol also cites the recommendation of the International Congress of Musicology held in Vienna in 1909. This Congress laid down the principle that 'The work must be transcribed from tablature to notation in such a manner that the resulting music heard by the listener is identical'. This axiom Pujol attempted to follow in his own transcriptions of sixteenth century music and for this reason his editions became increasingly popular with recitalists. It was indeed time that scholarly scrupulousness should replace the tendency to *adapt* early compositions rather than transcribe accurately note for note, as is possible for the vihuela though not for lute music.

Pujol's edition of Mudarra's Fantasia que contrahaze la harpa en la manera de Ludovico became one of the most popular virtuoso concert pieces. Its brilliant dissonances were to be exploited on many occasions until this particular work, like the limited stock of Segovia's Renaissance material, became rather jaded with repetition. Alirio Diaz, Julian Bream and John Williams took the Fantasia into their repertoire to the manifest delight of audiences, though Bream preferred to play it on the lute rather than guitar. This novel development on the part of a great guitarist, a genuine research of the lute's music (and its subsequent performance in recitals on a specially adapted lute) proved to be the spearhead for a vibrant interest in early music throughout the world from the 1960's onwards. This fascination for Renaissance culture sometimes produces, as we shall see, a need for guitarists to re-define their approach to the guitar itself, and challenged the Segovian basis of the guitar's habitual recital repertoire.

Julian Bream began playing the lute in the late 1940's, using an instrument made for him by Thomas Goff, the London harpsichord maker. Bream's lute was based on a Tieffenbrucker in the Victoria and Albert Museum and Goff used X-ray photos of this instrument in his preparations to construct a concert lute capable of sounding effectively in recitals.

Bream maintained that though the guitar was his profession, the lute was his hobby. Unkind critics remarked on how he seemed to play the guitar like a lute, and the lute like a guitar, a not entirely inappropriate comment considering the enormous originality Bream brought to his playing of both lute and guitar. He was the first player of truly virtuoso powers to bring the lute to a level of international concert significance. The immediate impact on audiences was to emphasise the obvious distinctions between guitar and lute, and in many countries of the world curiosity was stimulated about the nature of Renaissance music for fretted instruments.

The lute and guitar, it was observed, sounded quite distinct from each other, and the former with its attractive shape, multiplicity of strings, and a deeply rooted repertoire of its own, contrasted against the more familiar guitar contours with its wider variety of musical periods to choose from. By 1957 Bream was recording guitar and lute albums for the Westminster Company and for the first time a wide audience could listen to a complete record of Dowland's music performed on the lute.

Bream's repertoire of Dowland compositions both included and exceeded those already familiar to guitarists through the work of Segovia. As well as Melancholy Galliard, My Lady Hunsdon's Puffe and King of Denmark's Galliard, came some of the bigger solos such as the Fantasia No. 7 and Forlorne Hope Fancy. This was a tremendous step forward in general awareness of Dowland's music in particular and the high standards of the Renaissance lute in general.

What Julian Bream's concerts and recordings achieved moreover was a demonstration of how sixteenth century music could be entirely pleasurable, a fact owed initially to Bream's musical personality in which passionate intensity and sheer enthusiasm united with scholarly precision. He loaded Dowland's music with great personal involvement and an almost Romantic burden of utter expressiveness. The plaintive song-like quality of Bream's playing of the lute took the imagination back to the 'lascivious caperings of a lute' and a sense of Shakespearean richness; he revealed that the great emotional artistry of Elizabethan literature was more than complemented by the ardent yearnings of its musical life.

The realisation of Elizabethan achievement in the sphere of musical composition provoked not only a deep public response as

Bream's affinities with the Elizabethan art of the lute made their impact; scholars and artists were now stimulated to research sixteenth century music, aware that performance of these treasures was now possible.

Some years later, in the kaleidoscope of musicological fashion and progress, Bream, like Segovia, could be accused in his turn of departing from true authenticity and distorting the purities of Elizabethan lute music, perhaps by the very personal involvement which had introduced Dowland's music to a wide audience. The purist lutanists disliked Bream's lutes with their long string-length, metal frets (instead of tied gut) and the brilliant extrovert sound penetrating to the back of large concert halls. The new race of lutanists, playing lighter, smaller instruments, concentrated on the inward, restrained voice of the lute. Bream's passionate advocacy of a very demonstrative approach to Dowland was now challenged by Early Music groups who favoured more objective attitudes to interpretative problems. They maintained that the lute suffered from the recital hall, became brash and outward, and should instead draw the audience to itself by means of a tiny voice that was felt to be quite sufficient. Vast tonal contrasts in phrasing, characteristic of guitar style, were to be avoided like the plague, and the lute should be played close to the bridge. Bream's habit of attacking the strings with nails instead of finger-tips was also rebuked.

Such criticisms were not new, nor merely the back-biting of jealous musicologists or untalented players, though these are not altogether absent from the world of music. Professor Thurston Dart, a great authority on Renaissance music, put a strong argument as early as 1961 that Bream's lute sound was not the timbre of Dowland's instrument. To prove his point he lent me one of his lutes, constructed on Elizabethan lines without modification. While arguing his case against Bream's lute technique, Dart produced a booklet he himself had written to accompany the American edition of Bream's records, in which Bream was enthusiastically acclaimed as the foremost lutanist of the twentieth century. Thus the paradox was resolved; Bream's playing may not sound exactly as Dowland would have wished, any more than a modern production of a Shakespeare play at Stratford-on-Avon would have pleased the author himself. Dowland might have been, and probably was, a far better lutanist than Bream. But after all the arguments have been advanced, it was Bream's responsibility to take the lute to the people, and it is to his initiative that we owe our primary awareness of Dowland's music and the immense virtuoso capabilities of the lute. No other lutanist has yet emerged who is comparable with Bream in terms of virtuosity or musicianship or who possesses a significant proportion of Bream's undoubted charisma.

Bream's response to the scholarly furore was to carry on playing the lute in his own inimitable manner. As the twentieth century's foremost lutanist his technical prowess, interpretative resources and international appeal, remained intact and the demand for his concerts and records was insatiable world-wide.

But the concentration on the lute repertoire and the intense discussions about how this great treasure-house of music should be interpreted reverberated amongst guitarists with crucial effects. Following the appearance of the early Bream records of Dowland's music, guitarists proceeded in the traditional manner to adapt lute music to the needs of the guitar. If the larger compositions of the lute repertoire such as the Fantasia No. 7 were now available for the lutanist, then guitarists, both professional and amateur wished to lay their hands on suitable transcriptions of these items and perform this music on the guitar.

For a while guitarists disdained to notice the scholarly discussion, storms in tea-cups, and constant evaluation which stirred the esoteric world of early music specialists. Sometimes out of deference to the lute guitarists performed Elizabethan music with a quasi lute-like tone by playing the guitar near the bridge, thus inducing a Renaissance nasal dryness; this interpretative mannerism hardly fooled anyone and led towards sterile renderings of compositions which Bream's lute had made supremely meaningful. Other guitarists performing Dowland played lute transcriptions however with the usual approach of their craft, creating rich resonances, rubatos, vibrato, and tonal variation in phrasing, thus producing constant anachronisms of interpretation. Again they were using the music available to glorify guitar resonances in the Segovia manner. But unlike Segovia, guitarists were beginning recitals with the long Dowland pieces instead of the previous opening message of Milán or Narváez.

Slowly a revaluation of available resources and especially the problem of all kinds of transcriptions permeated the concert world of the younger players. It soon became very obvious that between the guitar and the lute was a great gulf of history, design, and tone. Not only did the lute possess more strings, but a real change absorbed lute music once it was transferred from the light silvery echoes of the lute to the rich golden sonorities of the classical guitar. Some players of the latter therefore abandoned Dowland on the guitar, whilst others dabbled with both lute and guitar imitating Bream but with vastly inferior results. They persisted in thinking of the lute as an instrument to be played with a guitarist's mentality and technique whilst lacking Bream's intuitive feel for the emotion of Renaissance music.

Gradually however it became clear to most recitalists that to fathom the depths of Renaissance music and to render true justice to the rigours of its demands involved more than just a willingness to fit lute music rather haphazardly into the dimensions of the guitar. The music's identity was so specific and powerful that only real dedication to the spirit of the sixteenth century could reveal the essential qualities of the lutanists' repertoire; this, on Bream's evidence alone, it was reluctantly acknowledged, would necessitate a return to the lute on its own terms. To play Dowland's music on the guitar was to sell the music short in more ways than one. To transcribe lute music was seen to be more difficult in many respects than performing the harpsichord sonatas of Scarlatti or even the violin music of Bach on the guitar.

At first guitarists could still cling to a belief that perhaps the vihuela was the guitar's true ancestor, and to play vihuela music on the guitar was to perpetrate less violence to the spirit of the music than was the case with lute material. This notion also crumbled like a dream. As far as researches could tell (on slender evidence admittedly) the vihuela with its double-strung courses and light construction probably sounded more like a lute than like the modern classical guitar.

Emilio Pujol's pioneering example of the 1930's recitals in which he used a replica of a vihuela was increasingly followed by serious-minded guitarists. The concert vihuelas obligingly constructed by luthiers for aspiring recitalists often possessed a somewhat timid voice but in the 1960's and seventies there were sufficient concert performers playing actual vihuelas to cause guitarists to stop and think about the implications of performing sixteenth century music on the powerful modern instrument. Some realised indeed that to play either lute or vihuela music on the guitar, though infinitely delightful to audiences and player, is analagous to playing Byrd's keyboard music on a twentieth century Steinway.

Many of the great players, following in the immediate tradition of Segovia, threw all concepts of historical thinking about authenticity to the four winds, and played how they pleased. Julian Bream initiated some essential metamorphoses in timbre by performing vihuela music on the lute; his precedent was later followed by the Austrian guitarist Konrad Ragossnig, whose extensive recordings of European lute and vihuela music were performed on an eight course Renaissance lute made by David Rubio of Oxford, England. But other players of distinction were either less scholarly or departed into their own world of tone-colours.

Alirio Diaz, one of the world's most esteemed players, continued to dazzle audiences throughout the world with his guitar rendering of Mudarra's Fantasia; he published an edition of this work which announced that he had 'modernised' the fingering, thus sending a frisson of horror through the groves of academe. Diaz' brilliant playing of this item won the plaudits of his public, who appreciated that good playing matters more in the context of a virtuoso recital than historical niceties. However, this kind of interpretation takes little heed of how the music sounded in the sixteenth century though it may well be more attractive than in its original form, capturing as it does the spirit of vitality and vigour, as Diaz' performances always do. A magnificent, full-blooded *tour de force* of this kind may however give a misleading and in the end, unsatisfactory, atmosphere to the refined exuberance of sixteenth century music. The cause of the classical guitar is advanced at the expense of the music's implications, a concept which carries more seriousness now than it did twenty years ago.

Another great guitarist, Narciso Yepes, introduced to the public some of the music for four-string sixteenth century guitar by Adrien Le Roy. Ironically Yepes played this on a specially designed ten-string guitar, which after a time he used in all his many recitals. Mudarra's Fantasia, Narváez's Guárdame las Vacas (transposed into a high key) and the music of Le Roy were thus projected on a totally novel instrument. Yepes also recorded a collection of songs from the sixteenth century with the singer Teresa Berganza, in which the ten-string sonorities imitated the plaintive echoes of the vihuela.

By and large therefore the finest guitarists of the world have not been so far unduly concerned about problems of authenticity in the presentation of early fretted music. They have not usually chosen to imitate Pujol and play the vihuela, and Bream's lute has resonated round international concert halls with a powerful vibrant tone that Dowland might have envied but did not necessarily produce. The choice of guitarists has been to provide living music for a wide public, expressing their respect for the music of previous ages by means of the tonal resources of the classical guitar. Their playing has indeed encouraged audiences to appreciate the Renaissance ideals of structure and aesthetic appeal.

Younger guitar players have become extremely sensitive to the specific needs of sixteenth century interpretative demands. The rapid spread of interest in Early Music groups and live performance of medieval and Renaissance ensemble music, as well as the proliferation of harpsichord and lute recitals, have all contributed to radical changes in musical tastes. Changes have occurred in all areas of musical thinking; in piano recitals the work of Scarlatti, Bach and Handel is now left more and more to the harpsichordists as pianists devote themselves increasingly to the nineteenth century repertoire indigenous to the grand piano. Such a profound change may ultimately drive the classical guitar into a reliance on its own original music, leaving earlier material to the relevant instruments.

It is now time to look more closely at the historical roots of Renaissance fretted instrument traditions as they exist in available sources, and to examine the problems such sources present to the player of today.

3. The Music of the Vihuela

*The vihuela was always the instrument of elegant and
aristocratic society.*

J.B. Trend: *Luis Milan and the Vihuelistas*

The principal composers for vihuela whose work still survives in the
modern concert hall are Luys Milán, Luys de Narváez, Alonso
Mudarra, Enrique de Valderrábano, Diego Pisador and Miguel de
Fuenllana. Only a small proportion of their complete output is
performed but it is with these names that the written literature of a
guitar-like instrument distinct from the lute begins. These composers
played the vihuela de mano, plucked with the fingers as opposed to
the vihuela de púa (played with a plectrum) and the vihuela de arco
(played with a bow).

Etymologically, the word 'vihuela' has clear connections with such
terms as 'violao' (the Portuguese word for guitar), 'viol', 'fiddle', and
'viola', and the instrument itself is quite distinct from the popular
four-course 'guitarra' of sixteenth century Spain and France.

The vihuela possessed six courses (i.e. six pairs of strings tuned in
unison) and they were tuned according to this relationship of
intervals.

Thus to perform vihuela music on the classical guitar is quite
simple in terms of transcription, and more convenient to the modern
player than the music of any other fretted instrument. By tuning the
third string of the guitar to F sharp the player puts the tuning into the
direct context of the vihuela's own tuning. Unlike the lute's music,
the vihuela did not have to resort to bass strings in excess of its normal
six-course stringing, and thus anticipated the eventual arrival of the six

string guitar, which appeared towards the end of the eighteenth century.

The vihuela was quite different in obvious ways from the classical guitar as we know it. Its 'courses' and the absence of the characteristic nineteenth century fan-strutting under the front of the instrument would be two powerful factors in giving the vihuela a resonance entirely of its own nature. Though this cannot be verified, as only one sixteenth century vihuela is still in existence, we might presume that the vihuela imitated the lute in respect of lightness of construction, perhaps being more reminiscent of a modern flamenco guitar of light cypress wood, rather than being made of heavier rosewood. With all fretted instruments weight is a crucial element in determining precise tone qualities. Also, being of a guitar-like waisted shape, and not pear-shaped like the lute, would have imparted to the vihuela distinguishing aspects of timbre; the vihuelistas would surely have enjoyed the tonal properties of the vihuela in their own right, and perhaps in most instances preferred them to the lighter timbres of the egg-shell inspired lute cavity.

Even if the vihuela was decisively heavier than the lute, it would have lacked the richer sonorities of the modern guitar. The twentieth century guitarists achieve many of their best resonances by exploiting the higher positions of the guitar, a technique established by Tárrega (and Segovia) once the full string-length of the modern guitar had been developed in the mid nineteenth century. But on the vihuela, with its limited number of frets, the concept of exploiting individual tonal colours was probably lacking.

The vihuela tablature makes instead a great use of open strings, the first, second and third positions on the instrument, and from the few pictures of vihuela playing from the period it can be observed (from for example the frontispiece to Luys Milán's *El Maestro*) that nine or ten frets seemed to be normal. J.B. Trend comments in his book on Luys Milán:

> Luys Milán and the earlier lutanists thought entirely in terms of counterpoint, and not in terms of harmony. They regarded music as made by a number of voices moving horizontally; they did not think of it vertically as a succession of chords.

This contrapuntal emphasis, then as now, demands a concentration on the linear flow of the music rather than on the interruptions of a rubato kind associated with Segovia's lavish display of instrumental tone colours. Renaissance timbres in keyboard, viol and other fretted instruments were quite different from modern concepts of what makes a good sound; even the principles of voice production of the

sixteenth century could well have been in very different directions
from the art of Caruso and Callas.

The only vihuela to have survived cannot necessarily be taken as
representative of the entire vihuela tradition. The enormously
extended string length of about eighty centimetres is in direct
contrast to the Italian four-course guitar still extant, whose
entire length measures about fifty-six centimetres. The larger
instrument would presumably have possessed more power,
more resonance, and thus would be suitable for use in ensemble work
and accompaniment for song, dancing, and other vihuelas (perhaps
of a smaller string-length).

As it is not possible to examine a multiplicity of extant vihuelas,
many questions concerning its structure will never be satisfactorily
answered. The secrets of its musical traditions are contained in
various collections published in Spain in the sixteenth century. All
vihuela music, like that of the lute and other fretted instruments until
the eighteenth century, is written down in that obscure musical
notation device known as tablature. It is an obscure method because
its language applies only to fretted instruments unlike normal
European notation which can be understood by any person who has
learned to read music no matter what instrument they play.

Ordinary notation moreover tended to become standardised once
its principles were established and music publishing had grown
popular. Tablature on the other hand became diverse and provincial
in its application; different eras of lute playing produced totally
different systems of tablature, not to mention the tablature systems
relating to vihuela, four-course guitar, five-course guitar, and
cittern, etc., each related to a specific geographical context.

Tablature is essentially a private language, joining together
aficionados of a particular instrument in a coterie from which other
musicians are excluded. Practitioners of tablature tend to make their
own modifications to the system as a matter of course, and so it is not
to be wondered at if many of these miniature traditions of tablature
publishing tended to vanish after the originator's lifetime or to
endure for the space of only thirty or forty years.

However, tablature undoubtedly possessed advantages for its
immediate practitioners. Certainly a notational method which
endured from the Renaisssance (and earlier) till the end of the
eighteenth century, and which is still used today in the setting down
of flamenco and other folk traditions, must have had much to
commend it. Thurston Dart praises the lute-tablature for its fidelity
to the requirements of the music and compares it favourably with the
less reliable part-books and choir-books which left out accidentals as

performers would have been aware of what the conventions of the music demanded.

> The notations used for lute tablatures were far more precise than staff notation in this respect, since each intersection of string and chromatic fret on the neck of a lute was represented by a separate and distinct symbol; lute-transcriptions of vocal music will thus supply many of the accidentals that were lacking from the vocal texts, and no scholar dare ignore the evidence they provide. But even these transcriptions have to be used with great care. It is as easy to make mistakes in writing or printing lute-tablatures as in any other kind of musical notation . . .
>
> Thurston Dart: *The Interpretation of Music*, London, 1954.

For the player of fretted instruments working within a specific tradition the tablature system is extremely convenient. The method can be easily taught and quickly absorbed, and pupils can instantly be directed to the actual performance of music without prolonged rituals of memorising. Tablature is a direct statement of the notes actually played on the instrument and thus the student need only concern himself with matters directly related to technical problems without reference to concepts of pitch or harmony.

Tablature, as has been commented already, tends over any length of time to become diversified. The fundamental principles may be the same, but the details of presentation show widely fluctuating ideas. The multiplicity of types of tablature between 1506 and the late eighteenth century is a complex assortment of methods, instrumental types, textures, traditions and degrees of virtuosity; each kind of tablature should be considered in the context of its own requirements rather than viewed as a continuous, abiding development of communication between composers and players.

Renaissance tablature systems are the easiest of all to understand, unlike the more cumbersome systems introduced in the late seventeenth century. Six lines representing the six courses of the vihuela (or the six principal courses of the lute) were drawn on the page. Numbers in the case of the vihuela (letters for the lute) denoted which fret was to be stopped by the fingers of the left hand. So the vihuelista was in effect putting a number on each fret, an extremely straightforward device. The lutanist would use the same system but instead of numbers letters were employed, *a* standing for the open string, *b* for the first fret, *c* for the second fret, *d* for the third fret, and so on through all the frets. (The lute did not use the letter *j*.) The student quickly began to associate a particular fret with its relevant letter.

Above the six lines of the tablature rhythm marks were written to indicate the values of the fastest moving line. If the same time value applied to several notes then the sign was placed only over the first note of the group. Bass notes of longer value than the fastest moving part were kept down for as long as possible, thus achieving a continuous pattern of sound, not a staccato delineation of time values indicated by the marks over the tablature. This imprecision in tablature, when it comes to showing the duration of the slower moving lines of the music, often leads to problems for modern editors who wish to translate tablature into conventional staff notation. Later sixteenth century tablatures introduced a system of drawing lines to show the exact duration of notes but vihuela tablature did not reach this degree of sophistication and perhaps did not need to.

Here is an example of the opening of a Milán pavana in tablature:

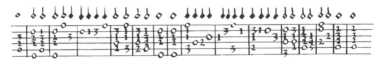

and in staff notation:

The literature of the vihuela which has survived is a compact collection of work unlike the more varied and diffuse lute books which were published in many countries over a far longer period of time. The vihuela tradition is represented for us by the following texts:

Luys Milán: *Libro de música de vihuela de mano, intitulado El maestro,* Valencia, 1535-1536

Luys de Narváez: *Los seys libros del Delphin de música de cifras para tañer Vihuela,* Valladolid, 1538

Alonso Mudarra: *Tres libros de música en cifra para vihuela,* Seville, 1546

Enriquez de Valderrábano: *Libro de música de vihuela, intitulado Silva de Sirenas,* Valladolid, 1547

Diego Pisador: *Libro de música de vihuela,* Salamanca, 1552

Miguel de Fuenllana: *Libro de música para vihuela, intitulado Orphenica Lyra,* Seville, 1554

These six publications represent the finest flowering of the vihuela tradition, and it is from these books that twentieth century recitalists such as Segovia, Pujol and Bream have selected the comparatively few works that are regularly performed in modern recitals.

Further publications relevant to the vihuela included scholarly works such as Juan Bermudo's *Declaración de Instrumentos Musicales* (Ossuna, 1555) and Thomas de Sancta Maria's *Libro llamado Arte de tañer Fantasia* (Valladolid, 1565).

Bermudo's treatise offers a considerable amount of information about the fretted instruments of his period. He mentions four-course guitars and vihuelas strung with five, six and even seven courses. He suggests that ten is a reasonable number of frets for a vihuela, though on bigger vihuelas there may be room for eleven or more; he also gives instructions to aid the placing of tied frets, delving into the complexities of scale structure and the relationships of semitones which could be solved ultimately only by the solution of equal temperament. The shift from the tuning founded on Pythagorean mathematics to Bach's 'well-tempered' klavier was certainly influenced by the tuning problems encountered by players of fretted instruments.

Three years after Bermudo's book, Gioseffo Zarlino's *Institutioni Harmoniche* (1558) explored the concepts of dividing the octave into twelve equal semitones. As the teacher of Vincenzo Galilei, a fine lutanist, Zarlino used the opportunity to demonstrate to his pupil his ideas of tonality on the fingerboard of the lute.

Vincenzo Galilei incorporated the fruits of his thinking about Zarlino's theories in his *Dialogo della musica antica e moderna* (Florence, 1581). In this book he expounds 'The Rule of Eighteen', a formula used for establishing where the frets should be placed. In this system the first fret is placed at one-eighteenth of the vibrating string length; the second fret is positioned at one-eighteenth of the remaining string length, and so on. Modern luthiers divide the string length by the exact measurement of 17.835, but it is fascinating to observe how the sixteenth century theorists had already solved the basic problem of European tonality by means of fretted instruments. In this evolution the line of theoreticians include Bartolome Ramos de Pareja who demonstrated in about 1480 the principles of equal temperament, and whose work influenced Bermudo.

In 1557 an anthology of music by Luys Venegas de Henestrosa was published in Alcala entitled *Libro de cifra nueva para tecla, harpa y vihuela;* this included compositions by Narváez, Cabezón, Mudarra and Pisador, though it regarded the vihuela as only one possibility of performing certain pieces within the selection.

A more central contribution to vihuela literature was Esteban Daza's *Libro de musica en cifras para vihuela, intitulado El Parnaso* (Valladolid, 1576). His work has not survived into the modern concert repertoire despite Daza's desire 'with that love that every father has for his children, even if they are ugly, that my work should endure and live for many years'.

The final curtain for a living vihuela tradition, as far as printed books are concerned, is represented by Antonio Cabezón's collection *Obras de música para tecla, arpa y vihuela* (Madrid, 1578). Cabezón (c.1500-66), one of the greatest of all Spanish composers, was described in his epitaph as 'the finest organist of his time, whose fame fills the world'. His keyboard diferencias were composed at the same time as the work of Narváez and Mudarra and he chose themes such as Guárdame las Vacas, loved by the vihuelistas, as a basis for his variations. As organist and clavichordist to Emperor Charles V, Cabezón represents the tradition of virtuoso organists extending through Frescobaldi to the great fulfilment of J.S. Bach. Like Fuenllana and Francisco Salinas (organist to the Duke of Alba, and later Professor of music at Salamanca), Cabezón was blind, a fact which did not prevent him from travelling to England, Italy and Flanders and thereby building up an international reputation which the vihuelistas themselves did not achieve.

The printing of texts related to the vihuela extends therefore from 1535 to 1578, a total of forty-three years, and, allowing for several years on either side of the appearance of publications, a reasonably firm tradition within the context of fretted instrument fashion. Unlike the lute's wide circulation throughout Europe, the vihuela remained rooted in its Spanish environment even though certain vihuelistas, such as Luys Milán, may have visited Portugal and Italy.

The natural habitat of the vihuela was that of the court, and the position of the vihuelistas as respected musicians in the service of dukes and princes was essential if their compositions were to be published. Luys Milán, for example, was favoured by Germaine de Foix, Ferdinand V's widow at the court of Valencia. *El Maestro* was dedicated to John III of Portugal (1521-1557); the dedication included the comment:

> La mar donde he echado este libro es propriamente el reyno de Portugal, que es la mar de la musica; pues en el tanto la estiman: y tambien la entienden.

> (The sea where I have launched this book is properly speaking the

kingdom of Portugal, which is the sea of music; for there music is so much esteemed and also understood.)

Luys de Narváez was court vihuelista of King Philip II, in whose service Diego Pisador and Miguel de Fuenllana also worked. Alonso Mudarra was brought up in the household of the Duke of Infantado, and later became a canon of the cathedral of Seville. Valderrábano worked for the Count of Miranda.

The effect of courtly service on musicians is a complex issue. Some restraints may have been imposed depending on the personality of the employer. For a composer the court could either provide a stimulating context or a means to creative frustration: an instrumentalist, however, would find it necessary to deploy the highest possible standards of his craft and working at the court would bring him into the competitive orbit of the nation's leading exponents of various fretted instruments. There might also be a demand for novelty, innovation and development, as well as for repetition of the most popular compositions of the day.

The professional court musician also confronted a high level of musical competence among the amateur players of the sixteenth century; every courtier wished to show himself a man of culture, and the court vihuelistas and lutanists were prized as the exemplars of all that was best in the national traditions. Musicians such as Cabezón travelled with their royal masters to foreign courts and their virtuosity was a source of regal pride and prestige.

Luys Milán was himself inspired by the ideals of Baldassare Castiglione whose *Il Cortegiano* (*The Courtier*) published in Venice in 1528, was translated into Spanish by Boscán in 1534. (Boscán's poem 'Claros y Frescos Ríos' ('Rivers Fresh and Clear') was included in Mudarra's vihuela book). Milán even wrote a book himself entitled *El Cortesano* (1561) which placed the Renaissance courtly ideals of Castiglione in the context of Valencia and demonstrated how the norms of aristocratic demeanour were enacted there in daily life. (Castiglione's book appeared in English in 1561, translated by Sir Thomas Hoby, an elegant tribute to the universality of Renaissance aspirations to courtly behaviour.)

Thus the vihuelistas of the Spanish courts could regard themselves not only as the leading instrumentalists of their country, but also as representatives of Renaissance civilisation, an integral part of aristocratic society. The sixteenth century represents the golden age of Spanish culture in music, poetry, drama and painting; in all this activity the sound of the vihuela was a small but significant aspect of a unique civilisation, and an aspect of which its major practitioners could be truly proud.

4. *El Maestro*, Pedagogues and Players

*. . . I am not pleased with the Courtier if he be not also a
musician, and besides his understanding and cunning
upon the book, have skill in like manner on sundry
instruments.*

Baldassare Castiglione: *Il Cortegiano*

Luys Milán's *El Maestro* represents one of the first examples of an
instructional method for a fretted instrument. The problems dealt
with in the text are those found in all guitar methods ever since, and
the extant volumes of tutors published between 1535 and the present
day constitute in themselves a rich pedagogic tradition dealing with
the central questions of learning an instrument like the guitar, lute
or vihuela.

Apart from the problem of notation (in this case the tablature, with
its associated requirement for the student to obtain both correct
notes and correct time-values), a difficulty of great significance to all
players is that of tuning the instrument. The question of tuning
troubles students of the guitar even in the twentieth century when
nylon strings have replaced gut. For the vihuela novice the spectacle
of six courses strung with a rather unstable material must have
seemed very daunting, and even to tune one course so that the two
strings of equal pitch were exactly correct would not have been an
easy task.

However, methods have a way of making such problems sound
easy enough to deal with. Milán's advice was to tune the first string
'tan alto quanto lo pueda suffrir' (as high as possible); this comment,
though valid to all sixteenth century instruments of the string family,
must have caused some small problems from time to time to those
who tried to carry out the instruction. The other strings were then
tuned to the top string. Presumably the top string itself would have
gone out of tune a little while the other courses were being adjusted
but most methods have chosen, in any age, to ignore little practical

difficulties of this kind. The exact placing of each fret would probably have added to the confusion felt by an unaided beginner. Then, as now, a more experienced player would be needed to achieve the best results.

Milán also has advice to offer on the intricacies of compás (a word greatly used by flamenco players to signify the rhythm or beat of the music) and mesura, the actual note-values. On fretted instruments the observation of a strict rhythm is not always easy for the student; once rhythm is lost, as the fingers move over the courses, it is more difficult than on a keyboard instrument to re-establish the musical flow. Milán chooses simple rhythmic patterns with great care, relying on repeated note-values to convey to the student in these early pages the essential principle to follow.

Disappointingly Milán does not attempt to deal with the actual hand positions. He specifies particular fingerings for scale passages, but seems to have found it unnecessary, unlike modern methods, to give detailed instructions on holding the vihuela and further intricacies relating to muscular ease of performance.

However *El Maestro* does explicitly set out to cater for the needs of the beginner.

> Este libro intitulado El Maestro esta partido en dos libros. El primer libro es para principiantes: y assi tiene la musica facil y conforme a las manos que un principiante puede tener.
>
> (This book entitled El Maestro is divided into two books. The first book is for beginners and therefore contains easy music and is appropriate to the hands of a beginner.)

The first book is sub-divided into several sections containing instructions and music in various 'keys' with difficulties that could hopefully be coped with even by a 'principiante'. In the fourth and fifth sections of the first book the scale passages can be played either with dedillo (index finger) or dos dedos (alternating thumb and first finger or first and second fingers, a more complicated technique with obvious affinities to modern guitar technique). Sections six and seven contain rather more difficult items, and the last section of the first book has vocal pieces with instrumental accompaniment, no doubt to be sung in many instances by the student himself. The book contains twenty-two fantasias, the famous six pavanas (later popularised by Segovia!), and a useful assortment of Spanish and Portuguese villancicos, with two Spanish romances and three sonnets in Italian.

Book Two includes eighteen fantasias, four tentos, and more songs. Milán delves into the current concepts of tonality much as a modern method might examine tetrachords and key signatures.

The technique of the vihuela involves a mastery of consonancias (chordal textures) and redobles (scale passages, now called picado in flamenco). Even if the overall texture is contrapuntal, Milán's compositions offer many contrasts between the heavier chord passages and sprightly running picado work. He also designates the general speed of each piece by such expressions as compás apressurado (rapid movement) or compás a espacio (slow), perhaps the earliest example of tempo indications.

Milán's music for beginners in Book One opens with the Fantasias. Fantasia I looks formidable enough in notation, and even in tablature would not be the ideal material for a modern teacher to offer as an opening gambit in a progressive system of tuition.

However this concept of plunging the student in at the deep end was customary in Renaissance instructional material. *El Maestro* contains no single string exercises, graduated sight-reading studies or exercises to develop the dexterity of the hands. The *gradus ad parnassum* of later eras is not included in sixteenth century vihuela or lute manuals: the student is simply presented with some reasonable music and left to get on with it.

Though this may seem harsh treatment for the 'principiante' it must be remembered that the vihuela books were used in the context of a living tradition in which the student was surrounded by active players of the instrument. A similar state of affairs exists today in the teaching of flamenco; flamenco methods often begin at a more complex stage of the proceedings than the corresponding classical guitar tutors. Moreover in both vihuela and flamenco where cifra (tablature) is the norm, the student need make no dissociation between the printed material and the processes of playing, unlike the student of staff notation where the traditional means often impose a barrier between the pupil and the actual musical texture.

Milán would not agree that his fantasias are particularly difficult. He advocates that 'to give beginners easy music will make them feel happy with what they do', and warns against that loss of interest which occurs 'if from the start the teacher gives music that is difficult to someone who has never played'. He adds caustically,

Y en la veridad todas las mas cosas son faciles al hombre de alcanzar . . .

(and indeed most things are easy when a man can do them)

One wonders here whether Milán is attempting to do what other methods have done, to appeal to both beginners and those with some knowledge of the instrument, by presenting good playable music which needs a little more skill than the novice possesses yet stimulates his desire to perform worthwhile music. A disparity between the tone of the written text and the actual difficulty of the printed music would not be entirely unexpected in the problematical publishing context of sixteenth century Spain.

Clearly the writer of a fretted instrument tutor in any period has a number of related problems to resolve. Not only must the teaching material be carefully organised but the music presented must be indicative of the ideal music that the pupil really wishes to perform. A humane and gentle approach, such as Milán shows, has the effect of soothing the troubled student and thus he can be led by the nose into the labyrinth of technique and musicality; here absorption in the task stimulates the pupil to wrestle willingly with the trials of learning. It is a pity that written records do not exist showing the degrees of success achieved by *El Maestro*.

Luys Milán's great work shows him to be a distinguished ancestor of later pedagogues and players. His music in *El Maestro* is attractive, characteristic, expressive, and playable. His written text denotes him as a true maestro aware of pupil psychology and the need to arouse enthusiasm. He possessed a good melodic inventiveness and a feel for the possible textures of vihuela composition. We must consider him to be a careful and conscientious composer, though not on this evidence, unlike Mudarra, a particularly flamboyant or florid performer. His virtues were conservative rather than innovatory, thorough rather than dazzling and his values were essentially musical rather than exhibitionistic, as can be seen in Fantasia No. XVI (another work which appeals to twentieth century guitarists).

Modern players have used the work of Narváez and Mudarra to demonstrate their own virtuosity. Milán's pavanas are played for their Renaissance stateliness and melancholy, not for their excitement or sense of dramatic climax. For these qualities one would look elsewhere to the work of Luys de Narváez and Alonso Mudarra whose work reveals other distinctive qualities of the vihuela tradition.

Luys Milán's book contains a picture of the composer in the role of a Renaissance Orpheus, delighting with his vihuela, a crowded landscape of birds (including an owl), a rabbit, a deer, a dog and a lion, whilst in the background a sinister boat plies across the River Styx. The maestro wears the laurel crown of classical artists. This must have seemed to Milán the perfect image for his haunting and elegant music.

Luys de Narváez chose a more turbulent image in the myth he selected to adorn his *Delphin de Música* of 1538. The book's title and the accompanying illustration are a reference to Arion, a lyric poet and musician of Methymna, on the island of Lesbos. Arion went to Italy with Periander, the tyrant of Corinth, where he became rich and famous through poetry and music. On Arion's return to Methymna, however, the sailors of the ship in which he embarked, tried to steal his wealth and planned to murder him. Pleading for his life, Arion played a melodious tune and then threw himself into the sea; a number of dolphins had been attracted to the ship by the sweetness of the music, and one of them carried him to Taenarus and the court of Periander. On their return, the sailors were crucified!

The illustration shows Arion still playing his vihuela as the dolphin carries him through choppy seas; the ship is also in the picture. Whether Narváez chose this story as an allegorical reference to enemies at court over whom his music triumphed, or whether the myth appealed to his sense of style, will never be known.

Narváez's position as maestro de vihuela for Philip II took him to the Escorial palace, a considerable distance from his native Granada, whilst his book was published at Valladolid, even further north. However, the art of Narváez has proved to be durable and several of his works have been played regularly in guitar recitals.

His principal claim to musical fame lies in the fact that he was the first composer to publish diferencias in a purely instrumental form. His diferencias on Guárdame las Vacas extend our awareness of the vihuela's dexterity and inventiveness. Here the sweep of the redobles would have been received with considerable admiration as they still are when played well:

Cristóbal de Castillejo (1492-1550) wrote a witty *glosa* on the original quatrain, (this being a poem that repeats the rhymes of its refrain, in effect a poetic *diferencias*). Narváez's music captures the humorous banter of the poem, the words of which should always be borne in mind by the performer:

> *Guárdame las vacas,*
> *carillejo, y besarte he;*
> *si no, bésame tú a mí,*
> *que yo te las guardaré.*

(Look after my cows for me, darling boy, and I will kiss you;
if not, you can kiss me and I will look after the cows for you)

Narváez's more emotional music has been represented in modern recitals by Canción del Emperador; these variations on Emperor Charles V's favourite song 'Mille Regretz' by Josquin des Prés (1445-1521) show us the solo vihuela at its most profound. The consonancias and the redobles have never been more finely contrasted, and the overall texture is a reconciliation between ponderously moving chords and light contrapuntal scale passages — a superb example of the vihuelistas' art:

A lesser played work of Narváez is Baxa de Contrapunto, a dance using contrapuntal textures. This composition, the last piece of *El Delphin de Música* shows immense skill in using fugal parts. After beginning with rapid scale brilliances, the music moves into a technically demanding climax of great intensity:

Narváez's fantasias, twenty-four in all, are quite neglected by modern players. This is a pity as they contain a wide variety of Narváez's native inventiveness and his delight in the unexpected pleasures of the vihuela. Take, for example, the elegant dance-like poise of Fantasia XIV which combines a strong rhythm with delicately sophisticated changes in note values to give a miniature instrumental work of real mastery:

Narváez shows himself to be a truly ambitious virtuoso of the vihuela in his pursuit of extended musical structures. As the great exponent of the diferencias form, Narváez might well have considered his twenty variations on the theme Conde Claros to be of equal or greater significance to the variations on Guárdame las Vacas. Modern players have preferred however to perform Alonso Mudarra's diferencias on Conde Claros.

Narváez's Conde Claros diferencias is a magnificently sustained work, unlike Guárdame las Vacas, in that the diferencias run into one another in a continuous organic growth of musical ideas; instead of putting each variation into its separate compartment as with Guárdame las Vacas, Narváez builds up the work with an ingenious musical use of repetition, imitation, redobles, notes of different values and interesting tempo changes. Each diferencia is only six bars long, although some are meant to be repeated. Variations sixteen and seventeen illustrate the control of mood and variety available to the vihuela player:

This desire of players to create larger scale works is reflected in
later periods of the instrument such as the early nineteenth century
and of course the twentieth century. The variation form has always
been popular with composers for the guitar, and Narváez's espousal
of the diferencias has continued throughout guitar history with
compositions by Sor, Giuliani, Ponce and Britten, to mention the
supreme examples.

Narváez was also (like Tárrega and Segovia) eager to absorb within
the repertoire of his instrument some of the fine music of other
composers of his day. The third and fourth books of *El Delphin de
Música* reveal Narváez as the first great arranger for a fretted
instrument, bringing the compositions of Josquin des Prés, Gombert
and Richafort, as well as numerous kinds of 'O Gloriosa Domina'
and 'Sacris solemnis' to the vihuela's attention. Of these arrangements
perhaps the 'Mille Regretz' quoted previously (see p. 37) is the most
appropriate counterpart to modern concepts of guitar transcriptions.

Like Luys Milán, Narváez included (in the fifth book) a suitable
selection of villancicos and two romances, for vihuela and voice. The
villancicos are particularly interesting as they offer more evidence of
Narváez's obsession with the diferencias; on the theme of 'Y la mi
cinta dorada', using the same words and melody, Narváez provides
six different accompaniments, a fascinating study in both stamina
and ingenuity.

The usefulness of this kind of musical exercise is shown however in
his marvellously varied and appropriate accompaniment to the
exquisite words of an unknown poet;

> ¿Con qué la lavaré
> La tez de la mi cara?
> ¿Con qué la lavaré?
> Que vivo mal penada.
> Lávanse las casadas
> Con agua de limones.
>
> Lávome yo cuytada,
> Con penas y dolores.
> Mi gran blancura y tez
> La Tengo ya gastada.
> ¿Con qué la lavaré?
> Que vivo mal penada.

(With what should I wash my face? With what should I wash it? Misery is my lot. The wives wash in lemon water.

I, the unfortunate one, wash in pain and sorrow. My pale face is already wasted. With what should I wash it? Misery is my lot.)

Narváez supplies this poem with a haunting, agitated accompaniment which contrasts the sustained notes of the vocalist with anxious quavers and triplets which finally fall into semi-quaver patterns of simple but moving empathy. It is perhaps one of the finest accompaniments of the vihuela literature, and points to a superb living tradition at Escorial of voice and vihuela.

The publication of Alonso Mudarra's *Tres Libros de Música en cifra* in 1546 brings us back to Seville, and that region of Spain which later produced the exciting colours of flamenco. Mudarra's work contains a diverse selection of fantasias, tientos, pavanas, romanescas (including variations of Guárdame las Vacas), and even two gallardas, (a unique inclusion in a vihuela book), as well as the beloved villancicos, canciones, romances, psalmos, etc. for vihuela and voice.

The sparkling brilliance of Mudarra's compositions is encapsulated for most modern players in Fantasia X, 'imitating the harp in the manner of Ludovico'. This remarkable work contains certain intended dissonances and under this passage is written the comment,

acerca del final hay algunas falsas; taniendose bien no parecen mal.

(from here to the end there are some false notes; when played well they do not sound bad)

Here is the passage, a piece of writing which recalls the jangling discords of Andalucian folk music:

Mudarra's compositions open with three fantasias that are the closest possible Renaissance example of the study; they are designed to promote 'agility in the fingers of both hands' and are one of the few instances of conscious attention to the building of technique. Some of the following fantasias are designated as 'easy' but Fantasias VIII, IX and X develop more complex contrapuntal patterns.

The demands of Fantasia X are followed by the consummate

structure of Mudarra's Conde Claros, which like the diferencias of
Narváez, is a fine extended composition, built up within the pattern
of six-bar phrases into an impressive and unified statement of what
the vihuela tradition at its best could achieve. From the bare dignity
of sustained opening chords, the music moves through many aspects
of the vihuela's voice, including intricate counterpoint, bravura scale
passages, organ-like chord progressions, and a bar of parallel tenths
before resolving into a dignified finale.

By the end of the first book Mudarra has increased the level of skill
necessary for successful performance to a virtuoso level. Virtuosity,
it would seem, in the vihuela tradition would reside not so much in
extrovert display, but in control, smoothness of execution, disciplined
dexterity, and a projection of the innate lyricism of the music; these
qualities can still be seen in the demands of flamenco at its best.
Mudarra's compositions rely particularly on fluent redobles and the
fretted instrument's ability to articulate rapid scale passages with
total clarity.

Mudarra also includes items for 'guitarra al temple viejo' (guitar in
the old tuning) and 'al temple nuevo' (in the new tuning). Miguel de
Fuenllana's *Orphenica Lyra*, also published in Seville, includes nine
pieces for the four-course guitar. Mudarra and Fuenllana thus appear
to link their high art of the vihuela tradition with the more widely
popular folk instrument of old Spain. Mudarra's four-course guitar
material is the earliest published collection for the instrument and
therefore of considerable interest. Fantasia XII shows the characteristic texture of four-course composition:

Mudarra's setting of various songs relates him to the mainstream
of Spanish sixteenth century lyric poetry. The works of Juan Boscán
(c.1490-1539) and Garcilaso de la Vega (1503-1536), two poets who
followed Italian influences, found in Mudarra a sympathetic musical
awareness when it came to matching the splendour of their words
with the sublime sonorities of the vihuela.

> *Por ásperos caminos he llegado*
> *a parte que de miedo no me muevo;*
> *y si a mudarme o dar un paso pruebo,*
> *allí por los cabellos soy tornado.*

(Garcilaso de la Vega)

(By harsh roads I have reached a place from which through fear I cannot move; and if I attempt to stir or move a pace, then I am dragged back by the hair)

Mudarra also returned to the work of Jorge Manrique (1440-1479) whose single poem 'Coplas por la muerte de su padre' ('Verses on the death of his father') established his eternal literary fame.

> *Recuerde el alma dormida,*
> *abive el seso y despierte,*
>   *contemplando*
> *cómo se passa la vida,*
> *cómo se viene la muerte*
>   *tan callando;*

(Let the slumbering soul revive its senses and wake up to contemplate how life passes, how death comes so silently)

But perhaps the most poignant of all the songs composed by Mudarra is his setting of one of the finest Renaissance poems.

> *Triste estava el rey David;*
> *Triste y con gran passión,*
> *Quando le vinieron nuevas*
> *De la muerte de Absalón.*

> *Quando le vinieron nuevas*
> *De la muerte de Absalón,*
> *Palabras Tristes dezía,*
> *Salidas del coraçón.*

(King David was sad, sad and with great grief, when they brought him news of the death of Absalom.

When they brought him news of the death of Absalom, he uttered sad words, utterances of the heart)

Mudarra's setting of such poetry can be fruitfully compared with Luys Milán's similar, if more restrained, achievement in such songs as 'Toda mi vida hos amé' ('All my life I have loved you'). In the sadly neglected realm of the vihuelistas' compositions for voice and vihuela are many exquisite gems of Spanish Renaissance culture comparable in one or two instances, despite the stylistic differences, with the intensity and power of Dowland's melancholy in such masterpieces as 'In darkness let me dwell' or 'I saw my lady weep'.

Though the songs of Milán, Narváez and Mudarra, may on the surface possess a courtly urbanity and even a polite dryness, closer listening reveals that beneath the elegant façade of discipline and order deep feeling unites words and music in a poignant marriage. The emotion within the music is not declamatory or extrovert, but inward, private and restrained; and the emotions are powerful, not needing outward drama or bravura to make the point, the feelings being allowed to radiate from the crucial nucleus of the poetry.

In the vihuela song tradition there is implicit a particularly well-poised sophistication and refinement of technique; the starkness of treatment, the austere, simple movements of melody, and the plaintive followings and promptings of the vihuela, indicate a true expressiveness that has perhaps been obscured by the rival popularity of the more extrovert English and continental Renaissance songs. However the increasing number of performances and recordings of the Spanish vihuela songs indicates that the long eras of neglect are now giving place to a genuine interest in the best examples of the work of these few composers.

The amount of lasting instrumental and vocal material left by the vihuelistas is admittedly not very extensive, and far more limited than the lute has to offer. Yet in those few masterpieces, flung up in a short time by a comparatively thinly rooted tradition, is distilled the essence of Spanish courtly music of the Renaissance. The music creates for its listeners a Utopian world of order, poetry and appropriate emotion, ignoring the turbulence of Spanish history and focusing on the inward world of peace, dignity, control and beauty, where the external chaos and cruelty of politics, torture, the Inquisition and the other inconveniences of Renaissance life were subordinated to a sense of its philosophical ideals. Though produced by public musicians the music of the vihuela reflects a somewhat private, intimate world. It is perhaps this atmosphere that has prompted twentieth century guitarists to appropriate vihuela music for their own recitals and pleasure, thus ensuring, after centuries of silence, that the inner vision of the vihuelistas will not be allowed to die like the instrument for which they created their music.

5.   A Digression Concerning the Lute

*. . . I think the viols and the lute represented the music of
the spheres; the gittern, cittern and hurdy-gurdy, the
instruments of the street.*

Julian Bream

The history of the relationship between the lute and the guitar is a
tangled web of misunderstandings and rivalry of one kind or another,
much of which has survived into the twentieth century. But whereas
nowadays the lute has become a historical, museum-like species of
instrument, able to perform only the music of the past, the guitar has
survived the long struggle of its perilous evolution and in this century
has received the benediction of a new and virile repertoire.

Certainly the lute and its great collection of musical treasures have
been revived; the silence of centuries has been broken and the lute can
speak again with the voice of the past in a way that the guitar cannot.
The lute represents previous civilisations whether medieval,
Renaissance, or Baroque. The guitar in the hands of its great modern
players has created the past in its own image and its repertoire,
through the efforts of composers of our own age who have been
irresistibly drawn to write for it, continues to evolve and expand.

Throughout the last five hundred years the guitar has assumed
many shapes and sizes. Segovia once compared the survival of the
guitar to the history of the dog which by constant adaptation to the
needs of humanity and by processes of development for specialised
demands has retained a central place in man's affections. In the same
manner, as in our own century, the guitar has been used throughout
its history for many musical purposes, whether for the sublime and
esoteric writing of classical composers, the rhythms of popular
dance, or the traditions of folk culture such as that of Andalucia.

The guitar developed in a very haphazard way. The four-course
guitar and the vihuela of the sixteenth century yielded in the fullness
of time to the five-course guitar. This was displaced by the six string

guitar of the nineteenth century which through appropriate modification became the versatile prototype of the modern classical guitar. Luthiers and players are still seeking perfection as new methods of guitar construction are attempted in the pilgrimage towards the ideal instrument. Such a guitar, the lyre of Utopia, would possess many qualities; sweetness and strength, the capacity to sustain notes for as long as possible, a perfect balanced clarity across all strings so that treble and bass are in perfect accord, loud enough to carry to the back of a hall but never strident or raucous, powerful but discreet — these are some but not all of the potential qualities of the twentieth century instrument.

Segovia has argued that the guitar has reached its finest hour:

> . . . the guitar has been aesthetically and acoustically perfect since the eighteenth century. I can make my guitar heard in any good concert hall provided I have a cooperative audience. As for the lute it has been dead for a hundred years; it was completely usurped by the piano in the last century.

The argument over the ideal guitar will continue. What is more certain is that the lute cannot, by definition, be developed either in structure or repertoire.

New forms of strutting, types of shell or ways of fitting the ribs, if invented to add lustre and volume, detract from the lute's authentic interpretation of the music of the past. Occasionally modern composers have attempted to write for the lute but the weight of the dead lutanist-composers such as Dowland and Weiss has so far inhibited composers from discovering a suitable idiom. A mass of material for the lute, of various periods, has been rescued from the oblivion of libraries and whatever the lute may lack it is not a repertoire. The lute-books that outline technique have been studied and published, and a true understanding of the instrument's demands, quite separate from those of the guitar, has at last been reached.

The lute has profited by a contemporary wave of nostalgia for the rooted values of the past; moreover the more avant-garde developments of twentieth century music, in which so often university musicians compose for other university musicians, has stimulated the musical public throughout the world to discover enjoyable areas of cultural activity on which they can rely. Julian Bream (interviewed by J.M. Thomson in *Early Music*, October, 1975) has commented:

> The search back to the values of early music is as vital, in fact may be more vital, than many musicians amongst us care to admit, and perhaps

of more consequence than much of the contemporary music being composed in our time.

In this search for values, the lute has been of crucial significance.

It is therefore singularly fitting that Julian Bream, as one of the greatest guitarists in the instrument's history, should also have been responsible to an enormous extent for the lute's popularity in the recital halls of today. Bream's work has demonstrated that the lute and guitar fulfil quite separate musical activities, and that the classical guitar as we perceive it in the twentieth century has its own destiny, which is more substantial than a mere imitation of other instruments whether fretted or keyboard.

Ultimately, the twin enterprises undertaken by recitalists this century — either that of playing Renaissance and Baroque music on the modern guitar or of using replica vihuelas or lutes — have led, by what James Joyce called in *Finnegans Wake* 'a commodius vicus of recirculation', to an awareness of the realities of all kinds of fretted instrument music, its basis in tablature and its authentic modes of expression.

Taken to a logical conclusion this awakening, and new levels of historical awareness in music, must inevitably lead to a revaluation of classical guitar traditions. As we listen more and more to lute music, vihuela music, and the four-course and five-course instruments of Renaissance and Baroque, the post-Torres classical guitar from 1840 is seen in a very different way. Its strength and versatility can now be gauged in its own terms; the classical guitar is supreme in the presentation of specific areas of repertoire, and other areas that were previously thought to be appropriate to the guitar are now, perhaps sadly, less convincing to our ears. The growth of interest in lute music has therefore metamorphosed our aural perception in quite a short time, just as the pioneering work of Wanda Landowska has reorientated and re-defined the proper scope of the nineteenth century grand piano.

The twentieth century development of interest in the lute and Renaissance music is itself of great significance and fascination; it did not emerge overnight or even with the appearance of Julian Bream on the concert platform. The father of the lute revival was undoubtedly Arnold Dolmetsch who wrote concerning his Haslemere Workshops:

> In 1889, in the British Museum, I found an immense collection of English instrumental music of the sixteenth and seventeenth centuries. I resolved to play these pieces which had so fascinated me. Fortunately I felt from the first that this music would only be effective if played upon the instruments for which it was written.
>
> Viols, Lutes, Virginals and Clavichords had not yet become the prey

3. *A modern copy of a Renaissance Lute:* a concert lute made by David Rubio. Courtesy of David Rubio.

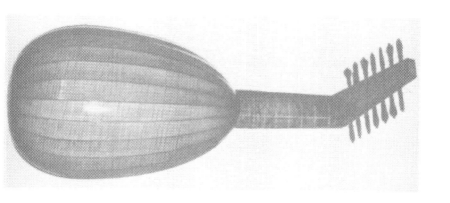

of collectors. I had no great difficulty in procuring some. Having failed
to find anybody who could put these instruments in sufficiently good
playing order to satisfy my requirements, I remembered that I was a
craftsman. I soon rigged up a workshop in the attic of my house and
began to work.

The problem was difficult. I could not tell how far an instrument was
out of order when I could not play upon it; neither could I learn to play
until the instrument was in good order. However, patiently, gradually,
my craftsmanship and my musicianship reacting one upon the other;
one day I found the instruments playable and my skill as a player well
advanced. Soon I had trained pupils to join me in concerted pieces.

Carl Dolmetsch: *Music and Craftmanship*

Arnold Dolmetsch's role of craftsman, recovering the secrets of
instrument making, was obviously of vital importance in the rebirth
of the lute. His work was complemented by the musicological
researches of other scholars. Oscar Chilesotti published a large
collection of transcriptions in staff notation from the lute tablatures
in 1891, including works by Newsidler, Galilei, Molinaro, Negri
and Besardo, among others. Conde de Morphy published his seminal
Les Luthistes espagnols in 1902 (Leipzig), and Felipe Pedrell's
Cancionero musical popular Español (Valls, 1921) centred attention
on much neglected Spanish traditions including the music of the
vihuelistas.

In 1920 Dr. E.H. Fellowes published all four volumes of
Dowland's songs and three more from *A Musicall Banquet*; he in-
cluded the original lute tablature. Peter Warlock's book *The English
Ayre*, one of the best introductions to the Renaissance fretted
instrument repertoire, appeared in 1926 published by the Oxford
University Press, to be followed in 1927 by his edition of Dowland's
Lachrimae or Seven Tears, and in 1928 by an anthology of fifteen
lute solos by Dowland entitled *The Lute Music of Dowland*.

The first recordings of the lute appeared in 1927, featuring the
lutanist Diana Poulton and John Goss in a performance of 'Flow not
so fast ye fountains', and 'Awake sweet love' sung by Cécile
Dolmetsch, accompanied by the lutes of Arnold and Rudolph
Dolmetsch. The work of Diana Poulton as one of the great pioneers
of interest in lute-playing was aided in the 1930's by the work of an
American lutanist Suzanne Bloch.

The efforts of Emilio Pujol to establish the vihuela have already
been touched upon in Chapter Two, whilst the first appearance of his
vihuela outside Spain was apparently his Paris debut of 1927.

The post-war years accelerated the number of those absorbed in
the art of the lute, though a public acceptance of it as anything more

than a rather arid academic pursuit would be postponed until the Bream recordings of the fifties. Diana Poulton in her monumental work *John Dowland* (London, 1972) remarks how the young Julian Bream, as early as 1951, 'astonished everyone with the brilliance of his musicianship and his complete technical mastery of the lute'. Bream had been tutored to some extent by Desmond Dupré, another earnest advocate of the lute, whose later recitals with Alfred Deller aroused considerable interest.

In 1956 the founding of a Lute Society, initiated by the lute maker and player Ian Harwood, laid the foundations of a following for the lute among amateurs world-wide, which the instrument definitely needed. Paradoxically the support for the lute in the sixties was propelled along by the phenomenal rise to international fame of Bream's lute recitals; many of the original members of the Lute Society had strong reservations about Bream's guitar-based lute technique and Bream retaliated by playing lutes that were some distance from the purist's concept of what a Renaissance lute should be. In the end some kind of equilibrium was achieved; the scholars and purists preserved their sense of authenticity, propriety and correctness whilst Bream kept his charisma, international public and the kind of instrument he wished to play in concert halls.

Every instrument, if it is to be truly popular, needs not only virtuoso players of the top rank, but a host of amateur aspirants. The lute's progress among amateurs, unlike that of the guitar, has been hindered by the prohibitive cost of buying an instrument; this has prevented the widespread playing of the lute in schools and universities and no great demand has arisen for lute teachers outside the main cultural centres. Thus a curious position comes about which recalls the Renaissance and Baroque dilemma of the lute; while the lute remains the instrument for divinely evocative music, the guitar, whether classical or electric, has become even more the instrument of the people.

Various outstanding performers on the lute apart from Julian Bream have emerged. The most well-known guitarist to espouse the lute, if only for two recordings, was Narciso Yepes, whose offering of a two-record album of all Bach's lute compositions was played on the Baroque lute. Konrad Ragossnig, an Austrian guitarist, embarked on a series of recordings in which the music of England, Poland, Spain, France, Italy and Germany, was each represented by one complete recording.

These three guitarist/lutanists have undoubtedly brought lustre to lute music. Other lutanists of international reputation include Eugen M. Dombois, on the Baroque lute, Michael Schaeffer, Anthony Bailes,

Anthony Rooley and Robert Spencer, who first made his name as a member of the Julian Bream Consort. The work of the late Walter Gerwig should also be mentioned as one of those earlier lutanists whose recordings helped to popularise the instrument.

With so many musicians intrigued by the lute, ranging from the very talented to those of virtuoso powers, the future of the instrument in recital contexts should be assured. One will expect to see more players turning to the relatively neglected areas of the Baroque guitar, where the music of Bach, Weiss and Baron, hitherto appropriated by guitarists on the whole, would provide a lifetime of fruitful study.

The lute and guitar are excellent bed-fellows, despite the lack of sympathy mutually sustained by some of the respective aficionados; it is now appreciated that each instrument represents a totally different musical experience, the various kinds of lute being only at home in particular periods, and the classical guitar being an anachronism before the nineteenth century. Yet the early species of vihuela, Baroque and eighteenth century guitars, have strong links with the development of the lute, and all the eras before 1780 owe allegiance to the high artistic standards established in the lute traditions.

The re-emergence of the lute as a part of our aural environment is a potent reminder of historical realities. The timbres of its voice and the riches of its long repertoire should surely complement rather than rival the velvet sonorities of its constant companion through musical history.

6. The Four-Course Guitar

Empieza el llanto
de la guitarra . . .

Federico García Lorca

The music written for the four-course guitar of the sixteenth century has been ignored by modern recitalists who have preferred to move on to the five-course Baroque repertoire. Of the leading guitarists on the international scene only Narciso Yepes and Turibio Santos have recorded four-course music on the classical guitar, and then but a few items from the collection of Adrien Le Roy.

Yet the four-course instrument is the most obvious ancestor of the classical guitar and there is a considerable amount of material for the Renaissance guitar extant, thus proving that it is a genuine branch of guitar tradition.

Mention has already been made in Chapter Four of the inclusion in the vihuela books composed by Alonso Mudarra and Miguel de Fuenllana of music for four-course guitar. Both of these books were published in Seville, perhaps bearing witness to a strong popular tradition of 'la guitarra' compared with the more aloof, courtly associations of vihuela and lute.

Juan Bermudo's inexhaustible *Declaración de instrumentos musicales* gives the tuning of the four-course guitar, distinguishing like Mudarra between the new and old tunings.

It will be observed how the new tuning follows the modern tuning of the top four strings of the guitar and not the vihuela or lute tuning with the interval of a major third between third and fourth courses. Thus the lowly four-course instrument is in the mainstream of later guitar developments. An unusual timbre is given to the instrument by the interval of an octave between the two strings on the fourth course, a device which gives the Renaissance guitar its specific identity.

Since the demise of the four-course guitar, plucked instruments with four strings have usually been relegated to the backwaters of musical art, though often popular in folk traditions. Bowed instruments have evolved towards the magical number of four, and the six stringed viols and the arpeggione have been discarded.

The ukulele (with its peculiar tunings reminiscent of the Renaissance guitar) and the banjo have never attracted serious attention. The mandolin, on the other hand, with its small lute-like proportions survives with its double-strung courses and its plectrum technique, (Beethoven composed several delightful pieces for it.) But the mandolin is not frequented so much by guitarists and is traditionally the recreation of players of the violin; the mandolin is tuned like the violin and its tiny fingerboard is not alien to the violinist's fingers.

In various South American countries four-course and four string instruments are still very much a part of the national identity of their respective musical traditions. The Spanish conquistadores took their vihuelas and guitarras with them in the sixteenth century; these instruments evolved into specific and recognisable types of guitar according to local trends, but the modern descendants still bear the obvious imprint of their Renaissance paternity.

Of these the Venezuelan cuatro is an interesting example. Its scale length of about fifty centimetres (compared with the sixty-five or sixty-six centimetres of the modern guitar) shows how it belongs to the tradition of the small guitarra. It is strung singly, thus achieving its own textures. At one time the Venezuelan Embassy in London employed a certain Señor Reyna who travelled the length and breadth of the country performing virtuoso recitals of Venezuelan music on the cuatro. His playing achieved the flair, colour and power of the larger flamenco guitar, and involved the familiar strumming and single note techniques characteristic of this size of guitar in any age. Thus four strings need not, it seems, be a crippling limitation to reasonable expressiveness, especially when operating within strong and vital ethnic traditions. The cuatro can be played either as a solo instrument or within an ensemble. Its voice, in the hands of a maestro, is remarkably powerful.

Another obvious relic of the four-course influence is the Colombian tiple, also played in parts of Argentina and Venezuela. However this instrument has three strings to each course, thus, once again, fulfilling an evolutionary principle, that each derivative type creates its own function and timbres. Other South American guitar-like instruments also represent another concept fundamental to plucked string developments — that five strings are better than four. In this category are the Mexican vihuelita, with five strings tuned like the top five of a guitar, the Bolivian and Andean charango, with five double-courses, and the peculiar jarana jorocho from Vera Cruz; the latter is again tuned like the guitar but the treble *e* and the bottom *a* are single strung, whilst the *b*, *g* and *d* are double strung courses in the best Renaissance tradition.

Thus the four-course guitar, for all its neglect since its demise in the seventeenth century, continues to exert an influence on the folk traditions of South America, proving that even despised and subsidiary fretted instruments can survive in one mutation or another when the courtly lutes and vihuelas have passed into silence.

In sixteenth century Europe the four-course guitar was greatly loved in Spain, perhaps especially in what is now Andalucia, as a popular instrument rather than a courtly and graceful adjunct to fashionable demeanour. The popular instruments pursue a less glamorous existence and sometimes are scarcely included in written sources, yet their power lasts longer than the miniature fads of courtly delight.

Musicology is an imprecise form of research, far more so than literary research. The published books in Renaissance vihuela and lute music emanate from the sources of political power. From the existence of a handful of vihuela books, and a few dozen lute books, one can conjecture the health, vitality and extent of those traditions in Spain and the rest of Europe. But in the Spanish tradition it is extremely difficult to estimate the pervasive influence of the people's love of the guitar at the grass-roots or the immense amount of excellent playing of fretted instruments throughout the centuries in Spain which was ultimately distilled into the music of Pedrell, Albéniz, Granados, Falla, Rodrigo, etc. There is no way of telling how far the vihuela tradition extended downwards into society from the courtly centres; one can only remark that the vihuela books of Mudarra and Fuenllana show that the four-course guitarra did penetrate, in a small way, the preoccupations of those two composers.

However the four-course guitarra, as well as being transplanted in the search for El Dorado, also took root in France. Its culture there may have been directly due to the experiences of Henri II who spent some years in Spain as a hostage. Moreover there must have been many musicians who preferred the less demanding four courses of the guitar to the more dazzling panoply of the lute with its problems of technique, stringing and upkeep.

The author of an anonymous method for lute and guitar, (*La manière de bien et justement entoucher les lucs et guiternes*, Poitier, 1556) charts the growth of interest in the guitar:

> In my earliest years we used to play the lute more than the guitar, but

for twelve or fifteen years now everyone has been guitaring; the lute is almost forgotten for goodness knows what kind of music on the guitar, which is much easier to play than the lute.

Henri II's reign, (1547-1559) saw the granting of the privilege of printing music to Adrien Le Roy and Robert Ballard following the death of Pierre Attaignant. (The latter published throughout his lifetime more than 150 volumes of music, both religious and secular, including over a thousand chansons and a remarkable quantity of lute music.)

Le Roy, a cousin of Ballard, began printing in 1551, and continued up to the end of the sixteenth century; Ballard's descendants then continued with the publishing business till the end of the eighteenth century. Le Roy was a lutanist and composer, and Robert Ballard probably concentrated on the administration of the firm, leaving the musical policy to his talented relative.

At least five books containing four-course music were issued by Le Roy (1551, 1552, 1554, 1556, 1557) including his *Briefve et facile instruction pour apprendre la tablature à bien accorder, conduire et disposer la main sur la guitare* of 1551, which has unfortunately been lost.

These collections contained the popular dances of the period such as the branles (called a brawl by Shakespeare and a brantle by Pepys), derived from the French verb *branler* (to sway); there were various forms of Branle from the energetic Branles de Bourgogne to the more sedate Branles Doubles and Simples. As well as the courtly pavanes and gaillardes, there were the instrumental fantasies, a form taken to its greatest heights by Dowland's lute compositions. There were also almandes, a dance derived from the German Dance of the early lute books, later to be metamorphosed into the exquisite instrumental textures of the suites of J.S. Bach.

Another publisher, Michel Fezandat, published tablatures for lute and guitar by Simon Gorlier, Guillaume Morlaye and Albert de Rippe (Morlaye's tutor). Between 1550 and 1562 seventeen volumes were published for lute, guitar and cittern, with eight collections for guitar, lute, cittern, transverse flute and keyboard. None of these composers has found favour with modern players of the guitar, but there is enough music in these anthologies to indicate that the four-course guitar was a worthy and vital form of music-making in sixteenth century France.

The transcription of four-course guitar music to the modern classical guitar destroys the timbres and atmosphere of the music. The lack of the double-stringing could be remedied, and usually is, by playing this body of music on its Renaissance competitor, the lute. However the appeal of the four-course guitar for its devotees was possibly its limited range and the utter simplicity of its musical structures. There was also the use of rasgueado in connection with the guitar of this species; to transfer the music to its larger great-grandchild means installing new basses on the fourth and fifth strings in performance, and this upsets the simple treble quality of four-course music.

Thus to 'improve' the music by transcribing it for the classical guitar is to destroy the nature of its appeal; it is moreover anathema for a modern player to perform an entire piece without playing on the fourth and fifth strings. The longer sustain of the twentieth century guitar also takes the rhythmic staccato tones of the smaller instrument and makes them into richer patterns of melody. In other words transcription from the four-course guitar to its modern descendant is perhaps the most fruitless and destructive of all possible types of instrumental change. What is left in such a transcription is the tune, the rhythm and essential beat of the original dance; what we lose are the sonority, the harmonies and the overall atmosphere characteristic of this tiny voice.

However the story of the four-course guitar is a delightful episode in the guitar's traditions. It shows how an enthusiastic group of players and publishers can immerse themselves in a vigorous tradition and capture in their compositions an essential aspect of the era's music. Even the guitar's most miniature tributaries can sometimes lead to an unusual significance and the creation of a cultural heritage of fascination. The soul of the four-course guitar survives not only in the folk music of the South American continent but also in the very existence of the guitar as we know it; the little four-course, as an early prototype of a larger instrument, gave birth to the five-course Baroque guitar, and its survival among the Spanish people of the sixteenth century transcends in time the higher aspirations of vihuela and lute traditions.

7. The Five-Course Guitar

DRYBOLE. *My melodious pipes are a little obstructed;*
but to serve you, I will chant forth
incontinently. But, Madam, I want a
Theorbo to pitch my voice.

LADY LOVEYOUTH. *Will not a Gittar serve?*

The Humorists (c.1670)

With the advent and establishment of the five-course guitar a
repertoire was established which twentieth century guitarists, often
with a certain amount of imaginative (if unscholarly) modification,
have been able to use to good effect in the recital halls of the world.
The addition of only one course to a four-course guitar is sufficient to
bring about a profound change in its expressive powers. Moreover
once a guitarist's friend possessed a five-course, it was probably not
according to human nature to be content with the limitations of only
having a four-course. On the five-course everything could be done
that was possible on the four-course, but other things could be
attempted musically which could not even be contemplated on the
smaller instrument.

Even with five courses the guitar was quite modest in its number of
strings compared with the six courses of the vihuela and the eight or
ten courses of the lute. The guitar thus evolved slowly and sensibly
and once the four course guitar was ousted from popularity, the five
course usurper remained for about two centuries.

To date the emergence of the five course is not easy. Fuenllana's
Libro de Música para Vihuela of 1554 contains pieces for a 'vihuela de
cinco órdenes', and a famous engraving by Raimondi shows a
performer with a guitar that is clearly strung with five courses
(c.1510). So the five-course guitar was familiar to aficionados early in
the sixteenth century. Once again, on turning to Bermudo's
Declaración de instrumentos musicales, information is gleaned about
the 'guitarra de cinco órdenes'; Bermudo's evidence is that the five

course guitar is fundamentally a four course instrument with the extra course added not below the fourth course, but above the first course. This could in some instances have been a single string or 'chanterelle'; we have seen in the previous chapter how some South American instruments combine double-strung courses with single strings, another legacy of the five-course guitar of the sixteenth century.

Thus the guitar's tradition as we can apprehend it in the sixteenth century, through a glass darkly, is obscure. The extant material lacks the brilliant outline of the vihuela and lute traditions. An instrument in any one historical period is as good as the music written for it, as far as later generations are concerned. The Renaissance guitar pursued an underground development. Some guitarists favoured the four-course instrument, others casually added a fifth string or course; the two types co-existed or could even be the same instrument variously strung. Improvisation both in construction and probably in performance was preferable to the polished masterpieces of the professional virtuosi. The four-course profited in France by entering a courtly tradition and even stealing some of the lute's popularity; the five-course guitarra seems to have bided its time, being used at the popular level, being mentioned and painted, but throwing up no respectable body of compositions which might give us a real lead on what the instrument represented to its supporters.

The early history of the guitar in the sixteenth century presents, therefore, an inchoate mass of conflicting information. On the one hand Fray Juan Bermudo will remark

> . . . if you want to make the vihuela into a guitar *a los nuevos* take off the first and sixth, and the four strings that are left are those of the guitar. And if you wish to make the guitar into a vihuela, put on the sixth and the first.

On the other, a lute book by Melchiore de Barberiis, *Opera Intitolata Contina* (Venice, 1549) refers to the 'chitarra da sette corde', meaning in this instance a four-course guitar in which the top string is single.

However, despite these early sources, guitar mythology, transmitted through the dramatist Lope de Vega (1562-1613) and Gaspar Sanz, persistently acclaimed Vicente Espinel (c. 1550-1624), poet and musician, friend of Cervantes, as the personality who inaugurated the five-course guitar.

This is characteristic of the confusion which surrounds an evolving instrument. The guitar did not exactly suffer from this prevarication concerning its ultimate function and destiny, for it did survive; but the general lack of specification, the guitar's chameleon-like ability to match its stringing and concepts to particular environ-

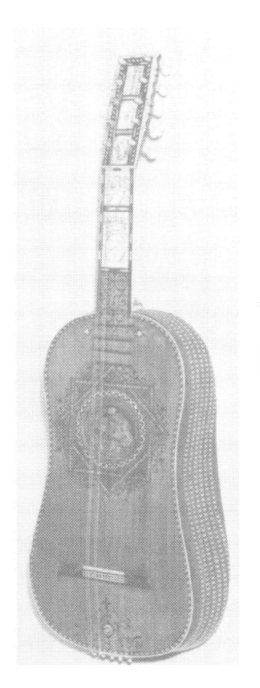

4. *Chitarra Battente,
1624:* an elaborate
example of exquisite
craftsmanship.
Courtesy of Castello
Sforzesco, Milan.

ments with none emerging decisively, robbed the guitar of a worthy Renaissance repertoire able to compete on equal terms with lute or vihuela. The guitar was the Cinderella of Renaissance instruments but on this occasion the two sisters prevented her from attending the Ball.

By the late sixteenth century the battle to define how many courses a respectable guitar should possess seems to have been won. The document which provides the evidence is Juan Carlos Amat's *Guitarra Española de Cinco Órdenes*, thought to have been published in 1596; the first extant publication of this work is dated 1626 as the original issue has not survived. This book was reprinted up till 1784, an extraordinary instance of how a guitar method can shape the destiny of an instrument.

Amat's tuning for his five course guitar follows the top five strings of the modern classical guitar except for the unusual timbre imparted by the split octaves on the lowest two strings:

The existence of double stringing on courses, as well as the early guitarist's delight in the curious effect of octaves on courses keeps the Baroque development of the guitar at a slight distance from the modern instrument. The double stringing also keeps the guitar in a certain precise relationship to the sonorities of both lute and vihuela, preserving that light nasal tang beloved by early fretted instrumentalists, echoes of which survive in the tender janglings of mandolin and country and western 'jumbo' guitars of the twentieth century with their derivative double stringing.

Amat's book goes into great detail concerning the playing of chords in rasgado (strumming) style; many later tutors of less repute have concentrated on this aspect, and guitarists have always admired the instrument's ability to sound chordal textures, right back to Luys Milán's *El Maestro*.

Amat teaches the fingering for 'taner rasgado todos los puntos naturales' ('playing rasgado all the natural chords'), a punto being a three voiced chord with root, third and fifth; of these puntos there are twenty four different chords, twelve major and twelve minor. Amat numbers these chords from 1 to 12, denoting the major chords by the letter 'n' after the figure, and minor chords by the letter 'b'.

A clever table is given in Chapter Five that designates which fingers should be used on each string to find the various chords. This system is the predecessor of the dozens of chord tutors which have appeared in the twentieth century. Unfortunately such books do not produce playable music; the onus is thrown on the student to employ the chords as best he can; thus Amat's treatise, whilst remaining one of the most fascinating and historically significant of all guitar methods, is also one of the least rewarding for those who wish to take advantage of music offered in the manual for the purpose of recital. However the use people such as Gaspar Sanz made of Amat's book is of a more special relevance to the twentieth century player.

Amat gave students of his book a variety of possible chords; these chords 'like the materials and colours of the painter' could then be used to perform 'vacas, paseos, gallardas, villabos, italianas, pavanillas, etc.' but it was left to the virtuoso performers of the Baroque five-course instrument to reveal just what effects the musical deployment of the rasgado technique might produce. Amat himself, like so many compilers of methods, had little to offer the world, it seems, in the way of composition. Like the writers of pedagogic material through the ages, he institutionalises and codifies the results of the tradition up to the time of writing; but it is the players and composers who refine and nurture the traditions of the guitar and Amat's work, though of enormous scholarly and musicological interest, is less musically significant than the subsequent history of the Baroque guitar. The *Guitarra Española de Cinco Órdenes* is to be considered however as perhaps the first of all guitar methods; as such it is an inviting 'sesame' to the sunlit and gentle pastures of the seventeenth century guitar.

As the five course guitar became more popular, it aroused the usual amount of opposition which always faces the emergence of new kinds of instruments. Praetorius in his *Syntagma Musicum* (published in three books 1615-20) complains about the 'cheats and swindlers' who perform on the five course guitar, 'singing their villanellas and other silly songs'. The disapproval was clearly intended for the kind of musician who took up the new instrument as well as for the shallowness of its available repertoire. (In our own age Andrés Segovia remarked about the ten string guitar made by Ramirez for Narciso Yepes: 'All this ten string monstrosity accomplishes is to transform the guitar from a voluptuous *femme* into a matronly hag'.)

Twenty years after Praetorius' book had appeared, Pierre Trichet in his *Traité des Instruments de Musique* (c.1640) argued fiercely on behalf of the lute, criticising those who slavishly imitated the fashions of Spain, and concluding that for the French the lute was 'the most congenial of instruments'. This shows, at least, that the lutanists felt their long supremacy to be threatened.

Luis de Briceño's *Método mui facilissimo para aprender a tañer la Guitarra a lo Español* (Paris, 1626) saw the guitar 'as the most suitable instrument for our time one could imagine. . . . It has none of the inconveniences to which the lute is subject. It is always fresh as a rose. If it gets out of tune easily, it is just as easy to tune it again . . . the guitar, whether well played or badly played . . . is pleasant to hear and listen to'.

Thus in the conflict between guitarists and lutanists, the former argued for the guitar's greater convenience and practicality. Pierre Trichet derided the guitar's simpler needs. Having complained, a little like Praetorius, that the Spanish 'know how to use the guitar more foolishly than any other nation', (particularly as they use ugly and ridiculous bodily movements as they sing and play their 'sarabandes, gaillardes, espagnolettes, passemezes, passecailles, pavanes, alemandes and romanesques',) Trichet comes to the nub of his argument. Surely people abandon the lute because the guitar 'is easier to learn to play' than the lute, 'which requires a long and arduous study'. He even accuses the guitar of some effeminate quality, quoting Ronsard's ode to the guitar:

> *Il est des dames pensives*
> *L'instrument approprié;*
> *Il est des dames lascives*
> *Pour les amours dédié.*

However, Trichet's attack is on the repertoire of the guitar which could, he admits, in time possess a more masculine kind of music, though 'it is necessary to wait for such an event'.

Several enduring prejudices against the guitar, some of which have even survived into the twentieth century, can be discerned in Trichet's angry prose. The onslaught against the actual music available to the guitar is a recurring theme in all ages, and critics often suggest that things could improve for the instrument but that at the moment the situation is unsatisfactory.

The linking of the guitar with Spanish shallowness, moods of feminine romanticism and the generally decadent atmospherics of *l'amour*, is still to be found in various forms in reviews of guitar recitals. Actually the association of the guitar with stories of mystery and imagination is not entirely an adverse criticism, even when the instrument is compared with the more intellectual flights of other forms of music. The guitar has always appealed to people's heart-felt

wish for more colour and vividness in their lives; for those who live in
the rainy temperate climes of northern Europe, intellectual stimulation is always available for those who need it, but highly exotic,
colourful and evocative echoes of the numinous world of the
imagination are more difficult to achieve.

Another fallacy in Trichet's discussion is the idea that a more
difficult instrument is somehow a worthier cause. The death of the
lute as a viable means of musical expression occurred when the
instrument's technical difficulty outran the amateur's desire to
pursue and conquer its music. Trichet, unknowingly but pro-
phetically, focused on the very fact which would ensure the lute's
ultimate demise little over a century later.

These storms in tea-cups at each stage of the guitar's history bear
testimony to the fervent enthusiasm of the aficionados of fretted
instruments. Each strand of the tradition produces a certain
defensiveness or aggressiveness as a writer or player identifies himself
closely with the instrument's destiny and engages in polemical war
on its behalf. Though sometimes irritating, these internecine
squabbles, even now not extinct among guitarists and lutanists, are
an essential aspect of the guitar's traditions and sometimes, by dint of
their strident repetitiveness, add a certain piquant charm to what
otherwise might seem rather trivial.

The five course guitar, despite Trichet's complaints, did achieve a
worthwhile tradition of both players and a suitable repertoire. If
Henri II had been the eminent patron of the four course instrument,
Louis XIV provided an equivalent service for the Baroque guitar. He
seems to have been an aficionado of both guitar and lute, though
Bonnet in his *Histoire de la Musique et de ses Effets* (1715) declares
that the guitar was Louis XIV's 'favourite instrument'. If the king
had been more inclined to play bowed instruments, the history of the
Baroque five course might have been very different.

However Louis was taught to play by a guitarist of genius whose
performances captivated other European courts including that of
Charles II of England. Francesco Corbetta, born in Pavia, Italy, in
1615, published his first book *Scherzi Armonici* in 1639 in Bologna.
His patrons included Ferdinand II in Vienna, and the Duke of
Mantua, to whom Corbetta dedicated his *Varii Capricii per la
Chitarra Spagnuola* (1643).

Jean-Baptiste Lully had been chosen in 1661 (when Louis XIV
assumed power) as *Surintendant de la Musique de la Chambre*, and
promoted to *Maître de la Musique de la Famille Royale* in 1662. How
friendly Corbetta was with his fellow countryman is not recorded,
though in 1656 Corbetta did provide an interlude to one of Lully's

ballets. It may seem a pity that Lully did not contribute to Corbetta's repertoire by composing for him, but no doubt he assumed that the court's guitar maestro was more than capable of providing music for his own instrument.

The dignity and esteem of Corbetta's position in the world of courtly music can be judged by the title given to two of his published collections — *La Guitarre Royale*; the first of these (1671) was dedicated to Charles II, and the later one (1674) to the French monarch. Count de Gramont described Corbetta as having 'a genius for music, and he was the only man who could make anything of the guitar', thus expressing an admiration shared by kings, dukes and other aristocracy for Corbetta's skill.

Corbetta delighted his lordly paymasters with a variety of dances, often forming a more satisfying musical structure by combining pieces in a suite, consisting of an almanda, a corrente, and a sarabande. The inclusion of a gigue would have brought Corbetta's suites into line with the keyboard works of Froberger (1617-67) and Buxtehude (1637-1707), two of whose suites, in transcription by Julian Bream, became popular with modern guitarists; it is an ironic twist of musical destiny that Corbetta's guitar music has been neglected and transcriptions from clavichord or harpsichord works have been heard more frequently. Segovia set a precedent here with transcriptions early on in his career from the works of Frescobaldi (1583-1644) and Kuhnau (1660-1722).

Though Corbetta's work has been edited and published this century, only Alirio Diaz, so far, among the great performers has deemed Corbetta worthy of being played in recitals, and even then it remains a very limited selection. Corbetta may have charmed his contemporaries but he has not captivated later generations.

Corbetta died in 1681. An epitaph was printed in *Mercure* of Paris in August of that year which expresses the profound respect and affection inspired by Corbetta and his guitar:

> Ci g'it l'Amphion de nos jours,
> Francisque cet homme si rare
> Qui fit parler à la guitare
> Le vrai langage des amours.
> Il gagna par son harmonie
> Le coeur des princes et des rois,
> Et plusieurs ont cru qu'un genie
> Prenait le soin de conduire ses doigts.
> Passant, si tu n'as pas entendu ses merveilles,
> Apprends qu'il ne devait jamais finir son sort,
> Et qu'il aurait charmé la mort.
> Mais, hélas! par malheur, elle n'a point d'oreilles.

(This was the Amphion of our days, Francesco, that extraordinary man, who made the guitar speak the true language of love. By his harmony he won the heart of princes and kings, and some believed that a spirit took care to guide his fingers. As you pass by, if you have not heard his miracles, understand that he would never have met his fate and would have charmed death itself, but, alas, unhappily, death has no ears.)

By this estimation, even allowing for the natural hyperbole of an epitaph, Corbetta should be considered as one of the greatest practitioners of fretted instruments, ranking with Milán, Narváez, Mudarra, Dowland and Weiss, in the great tradition of players who conquered the royal courts of Europe with their expressive mastery of plucked strings. In the highly competitive musical environment of the seventeenth century Corbetta was considered a true maestro, holding his own with keyboard players, lutanists and composers of the stature of Lully.

Corbetta's musical style, and its apparent lack of appeal for modern players, is perhaps due to the fact that he was clearly a surpreme player and less gifted as a composer. His work lacks the strong imprint of personality that marks the compositions of Dowland, Weiss or even Milán, yet as a performer his impact seems to have been as considerable as theirs.

The style of the Baroque guitar recalls the consononcias and redobles of the vihuela tradition. The basic and most primitive concept of guitar playing is to strum a chord; the more advanced player is adept at uniting chordal textures with smoothly running melodic passages in more complex musical patterns. Corbetta, throughout his career, experimented with the possibilities of the instrument, a process well represented in the types of tablature he used to notate his compositions.

At first he preferred an alfabeto kind of tablature in which the chords are set out by employing letters of the alphabet. This produces an emphasis on the rasgueado type of playing. Later on Corbetta mixed the alfabeto with single notes indicated by numbers until finally he adopted French tablature in which letters indicate where the notes should be played. All the Baroque instrumentalists were in the habit of embellishing their notation in actual performance with the ornate filigree and encrustations of mordents, trills, acciaccaturas etc.

The seventeenth century taste for an extravagant labyrinth of ornamentation seems insatiable. As Thurston Dart remarks, 'The ornaments which seem fussy on paper gave the greatest delight at the time they were written.'

Modern performers of the guitar tend in their playing to make ornamentation lose its spontaneity. The clusters of extra notes are carefully practised and their precision often draws an adverse attention to details so that the wood cannot be seen for the trees. One would expect the tight-rope improvisation of the Baroque player to be part of the suspense and the miracle of his playing. Today it is in jazz that the ornamented note still bears its weight of unpredictability. Guitarists who play Baroque music study the subject of decoration carefully (though not always carefully enough) and whilst applying most of the rules lack the essential spirit appropriate to the lost tradition. The modern players of the lute have attempted in their playing to recapture the nature of creating their own divisions, graces and sense of freedom with the instrument; in this area the guitarist has lagged behind.

Corbetta's music suffers more than most from the need for a thorough awareness of seventeenth century practical musicianship, and the timbre and resonance of the modern guitar does not serve the music particularly well. Small wonder then that not a few players have brought reproduction Baroque guitars into the concert hall in an attempt to do a higher justice to the five-course guitar's special nature.

On the other hand guitarists have usually entered the French tradition of the Baroque instrument by way of Corbetta's pupil, Robert de Visée (1660-1720). His publications which appeared in 1682, 1686 (two books of guitar works), 1689, and 1716 (lute and theorbo) offer an ample variety of 'suites' containing prelude, allemande, courante, sarabande and gigue, with other movements such as gavotte, bourrée, minuet, chaconne and passacaille.

Robert de Visée seems to have possessed a gift for lively melodic inventiveness and perhaps for this reason modern players have found his suites particularly useful for their recitals. Segovia popularised the Suite in D minor and various assorted dances in concerts and recordings, and Julian Bream recorded this Suite in 1966 on an album entitled *Baroque Guitar*.

De Visée's compositions are usually rendered less alien, less historical, and more familiar when parted from the customary Baroque timbres and transplanted on the single strings of the modern instrument. His guitar was tuned, like that of Corbetta, as follows:

5. *Two Ladies of the Lake Family* by Sir Peter Lely (1618–1680): the elegantly curved left hand and the relaxed right hand would seem to denote a true player of the guitar. Courtesy of the Tate Gallery,

One would expect a certain flexibility in the matter of tuning, just as nowadays guitarists employ scordatura or altered tuning to suit the varying needs of individual compositions. But the basic difference in timbre between the Baroque instrument and the modern guitar remains considerable. Even if the seventeenth century players had employed exactly the same tuning as later six string guitarists, there would be as big a distance between the two as there is between grand piano and harpsichord. The octaves between two strings of the same course is a crucial determining factor in the characteristic Baroque sound, just as it is with lute textures.

The notes of the tablature reveal a specific kind of musical imagination, adjusted to the needs of the instrument played and not to the rich tone colours of twentieth century players. The six string guitar exploits its greater range and transfers appropriate melodic passages to achieve maximum sonorities with the shorter string length in the higher positions where a lusher vibrato can be achieved. Often, too, the inclusion of extra basses support the melody line. Thus both treble and bass are suitably modified to achieve almost a new hybrid composition.

Here is an example of de Visée's tablature and its reduction to staff notation:

Prelude by Robert de Visée

So the music of de Visée has reached a wide audience and many amateur guitarists enjoy playing the various published transcriptions. Only slowly have guitarists appreciated that the medium is indeed the message and that the Baroque guitar tradition is further from the modern instrument than, for example, the harpsichord sonatas of Scarlatti (those that are amenable to transcription). Corbetta's music, by not being played, has thus remained obscure but uncorrupted. Guitarists of today, where they have touched the seventeenth century music, have shaped the delicacy of its voices for their own effects, and in so doing have lost the soul of its expression. The music has become bigger, less idiosyncratically textured without the double stringing and the peculiarities of Baroque tuning, and the strange otherness of the Baroque guitar has been moulded into a spurious familiarity that is not native to the composers of that period.

The same process of distortion has been applied to the Spanish Baroque of Gaspar Sanz. His *Instrucción de Música sobre la Guitarra Española* (Zaragoza, 1674) ran through eight editions up till 1697. In this vital text Sanz enters consciously into the five course tradition and cites his illustrious predeccessors, composers such as Pellegrini, Kapsberger, Granata and Corbetta (whom he regarded as the 'best of all').

The music of Sanz takes its strength more from the folk elements of the Spanish guitar than from the more rarified atmosphere of the French court. His españoletas, gallardas, caprichos, corrientes, gigas, pavanas and canarios are quite simply composed, yet are intrinsically energetic with powerful rhythms and attractive melodic impulses.

Joaquín Rodrigo (b. 1901) included many of Sanz's dances in his Fantasia para un Gentilhombre (1954) for guitar and orchestra, dedicated to Andrés Segovia. Later Narciso Yepes played a collection of these pieces in his solo recitals (including them in his London debut in 1961) and later published them under the title of Suite Española. A version of Folias, Españoleta, Marizapolos and Canarios, by Regino Sainz de la Maza published in 1963 also proved popular among recording artists. Emilio Pujol had performed various works by Sanz since at least the 1920's and eventually published editions of about twenty pieces.

Of the many editions, Pujol's was the closest to the tablature. Guitarists liked to thicken the textures, expand the range, and make the music appropriate to the more powerful demands of the modern guitar. The Spanish performer and musicologist Rodrigo de Zayas complained about the treatment of Sanz by players and asked for a return to an awareness of the original tablature. Once more guitarists had shown themselves to be more interested in the voice of their instrument than in a realistic and truthful approach to the documents of the past. This ensured the wide dissemination of the music of Sanz even though in some instances he might not have recognised his own music in its new clothes. Critics of guitar recitals have often complained about the banality of Sanz, but audiences and players have taken a warm interest in what he has to offer, though usually on their terms rather than the composer's.

Here is an example of Sanz's music in tablature and notation. A twentieth century arranger of many of the dances of Sanz would feel it necessary to strengthen the simple gaiety of the five course guitar by a more full-blooded use of the tonal resources of the modern guitar. The sweet strumming of the seventeenth century and its vigorous picado would be subjected to quite different timbres, levels of attack, degrees of sonorities, tone colours and dynamic shading. The result may be a gain in clarity, power and even precision, but it discards the resonances, overtones and colourings which gave the original work its authenticity and flavour.

In this process of 'transcription', the following Canarios is usually less metamorphosed than many other dances as it contains its own vitality which accords well with the temperament of the six string guitar.

How far can a guitarist interfere with the legacy of the past to mould its music to suit his present purpose? This question, once considered of no particular importance, now dominates the work of thoughtful and considerate musicians of all instruments. The guitarist, by tampering with Baroque music, brings its composers and players to life before twentieth century audiences; yet what is resurrected is not the actual sound of the past, but a distorted version. So long as the audience is made aware that the work presented is an

adaptation, perhaps no harm is done. But the historical awareness
that has grown over the last twenty years among both scholars and
laymen alike means that for an artist to counterfeit the past's
experience is to demean both his own integrity and that of the
instrument he plays.

This problem is particularly acute with the Baroque five-course
tradition. Guitarists should enter this region of music with the
respect it deserves, taking no edition entirely on trust, returning to
original tablatures and ur-texts, and making it their duty to follow
the latest lines of scholarship. The excavation of the past, whether
archaeological or musical, enriches understanding; the false
experience of historical reality helps no one in any of the arts,
whether performer or public.

The Utopian idealism of the purists may on occasion seem tedious.
It is always easy to be sloppy and unscrupulous about the demands of
the past on the present situation. There is even the possibility of a
happy compromise between pedantic scholarship and artistic
performance. What is certain is that guitarists have tended to be less
careful than many other instrumentalists in their editing of early
music. This situation is however beginning to change as the public
learns that what the composer actually wrote may be far more
exciting than the bogus 'improvements' of musicians living several
centuries later. The music critics, with their capacity and instinct for
seeking out the truth, even if artists may feel their manner of
expression is clumsy, have been quite right to feel uncomfortable at
the dramatic renderings of Sanz' music which have often entranced
audiences of amateur guitarists; the soul of Sanz is often elsewhere in
a different, firmer tradition of his people's voice than the exhibitionism
which so frequently ruins his music nowadays.

The music of Sanz with its danza de la hachas, folias, villanos, la
Minoña de Cataluña, gallardas, etc., does capture the imagination.
The titles alone enable us to enter a sparkling world of innocent
vitality, expressive music making and the lost vision of the Spanish
Baroque folk culture. This is indeed quite different from the elegant
courts of Europe and reflects the change in Spanish music since the
vihuelistas. The colour and the brilliance glitter like diamonds in the
music of Sanz; our only problem is how to cut and mount that
particular type of diamond in order to show it in its true splendour.

There are many other names in the tradition of the Baroque guitar
that deserve mention. Apart from the nomadic progress of Corbetta
around the various courts, the best known Italian guitarist of the late
seventeenth century is Ludovico Roncalli; his *Capricci Armonici*

sopra la Chitarra Spagnuola was published in 1692, and the nine suites contained in the book show an ideal union of the melodic punteado and the rasgueado. Roncalli uses the alfabeto and the designation of notes by numbers together, a useful mutation of tablature to synthesise the redobles and consonancias of the old fretted instrument traditions.

His suites include preludios, alemandas, correntes, sarabandas and giguas, and also gavottas and minuets, as well as an exquisite passacaglia. The latter was recorded by Segovia along with a gavotta and gigua, a somewhat restricted selection from such a wide range of choice. Roncalli's music continues the Italian vein of melodic inventiveness and ease, which runs right through the history of the guitar from Melchiore de Barberiis' *Opera Intitolato Contina* (1549) for four-course guitar through the five-course work of Granata, Pellegrini, Foscarini and Calvi, down to the compositions of Carcassi, Carulli and the great Giuliani. This Italian love of the guitar has continued in our own century with the work of Castelnuovo-Tedesco. An innate lyricism pervades all the music composed by the many Italian admirers of fretted instruments.

Here is the tablature and notation of the prelude from Roncalli's first Suite of Capricci Armonici. The texture of the music is elegantly cluttered with a truly Baroque intricacy:

Roncalli has a small but secure niche in the pantheon of those Baroque maestros who are still performed today for better or for worse. Many other ghosts haunt the five-course guitar, names that do not possess the aura of genius but whose publications display on the page abundant talent and a fervent enthusiasm for the instrument.

Of these Giovanni Battista Granata is the most prolific and (considering his immense output) the most unfortunately neglected. He published seven books between 1646 and 1684, including chamber works, all published in Bologna, Italy. His fourth book contains no less than sixty-nine compositions. Except for the indefatigable Pujol, none of Granata's works seems to have been taken up by the leading players. His books were as follows:– *Capricci Armonici* (1646), *Nuove Suonate* (undated), *Nuova Scielta di capricci armonici* (1651), *Soavi Concenti de Sonate Musicali* (1659), *Capricci Armonici Musicali* (1674), *Nuovi Soavi concenti de sonate musicali* (1680), *Armoniosi Toni di varie Suonate musicali* (1684). Although these span the salad days of the Baroque guitar they seem doomed to silence.

Obscurity shrouds so many others including Carlo Calvi, Eoscarini, Pellegrini, the Spanish Francisco Guerau and Orazio Clementi, amongst others. In musicological research they have their place among the debris of footnotes and the scratchings of scholars. Their music remains the silent tradition of the secondary composers who in their day enthralled their contemporaries. Even the greatest Baroque names of the guitar such as Corbetta, de Visée and Sanz do not loom large in the mainstream histories of seventeeth century music.

The line of succession slowly dissolves in the eighteenth century. In Spain only Santiago de Murcia's *Resumen de Acompañar la Parte con la Guitarra* (1714) offers a consolidation of the glories of Gaspar Sanz. Segovia's advocacy of his Prelude and Allegro (in Pujol's version) brought him briefly to life but his suites, though published, languish as the final heart-beats of the five-course tradition.

The guitar flourished in the Baroque era. Its voice was heard in many contexts, yet the appeal of its music is the most strangely muted part of the repertoire, neglected for the most part, and when performed it is subjected to some crude manipulations which more often than not destroy its spirit. After the Baroque vitality the guitar entered a dark age where once again it survived and emerged, transformed by three metamorphoses of significance. A sixth string was added, the tablature changed to notation, and the double strung courses of the antique instrument changed to the single stringing characteristic of the guitar as we know it. Thus the Baroque tradition was pushed further back not only by the passing of time, but by real changes in the nature of the guitar. The full richness of the five-course guitar is perhaps the least appreciated of all the many strands of the instrument's history.

8. Guitarists and their Repertoire: 1685 to 1750

I therefore declare that my pieces ought to be played exactly as I have marked them, with no additions or omissions; for otherwise they will never make their proper impression on persons of good taste.

Louis Couperin (1722)

The recital programmes of Andrés Segovia present a curious patchwork of transcriptions and arrangements when one considers the music he performed from the seventeenth and eighteenth centuries. In this area of musical history the guitar's standing is tentative. His transcriptions came from keyboard sources (Frescobaldi, Scarlatti, Purcell, Handel, Kuhnau, Couperin, Rameau), five-course guitar (de Visée, Roncalli, Sanz, Murcia), Baroque lute, (Weiss, Bach) violin, (various pieces from J.S. Bach such as bourrées, gavottes and sarabandes), 'cello (Courante, Bourrée, Prelude from Bach's First and Third 'Cello suites), string quartets and symphonies (Haydn, Mozart) and in one instance a suite allegedly from Sylvius Leopold Weiss' lute works, but actually composed by Manuel Ponce, the leading twentieth century Mexican composer.

Segovia's plan of campaign was simply to provide the guitar with as many voices and textures as possible, establishing its universality within the stylistic guidelines he imposed on most of his repertoire. Thus he experimented with a wide variety of possibilities for the instrument, offering new perspectives from which the music of the Baroque and Classical eras could be appreciated, and significantly setting the guitar in a context of important European traditions.

The guitar was viewed as a miniature orchestra, full of tone colour and expressive potential which in recital offered a satisfying experience to world-wide audiences. 'Authenticity', as scholars later conceived the idea, hardly, if ever, entered the Segovian orbit of consideration. What he needed was a viable repertoire for the guitar, and he set out to provide it. Every musical treasure chest of every period was ransacked and appropriate booty extracted.

In the early part of the twentieth century when the public were less historically aware than they may be now that the market has been flooded with many types of music variously interpreted, Segovia could feel confident that he was doing justice to the music under his fingers.

In particular his readings of J.S. Bach became world famous and remained throughout his career as one of the public's favourite reference points in Segovia's programmes. Great artists such as Paul Tortelier, the French 'cellist, were not ashamed to admit that Segovia's approach to Bach revealed fresh interpretative possibilities. Segovia's rendering of Bach actually owed much to the example of string players, and he played those few pieces he selected from their repertoire for his own instrument with their kind of phrasing and sense of freedom; exquisite vibrato would be enticed from some notes, others would race ahead unpredictably and even more notes would savour a subtle rubato and changes in accent and rhythm, inimitable and amazing.

The lack of bowed sonorities in the guitar's melodic line involved the addition of various bass notes to thicken the texture. All this was done in a fiercely individual way, and throughout his career Segovia clung to his ideals, yielding neither to fashion nor to academic dictates but charming audiences with the fruits of interpretation yielded by a lifetime's concert work.

His manner of presenting Bach was to select isolated movements which appealed to him. He did not play complete suites to his audiences and ignored the expansive areas of the lute suites, preferring to pick and choose with tremendous selectivity and deliberation. His greatest assault on the Bachian citadel was his monumental transcription of the Chaconne.

The transcription of the Chaconne (Schott, London, 1934) set new standards for the guitarist's art. It showed that a guitar recital could deal with one of the eighteenth century masterpieces with true seriousness. A precedent was also established for subsequent performers, who would henceforth be measured by this yard-stick, both musical and technical; newcomers to the arena of guitar ascendancy would have to attain a high standard in Bach's Chaconne before their credentials could be accepted.

Opposition was mounted in some circles to Segovia's abduction of this central jewel of the violinist's repertoire, but the perfection of his playing won over the public of the 1920's privileged to hear the maestro's first performances of this work. After Segovia's Chaconne the guitar would never be the same again. The disadvantages of the guitar when confronting violin solos were usually ignored by audiences, especially as many amateur guitarists had never heard the Chaconne in any other setting and did not particularly want to. They preferred the guitar's trick of smoothing out the angularities of the Chaconne's tortuously intense arpeggios and replacing the biting rasp of the bowed attack with a more mellifluous, less dramatic blandness.

As we have seen in the previous chapter Segovia did not play very much music written by the eminent Baroque guitarists. He preferred to concentrate his attention on compositions which could immediately yield the romantic richness of the guitar's sonorities and many of the Baroque works for the five-course lack the sensuous appeal of Bach as transmuted through the Spanish voice of Segovia's guitar.

The possibilities of the Baroque lute had no appeal either for Segovia's purposes. He unearthed a few items by Sylvius Leopold Weiss, including the remarkable Tombeau pour Monsieur le Comte de Logy, as well as an occasional Minuet of rather less staying power. The lute works of Bach yielded a few items for his use, including some movements from the First and Third Lute Suites, but on the whole he preferred the process of transcribing from violin music.

It is ironic that one of the few suites Segovia played in its entirety was fake Baroque, attributed to Weiss but actually written by Manuel Ponce. This Kreisler-like joke did not really help the guitar; even recently records have been issued attributing Ponce's pastiche to Weiss. Segovia's advocacy of this suite also exposed the shallow and opportunist nature of many editors of guitar music. Several versions of the suite were published (though never by Segovia) claiming to be transcriptions from the tablature of the eighteenth century. Counterfeit money may look attractive but in the end threatens the credibility of genuine currency. In this instance the same may apply to music; however, a by-product of Ponce's Suite Clásica was to encourage further interest in the work of the unknown Weiss, with the establishment eventually of a useful selection of Baroque lute works suitably transcribed for guitar.

As we shall see in later chapters, many of the transcriptions associated with Segovia's recitals were originally taken from versions by the nineteenth century guitarist, Francisco Tárrega. He initiated the tradition of adapting works from other instruments for recital purposes and found refuge from the usual material for guitar in the works of Bach, Haydn, Handel, Mozart, Beethoven, Chopin,

Mendelssohn and many others.

Segovia increased the number of available Bach items for guitarists and transcribed works by Purcell, Frescobaldi, Scarlatti and Rameau. Ralph Kirkpatrick in his great book *Domenico Scarlatti* remarks:

> As far as we know, Scarlatti never played the guitar, but surely no composer ever fell more deeply under its spell . . . Some of Scarlatti's wildest dissonances seem to imitate the sound of the hand striking the belly of the guitar, or the savage chords that at times almost threaten to rip the strings from the instrument. The very harmonic structure of many such passages that imitate the guitar seems to be determined by the guitar's open strings and by its propensities for modal Spanish folk music.

Scarlatti's link with the guitar was aptly sealed by Segovia's arrangements of several sonatas which sounded as if they had indeed returned to the source of their natural inspiration. He also borrowed from Frescobaldi's keyboard writings the Aria detta Frescobalda from the composer's second volume of 1624 (*Il Secondo Libro di Toccate, Canzoni, Versi d'Hinni, Magnificat, Gagliarde, Correnti et altre Partite d'Intavolatura di Cembalo et Organo*). This work became solidly established in the guitar repertoire often as a suitable opening gambit for a recital. Segovia also played a few more pieces from Frescobaldi including three correntes, a gagliarda and a remarkable Passacaglia, though these pieces (Schott, London, 1939) did not achieve the universal popularity of La Frescobalda.

Segovia's emphasis therefore, as far as the seventeenth century is concerned, lay in suitably appropriate keyboard textures, which seem to have attracted him far more than the compositions for five-course guitar. He continued this pattern by transcribing a suite by Kuhnau, minuets by Rameau, various pieces by Purcell, as well as further keyboard pieces, including a number from the eighteenth century, by Handel, Bach (from *Anna Magdalena's Notebook*), Vanhal, Schale, Benda, Couperin and Wenkel. Most of these were published by Schott in the 1930's and illustrate how Segovia's concept of the guitar made good use of intimate, often obscure, keyboard compositions.

His use of the Baroque and Classical repertoire was in essence small-scale. All these items tended to delight rather than move, and even the works of Bach (with the resonant exception of the Chaconne) skimmed the cream off the top rather than analysing the profoundest depths of Bach's genius. Again following Tárrega's precedent, he adapted the violin version of Bach's A minor Fugue (BWV 1000) and published Prelude and Fugue in D (BWV 998:

6. *The Guitar Player* by J. van Schuppen: the animated dancing of the girl, and the lute on the table, as well as the player's excellent hand positions, show evidence of skill and enthusiasm. Courtesy of the Walker Art Gallery, Liverpool.

Schott, London, 1935) which, with the inclusion of its proper
Allegro, later became one of the great warhorses of recitalists, though
Segovia never recorded this work. Segovia did, however, lay the
foundations of a workable repertoire and also prepared the way for
considerable changes in the structure of guitar recitals by his practical
demonstration of how the guitar could successfully involve itself in
areas of music not specifically created for it, and yet not at all alien.

Segovia's recitals tended to offer clusters of brilliant miniatures in the
first half of the programme. Complete suites were played only if they
were not too extended. La Frescobalda is an early example of a suite
as its variations included a galliard, an allemande and a courante
(which Segovia for some reason omitted), but its structure is still
that of an unpretentious piece of private music making.

Groups of dances by Bach, de Visée, Handel and Purcell preserved
this sense of contrast and variety, as the soloist moved quickly from
one mood to another in works not organically related within
spacious musical forms.

Later guitarists found the need to incorporate more substantial
pieces in the first half of their programme, providing for their
audiences not only complete lute suites by Bach, but often two suites
and a Prelude and Fugue.

The early twentieth century had not encouraged the complete
performance of a suite by J.S. Bach. In his autobiography, *Joys and
Sorrows*, Pablo Casals explains the prevailing fashion of the day in a
description of his discovery of Bach's 'cello suites, when he was
thirteen years old:

> These became my most cherished music. I studied and worked at
> them every day for the next twelve years. Yes, twelve years would
> elapse and I would be twenty-five before I had the courage to play one
> of the suites in public at a concert. Up until then no violinist or cellist
> ever played one of the Bach suites in its entirety. They would play just a
> single section, a Sarabande, a Gavotte or a Minuet. But I played them as
> a whole; from the Prelude through the five dance movements, with all
> the repeats that give the wonderful entity and pacing and structure of
> every movement, the full architecture and artistry.

Thus the world had to wait until 1901 before a musician performed
a whole Bach suite in public. This was the musical environment in
which Segovia developed, a tradition to which he remained constant
in his own recitals. His public expected varied diversion and not the
deployment of large aesthetic and intellectual forms, although this
does not seem to have applied to piano recitals or symphony concerts.

It has been said that Agustín Barrios (1885-1944) was the first guitarist to play an entire lute suite by Bach in his concerts; he was also the first to make records. Between 1915 and 1927 Barrios recorded over fifty pieces, though among them we find only the isolated work by Bach, most of the playing being devoted to the Paraguayan guitarist's own compositions. It is also apparently impossible to locate anybody who actually heard Barrios play either a complete lute suite or attended one of his recitals, though his records reveal that for him no flights of technique were impossible.

Apart from his claims however, it is not clear who really pioneered the inclusion of entire Bach suites in classical guitar recitals until the late 1950's. The first complete recording of a suite was scooped by the seventeen year old John Williams in his first album (recorded December, 1958) when John W. Duarte's transcription of the First and Third 'Cello Suites made a brilliant start to Williams' recording career.

John Williams' Wigmore Hall, London, debut on 6 November 1958 reflected the usual views of that time about the make-up of a programme. The Baroque and Classical part of the recital included three pieces by Bach (Prelude, Allemande and Bourrée), the notorious fake 'Weiss' by Manuel Ponce, a Gavotte allegedly composed by Alessandro Scarlatti (also, alas, composed by Ponce) and a single Gallardas by Gaspar Sanz. This continued the inherited tradition that the voice of the guitar mattered more than the song itself, a regime which Williams later repudiated in no uncertain terms.

In 1961, Andrés Segovia also recorded Duarte's transcription of the Third 'Cello Suite, though there is no account of his ever performing this suite in its entirety in a recital. In 1968 Alirio Diaz recorded the same transcription and frequently played the suite in his concerts throughout the 1960's and 1970's.

Julian Bream began playing complete Bach lute suites from the outset of his performing career in the mid 1950's. The remarkable pioneering nature of this achievement went almost unnoticed at the time though his excelling talent did not. In 1966 Bream became the first to record Lute Suites Nos. 1 and 2, a decade or so since he first introduced them to his international audiences.

Bream continued the Segovian tradition of transcribing Scarlatti's sonatas for the guitar by recording not only L. 352, but also L. 33 (in his own version). The guitar's traditional affinities with Baroque keyboard textures were enhanced by Bream's transcriptions of Cimarosa, Froberger, Buxtehude and Purcell.

Prior to this systematic expansion of the guitar's horizons however Bream won his spurs with a remarkable recording of an all-Bach album, (including the Chaconne, Prelude, Fugue and Allegro and Prelude and Fugue from the Second Lute Suite), which established his immediate claim as a worthy successor to Segovia.

Bream embarked on a musical pilgrimage which in depth and feeling rivalled that of Segovia. His playing of a suite for Baroque lute by Carl Kohaut (c.1780), and some elegant Mozart transcriptions, coincided in the 1960's with a fine advocacy of various works by Weiss including the Tombeau pour Monsieur le Comte de Logy, Fantasia (both previously recorded by Segovia) and a Passacaille of Bach-like magnificence. Bream steered well clear of the counterfeit Baroqueiana of Ponce, though his playing of de Visée's Suite in D minor followed very closely the adaptation and consequent distorted sweetening of the Segovian tradition in respect of five-course guitar music.

John Williams' contribution to our understanding and appreciation of seventeenth and eighteenth century music soon equalled that of his two illustrious companions of honour. He introduced an all-Bach recital in the 1960's and later (following on the heels of Narciso Yepes who managed to get there first and record all of Bach's lute works on both Baroque lute and guitar) issued his own complete recording of Bach's lute compositions in 1975.

Williams introduced into his recitals a considerable number of Baroque works that had not been heard before including more suites by de Visée (and not just the hackneyed and inaccurate D minor adaptation), pieces by Esaias Reusner (1636-1679, a Baroque lutanist who published Delitiae Testudinis in 1667 which included several suites) and the familiar arrangement of Sanz' Canarios.

He also played a brilliant range of Renaissance music on the guitar, an area which Julian Bream preferred to deliver through the medium of the lute. Williams' renderings of Narváez, Mudarra and (in the early days) Milán, were later displaced in his concerts by a preference for a transcription of various dances from Praetorius' Terpsichore. All these were played with the remarkabe fluent virtuosity which makes Williams perhaps the greatest technical phenomenon in the guitar's history.

The small circle of international guitarists of the 1960's remained fascinated by the Baroque era. Alirio Diaz championed the four Sanz dances arranged by Sainz de la Maza, introduced the suites of Corbetta to his adoring public, and persisted in performing Ponce's Suite Clásica under its true colours.

Narciso Yepes brought to his 1961 London debut a collection of Sanz dances which broadened the perspectives of Sanz' work, as well as being one of the first to play Mudarra's Fantasia X and the music of

Adrien Le Roy. With his ten string guitar, a significant mutation of its six string relative, Yepes felt better equipped to play the Baroque lute music of Weiss and Bach and thus became the first guitarist to record a Weiss suite.

In this way the canvas of Baroque music has been steadily expanded by the united efforts of many guitarists. There have also been other developments which have yielded significant results in the production of a wider range of material. Among these are the extension by John Williams and Carlos Barbosa-Lima of the number of Scarlatti sonatas playable on the guitar; the transcription by Alexander Bellow of a suite by the eighteenth century lutanist Ernst Theophil Baron (1696-1760); Karl Scheit's edition of a Partita by Johann Anton Logy, or Losy (c.1643-1721), a transcription published as early as 1952 by Universal Edition though it has not received many performances until recent years, and many other indications of a growing awareness of the Baroque treasure-house of music.

The guitarist's repertoire has thus developed in volume, in seriousness and in discrimination. A development which has been accompanied by a great interest in tablatures and Baroque musical techniques. The arc of possibility is very wide and guitarists have thus contributed to keeping this music alive and well.

In practical terms much of the music transcribed onto the guitar is still rather a compromise, caught somewhere between the Segovian licence to use music of previous ages according to the player's own needs and the scholarly purity of researchers whose earnest endeavours have at last begun to make a real impact both on the quality of edited material, and, more important still, on the attitudes of players.

As time goes by and research deepens our response to the music of the past, it becomes less easy, though not impossible, to perform Baroque music on the guitar in a cavalier or slipshod manner. Audiences have now been exposed to a wide range of lute, clavichord, harpsichord, and early piano textures, as well as much medieval and Renaissance music, in concerts and on record. Guitarists have constantly to evaluate their response to the repertoire of various periods in a hitherto unaccustomed manner. The process of self-analysis is sometimes quite painful as players discover the cost of doing the highest possible justice to the priceless legacy of great musical cultures of the past.

Segovia's ambition was to do justice, first and foremost, to the guitar itself, and to enable it to be respected as a suitable musical medium which could range at will over the entire span of European music since 1535. Now that the validity of the guitar in serious music has been irrefutably consolidated, guitarists can use their creative energies to ensure that enthusiasm for their chosen instrument does not distort the essential requirements of Renaissance, Baroque and Classical interpretative principles. It is increasingly recognised that transcription onto modern types of instrument may be difficult; just as the delicate precision of a Purcell lesson or a Rameau suite can be overwhelmed and submerged by the grandeurs of a Steinway grand piano, so the twentieth century guitar will, in the wrong hands, clumsily abuse the spirit of Baroque and Classical music.

At the same time as reservations are expressed, it should be acknowledged that the guitarist's determination to seek out suitable material for his own performance has brought into the concert hall many valuable compositions that would otherwise have remained dormant or merely of academic interest. Without the classical guitar, it seems unlikely that twentieth century audiences would have enjoyed the opportunity to come to grips with Bach's lute works or the less well-known composers such as Sanz, de Visée, Weiss, Baron and many others whose work is undoubtedly worthwhile even if it does not reach the summit of Parnassus.

Segovia's influence in extending and refining our awareness of the music of many obscure backwaters continues and his distinguished disciples have continued to follow his tradition. From the player's curiosity about a suitable recital repertoire emerge profound lines of research and a deeper understanding of the demands of musical performance in the various strands of the fretted instrument legacy. Through the living example of the great guitarists' interpretations in concerts and recordings, amateur players now feel that the Renaissance and Baroque periods have great musical experiences to offer. By means of the guitar, rightly or wrongly, many feel they have achieved a true link with earlier musical activities characteristic of the sixteenth century onwards. Thus, in a very direct way, the twentieth century guitar has contributed immeasurably to a real understanding and enjoyment of hitherto unexplored music.

9. The Extinction of the Lute

The woes of hopeless lovers,
Whose dirge is whisper'd by the warbling lute.

Dryden: *A Song for St. Cecilia's Day, 1687*

Before the guitar could flourish as the instrument we now know, its sister, the lute, had to suffer a slow extinction. Phoenix-like, the lute rose eventually from the forgotten ashes of its great repertoire, but after the eighteenth century it was no longer an instrument which attracted composers.

The lute's decline is a melancholy fact of musical history. Its rebirth in the twentieth century is a good indication that humanity will not let something of value disappear for ever; even if the period of oblivion lasts for centuries the sleeping princess can still be brought back to life with the kiss of love.

Throughout the long reign of its popularity the lute indeed inspired tremendous devotion. By comparison with the lute, the guitar was the despised relative, subject to fits and starts, small coteries and musical cul-de-sacs. The lute was the domain of composer-performers of genius whose ability commanded high salaries from the royal courts of Europe, a supremacy rarely challenged by the appearance of the equivalent guitar virtuosi. Occasionally the lute was temporarily ousted from popular appeal, and in Spain the guitar ruled triumphant, but in most musical contexts the hierarchical superiority of the lute was unquestioned.

The first lute books of printed music appeared in Venice (1507-8), published by Petrucci. Following Joan Ambrosius Dalza's *Intabulatura de Lauto* (1508) dozens of lutanists and published books bear witness to the crowded greatness of the lute tradition. The roll-call of fine players includes Francesco de Milano, Valentin Bakfark, Periono Fiorentino, Antonio Castelione, Vincenzo Galilei, Giulio Cesare Barbetta, Gastoldi, Giovanni Terzi, Simone Molinaro, Cesare Negri and many, many more.

The English lute tradition culminated in the genius of John Dowland, but also produced Philip Rosseter, Francis Cutting, John Johnson, Thomas Robinson, Robert Dowland and the lute arrangements of William Byrd. The Renaissance instructional texts are superb examples of the enthusiasm of fretted instrument players, encouraging and guiding with that piquancy of expression which is associated with the Elizabethan use of language. We hear in the words of these books the tone of voice of a teacher speaking in caring terms to a beloved student, quite unlike the more objective and scientific pedagogy of later methods:

> Take therefore this worke of mine in good part, whosoever thou art that readest it, with a minde to profit thyselfe: yet thinke not I set it forth to the end to draw thee away from the lively teaching of thy Maister, (whose speach doth farre exceede all writing,) or presume to teach those which are Maisters in the ART these triviall wayes, but I offer helpe to young beginners, and such as oftentimes want a Teacher. . . . I would with all my heart have given thee the habit and power to play well, rather than the meanes of learning to play, if it were possible to be had without labour.

> Jean Baptiste Besard: *Varietie of Lute Lessons*, 1610

Like guitarists of later ages, lutanists found it necessary to defend the purity of the legacy, driving out heretical notions and making it clear to the student what was not acceptable in the great tradition:

> . . . for in older times they strouve (onelie) to have a quick hand upon the Lute, to runne hurrie hurrie, keeping a Catt in the gutter upon the ground, now true then false, now up now downe, with such painfull play, mocking, mowing, gripeing, grinning, sighing, supping, heaving, shouldring, labouring, and sweating, like cart Jades, without any skill in the world, or rule, or reason to play a lesson, or finger the lute, or guide the bodie, or know anything that belongeth, either to skill or reason.

> Thomas Robinson: *The Schoole of Musicke*, 1603

Robinson tells the beginner how to hold the lute in terms which look forward to Fernando Sor's *Method for Spanish Guitar* (1830):

> First sitting upright with your bodie, leane the edge of the Lute against the table, and your bodie against the Lute. . .

> Thomas Robinson

> Yet in proportion as I have required more and more of the instrument, I have found it necessary to have it better fixed in its position, from which it should not deviate but when I wished. To effect this, I have found nothing better than to have before me a table, presenting one of its corners opposite the 12th fret, allowing me to rest

the point B of the instrument on the right knee. . . .

Fernando Sor

Another corresponding detail between the lute tradition of the Renaissance and the early nineteenth century guitar is in the instructions given by Robinson and Matteo Carcassi for the placing of the right hand; Carcassi here provides an unconscious link between guitar techniques of the nineteenth century and the age-old hand positions of the lutanists:

> Now for your right hand, called the striking hand leane upon the bellie of the Lute with your little finger onelie, & that, neither to far from the Treble strings. . . .

Robinson

The right forearm has to rest on the curve of the Guitar's upper side and over the sound board towards the bridge. The little finger, thrown a little backwards, has to rest lightly on the sound board near the first string at a little distance from the bridge.

Carcassi

Three centuries after Robinson, the guitar thus remained a prisoner of lute techniques. The implications of the guitar's freedom from this bondage will be discussed more fully in the chapter on the early nineteenth century guitarists. What must be stressed is that so often guitar technique in four-course, five-course and vihuela traditions, followed automatically the dictates of the lutanists; it was a principle which restrained the guitar from developing its own lines of technical enquiry till after the demise of the lute.

The lute's road to dusty death can be related to the fact that its development consisted in the addition of more and more strings. Dowland wrote for a six course lute to which could be added a seventh course (intended to be fretted) and three further basses. The precise steps by which the lute grew are of labyrinthine complexity. Vincenzo Galilei was sensibly opposed to the extra strings which in the second half of the sixteenth century appeared on a lute type known as the theorbo; this possessed between fourteen and sixteen courses.

Later the chitarrone, with its enormously extended string length and peg-box for more basses provided an instrument for use in ensembles and song accompaniments. But this instrument, too, made its first appearance in the sixteenth century.

The precise naming of the lute type becomes increasingly complicated as the seventeenth century progresses. One becomes rather

7. *Man with an Arch-Lute* attributed to Isaac Luttichuiss (1616-1673): this man has the appearance of an experienced player — with an instrument as complicated as this he would need to be. Courtesy of the Glasgow Art Gallery.

submerged in a plethora of théorbes, tiorbinos, liutos attiorbatos, archlutes, theorbo-lutes, the French lutes, German Baroque lutes and so on. What matters more than precise naming of sub-species is perhaps the fact that there was during this period an eminent tradition of virtuosi willing to subdue the lute with their mastery. Unfortunately it seems that the more they conquered the lute's enormous technical problems, the less competent an amateur would be even to begin lessons.

In the eighteenth century the lute's monstrous growth began to provoke grievances. The lute's historian, Ernst Gottlieb Baron in his · *Untersuchung des Instruments der Laute* (1727) quotes Johann Mattheson, one of the lute's most articulate critics:

> We pay twice for the best lute pieces for we have to hear the eternal tuning that goes with it. If a lutanist lives to be eighty years old surely he has spent sixty years tuning. The worst of it is that among a hundred (especially amateurs) scarcely two are capable of tuning accurately. In addition there is trouble with bad or spliced strings, especially the chanterelle, and trouble with frets and tuning pegs, so that I have heard that it costs as much in Paris to keep a lute as it does a horse.

Baron, in a gallant rear-guard action, which failed to secure the lute's ultimate survival, defends his cherished instrument, especially on the vulnerable point of tuning:

> The annoying and wearisome tuning is not all as Herr Mattheson has represented it. A master must be able to tune his instrument instantly while playing so that it is scarcely heard even when a peg has slipped. It also does not happen (except when an instrument has been newly strung and the strings have not yet been sufficiently stretched) that all the strings are out of tune when it is taken out of the case. That there are from time to time amateurs who cannot handle it very well is a flaw in their own nature, and this cannot detract from the instrument in the slightest, since there are few of these people. If something is wrong with a peg, it can be cheaply replaced in a day and will last another fifty to sixty years. . . . The expense of maintaining the lute with strings is not at all true, let alone so precarious. Thus I think that the Parisian horses, if someone tried to maintain them for a year with two thalers' worth of feed, would very shortly look like one of the seven scrawny, emaciated cows, that the pharoah saw in his dream. . . .

Baron's final verdict is that even where the lute's strings are made of inadequate material, or subject to inclement weather, 'the player must occasionally accept a small inconvenience for the sake of the greater good'.

The entire discussion is like two medical opinions over a dying patient, and Baron's defence is not entirely convincing. The attack on the lute centres on its lack of practicality and the underlying assumption that the amateur cannot come to grips with the instrument. Once grass-roots support for the lute was no longer possible, the instrument inevitably withered into neglect as musicians chose to devote their energies to the easier pursuits of the keyboard.

Baron's advocacy of his musical dodo is in sharp contrast to the girlish ardour of Miss Mary Burwell in her *Instruction Book for the Lute* (1668-1671?); she evokes the glorious tradition of 'vieux Gaultier':

> It is the first Gaultier (who is named, in regard of his age and his merit 'old' Gaultier) to which fortune, not so deaf as blind, hearkened and, through the liberality of kings, queens and other princes, crowned with honour and fulfilled with riches. . . He played of the lute before the king and queen (of England). Their majesties made him presents worthy of kings and of the king of the lute, and the late Duke of Buckingham (before whom he played also) in embracing of him made slide in his pocket five hundred pounds of gold, to stop him — as Atlanta did her sweetheart with the golden apples — some few days longer in the court of England with this precious burden.

Mary Burwell then provides the lute with one of its most eloquent tributes, as well as offering a little musicological history of her own:

> By this it is easy to see what vast capacities the lute hath, what abundance of music, what variety both of things and manners, of fashions of playing and composing, the lute being like an ocean that cannot be emptied but is full of so many riches that the more we take from it the more remains to take, and in such sort that all his beauties are different according to the genius of the lute master that composes our plays and dives in that spring of science and charms. It is easy to find by this discourse that the French are in possession of the lute, that it is their instrument, as the viol is the instrument of England, the guitar that of Spain, the theorbo that of Italy, the virginall or harpsichord that of Germany, the harp that of Ireland, and so of others according to the genius of each nation.

It was, apart from the problems of tuning, the 'genius of the lute master' which paradoxically brought about the end of the lute tradition. The lute's history ended with the work of Sylvius Leopold Weiss, a player to rival the virtuosity of Dowland or Gaultier. Baron describes him in these terms:

> He is the first to show that more could be done on the lute than was hitherto thought possible. . . In arpeggios he has an extraordinary full-voiced texture, in expressions of emotion he is incomparable, he has a stupendous technique, and unheard of delicacy and cantabile charm.

It is said that J.S. Bach travelled a long distance to hear Weiss perform, and might even have composed some lute works for him. Weiss (b. 1686, Breslau), the son of a lutanist, played at several European courts including the palace of the Palatine Prince of Dusseldorf, the court of Berlin, the coronation of Charles VI and the palace of the Polish monarch. He died in October, 1750, one of the last and greatest representatives of the lute's tradition.

It is gratifying that such a noble instrument as the lute should have expired through a surfeit of expressive complexity. Its swan-song is the music of Weiss, Bach and Baron, the zenith of its glory and not an inert decline into silence. After a suitable period of mild retreat, the guitar would emerge once more, rid at last of its glamorous courtly rival. By adding approximately one course every century, the guitar's evolution was appropriately gradual. The explosive disintegrating brilliance of the lute's last decades loaded the instrument with a destructive beauty.

The guitar was to be slowly liberated from the shackles of past similarities to the lute in timbre, repertoire, and technique. It would begin, slowly but effectively, to forge its own identity, shedding the double-strung courses, adding a sixth string, and finding players who did not have to choose between guitar or lute. Once its emancipation was complete, the guitar would even return, perhaps nostalgically, to the glorious music of the eighteenth century by J.S. Bach and others, which coincided with the lute's fall from grace. The extinction of the lute preceded the spring time of the classical guitar as we know it today.

PART TWO

THE SILVER AGE

10. The Six String Guitar

Acaso de una reja florida una guitarra triste
cantaba la súbita canción suspendida en el tiempo . . .

Vicente Aleixandre

In the eighteenth century all fretted instruments suffered a partial eclipse. The guitar certainly did not disappear from view but for a while it took leave of any higher musical destiny and became once more a fashionable toy mildly haunted by the ghosts of Corbetta and Sanz.

As we have seen, Scarlatti (1685-1757) was influenced by the guitar but never wrote for the instrument, another missed opportunity in the guitar's history. Watteau (1684-1721) as a painter of 'fêtes galantes' used the guitar in many of his pictures as an essential component in a world of make-believe and idealised nature:

> What exactly is a fête galante? . . . it is the new form that Watteau gave to mankind's abiding dream of a golden age, a refuge of happiness where time will pass in a perpetual carnival. Couples stroll and talk together; in the Gamme d'Amour (Gamut of Love) they sing or play the guitar; they dance; and above all, they just idle. Watteau has caught all the attitudes of relaxation, graceful detachment and nonchalance; the dresses with their folds broken over a knee or spread upon the ground; the poses that indicate whispered secrets, fond confessions, groundless anticipations and aimless departures.

Luc Benoist: *Handbook of Western Painting*

As mentioned before, it is not entirely uncomplimentary that the guitar's identity should be associated with Utopian ideals; languor and unreality, dream, romance, an escape from the mundane world — these qualities are part of a certain kind of poetry, and the guitar also belongs to the realm of the imagination in much of its repertoire. But this consignment of an instrument to the pastures of an ideal Paradise is accompanied by a decline in the strength of its musical existence. The guitar, despite the powerful associations with mystery

8. *La Gamme d'Amour* by Antoine Watteau (1684-1721): once more the playing posture denotes competence. Note how Baroque guitarists in these pictures play with the right hand well up beyond the sound hole. Courtesy of the National Gallery, London.

and love that the instrument possesses, deserves more than this, exquisite as Watteau's vision is.

Thus the eighteenth century seems in retrospect to becalm the guitar in the musical doldrums. And this phase of guitar history bears the same relationship to the intense activity of the early nineteenth century as the pastoral poetry of late eighteenth century England does to the great Romantic poetry of Wordsworth, Byron, Keats, Shelley and Coleridge. It is in some ways the lull before the storm, and yet the signs are there that out of this something could grow. Under the apparently placid surface there were definite currents, happenings, tidal pulls.

It is difficult in the early nineteenth century to chart the progress of the guitar by its publications. With the earlier traditions of vihuela, four-course, and five-course guitars, (and the lute), reference to the steady flow of instruction books points implicitly to the vigour of the heritage which gave birth to these texts. By the early nineteenth century the printing of music and tutors became an extensive industry showering a mass of material for all instruments, including the guitar, onto an enthusiastic public.

The eighteenth century guitar methods are few and obscure, rarely reprinted in modern editions and unknown to many guitarists of today. But a quiet process of evolution was taking place though its principal lines of development were not clear until the virtuosity of players such as Sor and Giuliani brought out the strengths and values of new ideas about guitar playing.

These few works published between 1750 and 1800 take on in retrospect a luminous significance akin to that of the early lute texts of the Renaissance from which dark tradition Dowland's genius emerged like a bright comet. Unlike the sixteenth century, however, no music of particular value was given to us by the eighteenth century guitarists. But like Juan Carlos Amat and the five-course guitar, influence on subsequent generations of players is not confined merely to writing excellent music. The humble pedagogues and theoreticians inaugurate lines of enquiry which more talented musicians can later utilise. These writers represent the foundations of musical thinking which inspired the virtuosi of the six string guitar in the era of Napoleon.

Mention has already been made of Santiago de Murcia's *Resumen de Acompañar la Parte con la Guitarra* (1726), a document in direct line of succession from Gaspar Sanz. François le Cocq's *Recueil de Pièces de Guitarre* included a tribute to the French five-course tradition by anthologising works by Corbetta and de Visée, as well as selections

from Granata and le Cocq's own compositions. Murcia, guitarist at
the court of Queen Maria Luisa Gabriela of Savoy, and le Cocq, a
violinist in the court orchestra at Brussels, represent some of the
ultimate examples of the Baroque guitar's survival in aristocratic
cultural circles.

The trail now becomes somewhat confused, indicating the decay
of former customs and the gradual emergence of the six stringed
instrument. Joseph Majer's *Neu-eröffneter Theoretischer und
Praktischer Music-Saal* (1741) makes a reference to a strangely tuned
six string guitar but this seems to bear little relevance to the
mainstream development.

Another instruction book, Pablo Minguet y Yrol's collection of
1752 included Spanish dances in the Sanz style and the beloved
Folias. Sanz also influenced the work of Andrés de Sotos, whose
book entitled *Arte para aprendar con facilidad, y sin maestro, a
templar, y tañer rasgado la Guitarra de cinco órdenes, o cuerdas; y
tambien la de quatro, or seis ordēnes, llamadas Guitarra Española,
Bandurria, y Vandola, y tambien el Tiple,* appeared in 1764 in
Madrid.

Michel Corrette's *Les Dons d'Apollon: Méthode pour apprendre
facilement à jouer de la Guitarre* (1763) is a milestone in the liberation
of the guitar from its private means of notation — the tablature.
Corrette included tablature and staff notation, with the remarkable
step of using the treble clef with the music written an octave higher
than actual pitch; the device proved to be of lasting benefit to the
guitar and its players.

The tyranny of the tablature, lasting from the early lute and vihuela
books up to 1763 had at last been smashed. There could be no
possibility of leading the guitar out of the prison of narrow preoccupations until it could share the same language of musical literacy as
other instruments. Instead of the eccentric and easily individualised
habits of tablature, a more objective system of notation would ensure
(after a suitable transitional period) that the guitar would move from
the small backroom of musical culture into environments where
many composers, and not just players, would exploit the timbres of
guitar sound.

This movement did not occur for another century and a quarter,
but at least the first step had been achieved. At this point the validity
of writing in a private language in which actual pitch and sound were
subordinated to the whims and peculiarities of tuning, instrument
type and player's awareness of a limited and localised tradition was
being severely questioned. Tablature now lost its intellectual
respectability; what was gained by the disappearance of tablature

infinitely outweighed what was lost in the light of the instrument's development from the late eighteenth century onwards.

Another French aficionado B. Vidal published a new method for the guitar, written for the use of amateurs (Paris, 1778), and also composed concertos for guitar with orchestra or string quartet, as well as various sonatas for guitar and violin and guitar and 'cello. These compositions, like his sonatas, variations and other works for solo guitar, have not been resurrected, but show the kind of direction in which the instrument was moving.

Antoine Bailleux's *Méthode de guitarre par musique et tablature* (2nd edition published 1773) and Pierre-Jean Baillon's *Nouvelle méthode de guitarre selon le sistème des meilleurs auteurs* (1781) are two more examples of the quickening tempo of guitar activity in Paris, which later became the central focus of so many guitar activities when Fernando Sor settled there.

A further sign of the increasing importance of the six string guitar is given by Antonio Ballesteros' *Obra para guitarra de seis órdenes* (1780). An even more significant text from Spain was *Principios para tocar la guitarra de seis órdenes* of Federico Moretti, published in Madrid in 1799. Moretti, a naturalised Spaniard but of Italian origin (born in Naples) influenced Sor and Aguado with his concepts of the guitar. In *Méthode pour Guitare* (1830, later translated by Alan Merrick, who also published an English version of Moretti's book), Sor writes in a footnote:

> At that time I had not heard of Mr. Frederic Moretti. I heard one of his accompaniments performed by a friend of his, and the progression of the bass, as well as the parts of the harmony which I distinguished, gave me a high idea of his merit. I considered him as the flambeau which was to serve to illuminate the wandering steps of guitarists.

Another fascinating guide to the late eighteenth century's development of the guitar in Spain is Fernando Ferandiere's *Arte de Tocar la Guitarra Española* (Madrid, 1799). This text tells us that Ferandiere played a six-course guitar with the traditional, lute-like, double stringing familiar to all types of guitar up to this time. Moretti, in the same year, mentions that the French and Italians preferred single strings on their guitars. Sor may have grown up playing the double strung guitar, but by the time of his maturity the idea of courses had become as outmoded as the lute.

Once double stringing had been dispensed with, the guitar could really become an instrument *sui generis*. The courses imposed on the instrument a timbre that looked back to lute textures, and put a weight on the guitar's structure tht would only serve to deaden the resonances of the instrument. The lute's lightness and strength was a combination which could deal with courses without inflicting damage on instrumental sonorities. The guitar operates best as a vibrating medium with the fewest possible strings.

Pujol in *Escuela Razonada de la Guitarra* cites the various guitar notions which came and disappeared in the eighteenth century. Guitarists envisaged instruments with seven strings (1788), eight strings, ten strings, eleven strings, and twenty strings. Fortunately, and perhaps inevitably, none of these monstrosities persevered in general popularity. Only in Russia did the seven string guitar take root, and this type of instrument was also played in the nineteenth century by Napoleon Coste. It was left to Narciso Yepes and the twentieth century maker Ramirez to create a ten string guitar of recital capabilities, and opinions remain divided on the qualities of even this superb example of the luthier's craft.

The eighteenth century is often dismissed as a negligible and distressing period in the guitar's history. In some ways the progress of the guitar was retarded during these years when European music flourished as never before and Bach, Handel, Haydn and Mozart dominated the musical scene.

But the guitar did advance. In a confusing environment of change the guitar slowly accepted a sixth string, cautiously lost its double strung courses, steadily altered its tradition of notation away from tablature, and kept alive to some extent the music of Corbetta, Sanz and Granata. By 1799, when Fernando Sor was twenty-one and Mauro Giuliani was eighteen, the guitar, though not yet a perfectly evolved expressive medium, was rapidly absorbing its processes of growth and would soon emerge spectacularly from its neglected chrysalis. What the dictionary defines as 'the torpid encased stage between larva and imago' proved as important to the guitar as it is to the generation of butterflies; the evolution to the golden age was only one mutation away.

Fernando Ferandiere provides a fitting last word to the eighteenth century development of the guitar:

> And because music is, has been, and will be, the comfort of the wretched, the recreation of the scholarly, and the strength of great heroes, this instrument should be preferred, and you should dedicate yourself to it more than to other instruments . . . then because I am one of those who has found out more about it, I know that there is still much more to be discovered, and that other men will find out more with the passing of time.

11. Guitarists and their Repertoire: 1800-1850

> *From that day on we surrendered ourselves to searching in shops, libraries and even private homes for music written for the guitar. We found some compositions by Arcas, Sor and Giuliani, in poor and often well-worn editions.*
>
> Andrés Segovia

Both recitalists and amateurs of the twentieth century have applied themselves with considerable zeal to the task of playing the extensive guitar repertoire of the period between 1800 and 1850. Guitarists see this time as a miniature golden age of the instrument and consequently the resources of El Dorado have been incessantly quarried and players of all levels of ability are now very familiar with its riches and deficiencies.

The early nineteenth century explored two vital aspects of the guitar — the pedagogic and the creative; the great teachers of the age developed the techniques, methods of study and theoretical bases of the instrument in a manner appropriate to the era of Czerny (1791-1857) and Paganini (1782-1840). The leading guitarists also endeavoured to compose extended musical structures which could bring the guitar into the orbit of true seriousness.

The six strings of the guitar represented the ideal number for expressive writing. The instrument now assumed an aesthetic and mathematical appearance of logic; between the first and sixth string two octaves range provided a balanced harmonic foundation of symmetry and flexibility, being suitable for the forming of chords, scale passages, and a combination of the two.

The logic of the fingerboard is a fascinating study. Composers could now use these possibilities to release the guitar's latent energy, a process that perhaps reached a special kind of climax a century and a quarter later in the inspired patterns of Heitor Villa-Lobos.

The elimination of double-strung courses not only created a characteristic guitar timbre as single string sound came into vogue. It also affected the whole technical approach to the instrument. Left and right hand positions, scale passages, arpeggio playing, chordal textures, slurring, phrasing, higher positions and use of vibrato, would all now be developed in different ways. This was a critical moment in guitar history, analagous possibly to that time when the violin was first placed under the chin and a new technique evolved from that posture.

At first composers (all of whom were players as well) seemed a little unsure of what to write for this new type of guitar, and in some respects the native voice of the guitar would not emerge for some time. The guitar's small body size of about forty-four centimetres (compared with the post-Torres guitar of about forty-nine centimetres) and string length of approximately sixty-two centimetres (nowadays between sixty-five and sixty-seven centimetres) though it encouraged dexterity, inhibited production of rich, sensuous tone colours. Its aptitude was for solo work within the salon, rather than for extended use in partnership with string ensembles, though its long tradition of being an ideal medium for voice accompaniment still persisted.

The guitarist/composer of this period was particularly aware of the need to bring the guitar into an appropriate relationship with the music of his environment; this included not only exciting developments in the solo instruments (and especially keyboard) but also the composition of extended works such as sonatas, which the guitarist very much coveted. Guitarists like Sor and Giuliani were very responsive to orchestral textures and themselves wrote for other combinations of instruments, as well as attempting to place the guitar in the context of serious music making; furthermore, they tried, where possible, to make the guitar resemble a miniature orchestra.

For the first time in musical history, guitarists were looking outward at the repertoire of pianoforte, violin and symphony orchestra, instead of comparing their efforts at composition with the traditions of the lute and other fretted instruments. The guitar composers now set their sights high, wishing to give to the world a body of work capable of being compared favourably with the great music of the age. To fulfil this ambition they wrote sonatas, variations, overtures and fantasias, and in order to bring players up to the standard of virtuosity required they offered a wide range of technical studies. The functions of virtuosity and pedagogy carried out by the leading players were always totally complementary. They dazzled the public with their brilliance and prepared the way for amateur

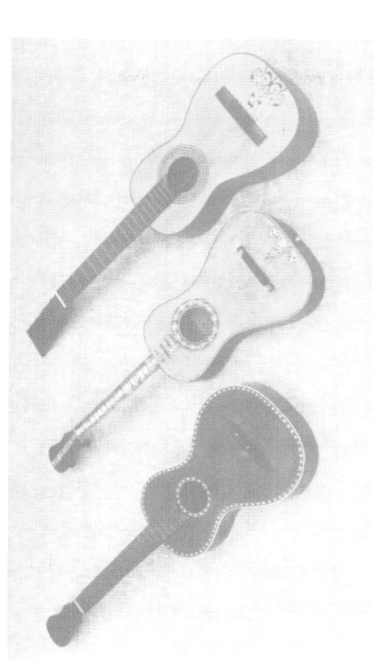

9. *Nineteenth Century Guitars*: these small instruments are attractive and informal, caught in the evolutionary process between ornamented *objets d'art* and genuine musical instruments. Courtesy of the Victoria and Albert Museum, London.

interest in the guitar with methods, divertissements, minuets, waltzes and studies which catered to the needs of the raw novice.

The personalities involved in this renaissance of the guitar were comparatively few in number for our purposes. Their work no doubt spawned hundreds of imitators, teachers and minor practitioners, in the same way as the modern stimulation of enthusiasm for the classical guitar has allowed many besides the magic circle of great players to spread with missionary zeal, the delights of the instrument and its music.

On the performing and composing level two men of genius emerged — Fernando Sor (1778-1839) and Mauro Giuliani (1781-1829) — who represent respectively the Spanish and Italian temperaments and musical disposition. Sor's countryman Dionisio Aguado (1784-1849), and the Italians Matteo Carcassi (1792-1853) and Ferdinando Carulli (1770-1841) were considered fine players in their day but have come down to us primarily as the writers of pedagogic material.

Much insignificant music has been left over from the period to provide suitable fodder for the amateur player. This includes pieces by well known musical figures such as Anton Diabelli (1781-1858), a music publisher immortalised in Beethoven's Diabelli Variations Op. 120(1823), and relatively obscure figures such as Don François Molino (1775-1847), Wenzeslaus Thomas Matiegka (1773-1830), Leonhard von Call (1768-1815), Joseph Küffner (1776-1856), Luigi Legnani (1790-1877), Simon Molitor (1766-1848), Christian Gottlieb Scheidler (c.1752-1815) and many others; of these only Diabelli and Scheidler have emerged into the modern concert hall and even in their case it is only one or two works which are regularly performed.

Several of the great players of other instruments and famous composers were peripherally involved with the guitar to the extent of writing for it or including it in one of their works, such as an opera, or merely being known to play the guitar. These included Weber (1786-1826), Boccherini (1743-1805), Berlioz (1803-1869) and Rossini (1792-1868). As is well known, the guitar's most renowned advocate as a player was Paganini (1782-1840) who fell heavily under the instrument's spell and wrote many solo and ensemble compositions for it. Schubert (1797-1828) also loved the guitar but unfortunately did not compose for it.

Beethoven (1770-1827) dominated the ears of composers such as Sor, who has even been called the 'Beethoven of the guitar'. Beethoven himself wrote nearly twenty pieces for the mandolin, exquisite miniatures of a recreational kind, but seems to have had better things to do than augment the guitar's repertoire. Even one small work from his pen would have been a triumph for the guitar. Beethoven knew Giuliani in Vienna but, as with Lully and Corbetta, the great composer left the guitarist's task to the professional players to the everlasting chagrin of aficionados.

Even before he was able to read music properly and with only a poor knowledge of the rudiments, Andrés Segovia discovered the works of Sor and Giuliani. At this point one of Segovia's friends 'unearthed a guitar manual of sorts', and Segovia began a long process of self-education. Thus, if indirectly, Sor's influence on the development of the twentieth century guitar has been crucial. His work, along with that of Giuliani and Arcas (1832-1882), provided evidence that the past contained musicians whose vision of the guitar extended far beyond the abuse of the instrument as little better than an accompanying medium, which was current at the time.

Segovia remained faithful to Sor's compositions throughout his career, though, as with Luys Milán, John Dowland and Robert de Visée, his principles demanded a ruthless selectivity, bringing forward those works which best exploited the guitar's capabilities as he saw them. His first recording of a piece by Sor was that of Opus 9, the famous 'Variations on a Theme of Mozart'. The composition is a remarkable demonstration of the guitar's ability to express many moods from gentle cantabile to violinistic slurs, from introvert melancholy to dazzling arpeggio passages.

These Variations on 'O Cara Armonia' from *The Magic Flute* tell us a great deal about the inventiveness of Sor's approach to the guitar. By writing such a brilliant showpiece he surely astounded the audiences of his day for whom the guitar meant no more than the routine chordal accompaniments and rudimentary romantic melodies of inferior strummers. There are no precedents in guitar literature for this kind of *tour de force* in which all the technical devices of the guitar are developed with such gusto.

Fernando Sor's 5th Variation from Variations on 'O Cara Armonia' from *The Magic Flute*.

Since Segovia's early recording of Opus 9, the composition has been played hundreds of times in recitals until its brilliant novelty has become jaded by constant repetition. It still remains however in the pantheon of those guitar works which break new ground in the instrument's history, uniting true lyricism with exciting virtuosity.

Fernando Sor was in the vanguard of those composers whose ambition it was to emulate the grandeur of the instrumental masterpieces of his day within the compass of his guitar. Sor tried his hand at concert studies, expressive fantasias and grandiloquent duos which he performed with Dionisio Aguado.

His composition of studies is superior to that of nearly all his contemporaries. In this sphere he is a true counterpart to the keyboard pedagogues of his day such as Clementi (1752-1832) with his *Gradus ad Parnassum*, Cramer (1771-1858), Hummel (1778-1837) and Czerny (1791-1857) famous for his School of Velocity, Op. 365. Virtuosity was in great demand and the frantic scramble on the part of teachers to develop their students' technical prowess was a corollary of the high standards of attainment in all branches of music in the age of Mozart and Beethoven.

Gifted with great technical ability and using their own studies to reach new levels of brilliance, it is not surprising if the larger compositions, and especially the sonatas, veer towards the grandiose, the long-winded and the rhetorical, in the work of Sor and Giuliani. To later ages, what must have seemed like a miraculous revelation of the art of guitar to early nineteenth century audiences (hearing the composers perform), became a spectacle of empty exhibitionism. The guitar as a showcase of dazzling pyrotechnics does not and should not try to compare with the colossal power and energy of the pianoforte in terms of Beethoven's achievement or Paganini's mastery of four bowed strings. The guitar is capable of technical display but it is a limited virtue, and a surfeit of exhibitionism destroys real musical expressiveness.

Moreover Sor, Giuliani and their fellow guitarists, were unfortunately inferior to the compositional genius of the great composers of the time. Sor discovered the true enduring voice of the guitar when he created a lyricism natural to it. To ape the expansive gestures of other solo instruments, such as the piano, was not good for the guitar's health.

Segovia was aware of the danger of Sor's grander ambitions and trod warily. As with other prolific composers (such as J.S. Bach) Segovia institutionalised the repertoire of Sor by concentrating his fire on what he thought were the most rewarding compositions. He did not take too many chances with his audience's stamina; for

Segovia, as for Sor, the guitar was in a volatile evolutionary state and to move too quickly onto large scale nineteenth century structures might not help his cause. Having found that the Variations Op. 9 worked magnificently on audiences, Segovia stripped the pretentiousness from Sor and emphasised the Mozartian charm to be found in both his small and large works.

In practical terms this meant that lyricism was stressed, pomposity left unplayed. Twenty of the many studies were collected and several of them made frequent recital appearances; these developed such aspects of technique as playing in thirds, bringing out a melody over an accompaniment, arpeggio playing, staccato chords, barrés and so on. All contained a reasonably firm musical basis and none could be said to appeal only to the gallery.

Segovia performed only individual movements from Sor's sonatas. The long work he most favoured was the grandiloquent Introduction and Allegro Op. 14. The episodic brilliance of this composition is more inventive than the formal longeurs of structured sonatas, and while primarily a showcase for guitar virtuosity does exploit the guitar's melodic qualities as well as plunging into quasi-orchestral textures which are extremely successful in this work.

Segovia did not play Sor's sonatas in their entirety. With Op. 22, Grande Sonate, he omitted the first movement but played the magnificent Largo (originally published written in two clefs and even alto clef as Opus 7, by Sor), Minuet and Rondo, sometimes as a group but frequently as separate items; it was this Largo which prompted a writer in *The Giulianiad* in 1833 to comment,

    . . . if it is said of Giuliani, that 'he must be considered as the inventor of

a new method of *playing'* — perhaps I may be permitted to say, that we
ought to consider Sor as the inventor of a new method of *composing*.
Let me point out to you, as a specimen, his delightful fantasias opera 7;
the introductory largo, in C minor, with its heart-thrilling combinations
of chords (although rather spun out too long) which abounds with
elegance and beauty from beginning to end, leading to the tender
floating theme in C major and its variations: all these beauties must be
highly relished by the proficient, as they must likewise fascinate every
sincere admirer of the guitar!

Later in his career Segovia brought in two more sets of variations —
Malbroug va t'en guerre, Op. 28 and Folies d'Espagne Op. 15(a).
Apart from Siciliana in D, several minuets and the magnificent
Allegro from the Sonata Op. 25, this concludes Segovia's selection
from Sor. His disciplining of the prolific creativity of Sor is a
fascinating example of Segovia's desire to present to the public's ears
only the most resilient and lyrical of Sor's output.

The next two generations of guitarists consolidated Segovia's
work. If Sor had been lavish in the multiplicity of his works, concert
guitarists constrained his efforts, putting the voice of the instrument
before the temptation merely to play anything from the treasure-chest
of the Napoleonic decades. Any process of expanding the stock of
Sor available on record was at first carried out along strictly Segovian
lines. John Williams recorded all twenty of Segovia's selection of Sor
studies very early on in his career; Narciso Yepes later recorded these
and some of his own choosing in an album of twenty-four studies.
Julian Bream, again as if in homage to Segovia, first of all recorded
five studies from the established set, the familiar Rondo from Op. 22,
and later the Grand Solo and the whole of Sonata Op. 25. Alirio Diaz
followed the same ritual of playing various studies, the Rondo
Op. 22, and the Op. 9 Variations, all of which were duly recorded.
Nearly all the great guitarists felt it important to record Op. 9, with
the exception of Bream, who however at one stage in his career
frequently included it in recitals. (Williams and Yepes even recorded
Op. 9 twice.)

Sor's material has therefore been used very much in the Segovian
manner, a handful of compositions having formed the essential
stockpile for recital purposes. A further dimension was added by the
popularity of Sor's music for two guitars. Pieces such as L'Encouragement, Op. 34, frequently performed by such eminent artists as the
Presti-Lagoya Duo, showed another side of Sor's genius. But overall
the approach to his output has been exceedingly discriminatory and
partial, a situation which may now be remedied by the appearance of
his complete guitar works in facsimile, published in 1977 under the

editorship of Brian Jeffery (Shattinger International Music Corp., New York) in five volumes. Already players are aware that Sor has more to offer than merely the traditional favourites.

Segovia's selection of Giuliani was even more drastic. He chose only the first movement of Sonata Op. 15:

Bream and Williams also recorded just the first movement of Op. 15. Though some guitarists, notably Rey de la Torre, performed the entire sonata, it was never a usual feature of the guitarists, few in number, who inhabit the Olympian slopes. Segovia's recording of a few negligible studies that he first played as a youth hardly deserves mention.

The massive advance in Giuliani's reputation came with Bream's discovery of the Grand Overture Op. 61, and Les Rossinianes Op. 121 and 119. These three works require enormous virtuosity and do indeed sound like the miniature orchestra the guitar is often said to resemble in its range of colour and timbre. Bream's playing (and subsequent recording) introduced a certain Lisztian bravura into the repertoire, a sense of the epic and the spacious, something that several nineteenth century works aspired to but did not quite achieve.

Les Rossinianes are impressive, if not entirely for their deep musicality, at least for the glimpse they give of the kind of music Giuliani played in Vienna in the company of Hummel, Moscheles and, possibly, even the great Beethoven himself. The textures, the amount of notes, the pushing of the guitar to the limits of its possibility and the overall length are a remarkable instance of what a guitar can be expected to do in the hands of a great player. Unfortunately under the glare and shimmer of the technical wizardry, the musical content is banal, despite the connections with Rossini.

Le Rossiniane, No. 1, Op. 119 by Mauro Giuliani

Thus the fertile pages of Sor and Giuliani, the two maestros of their age, yield far less in the way of regular concert repertoire than might be expexted. Attempts have been made by some guitarists to establish Giuliani's Gran Sonata Eroica Op. 150 as a suitable recital piece; on one occasion when it was played in London a critic acclaimed it as a 'masterpiece of parody', which was not the performer's or Giuliani's interpretation. Thus so much of their work, unsupported as it was by a strong tradition, runs into the sand or becomes the preserve of the amateur in the practice room. This may be better than oblivion, but it is a rather slender legacy from such an explosive outpouring of energy.

Other nineteenth century guitarists of this period have fared considerably worse in terms of concert performances, but they remain the staple diet of students. Segovia has openly criticised the banality of Carulli's feeble imagination, a judgement which surely should not apply to pieces such as his Serenade in A for two guitars, Op. 96. (In the same manner Giuliani's Variazioni Concertanti for two Guitars Op. 130, and his Guitar Concerto Op. 30 soar above the level of his solo creations). Carcassi's music is never considered serious enough for recitals, but is played daily throughout the world by beginners and less skilled aficionados.

Even the brilliant Dionisio Aguado, with whom Sor played duets, has made few inroads into the awareness of players beyond that of being a superb writer of inventive studies. His ability to see unusual possibilities in guitar composing never developed into the gift of writing more expressive works. Aguado seems to have been tied to the vision of the guitar as a technical box of tricks, though here lies his great strength for the development of a player's dexterity:

Study by Aguado

The benefits of the technical exercises of the nineteenth century pedagogues are considerable. Occasionally guitar teachers mount a reaction against the tyranny of Sor, Giuliani, Carcassi, Carulli and Aguado, preferring to present more modern music to their students, and by-passing the tortuous familiarities of the classical era; it is a posture not shared by the great players, all of whom developed their early skill in the art of Sor and his contemporaries. You can still estimate a player's capabilities by his rendering of a Sor study. Sor and his partners still challenge each and every player of the guitar and their searching enquiry cannot be denied. They lived and breathed the guitar, catering for all levels of ability in a way that has not been equalled by any composer except Tárrega.

The most extraordinary personality who played and wrote for the guitar was of course Paganini. His devotion to the instrument and his friendship with Legnani (a good player who toured Europe giving recitals), represent a superlative instance of a musical genius of the highest order giving himself to a whole-hearted study of the guitar's mysteries. Twentieth century players have performed various works of his for guitar and string ensemble, and guitar and violin. His most popular creation has however been the Grand Sonata, originally for guitar and violin, but suitably edited into a magnificent solo.

Segovia's recording of this included variations actually written by none other than Manuel Ponce. Williams and Bream rescued Paganini from Ponce's attentions by performing and recording the original work. There is considerable difference between various editions of this piece, but it remains one of the finest extended works of the period, requiring both a superb technique and a mastery of interpretation.

Diabelli also wrote copiously for the guitar. Julian Bream considered that none of his sonatas was truly worthy of a recital, so by transposition coaxed three movements from separate sonatas to form one sonata, a prime example of the triumph of mind over matter when it comes to discovering a suitable concert repertoire. Needless to say, Bream's skilful manipulations served to enhance Diabelli's somewhat faded glory.

12. Personalities and Pedagogues

Yet I think the day will come when learners of the guitar
will form their ideas by correct music. I am not the only
one that writes such music.

Fernando Sor

The guitar virtuosi of the early nineteenth century enjoyed the benefits
and adulation given to great instrumentalists of other ages. The
successful performer pursued a cosmopolitan path with good
rewards from the powerful and aristocratic, extensive travel throughout Europe and the following of an enthusiastic public and devoted
disciples. Mauro Giuliani even had a special magazine, *The
Giulianiad*, founded in his honour. The finest players could also
expect to see their compositions and methods in print, thus establishing the guitar as a serious musical study worthy of comparison
with violin and pianoforte, and ensuring a lasting memorial to their
work.

Sor and Giuliani represent the twin peaks of guitar achievement in
the age of Napoleon and Beethoven. Their careers illustrate the
spectacular possibilities of a great guitarist at that time and fulfil the
long traditions of Spanish and Italian involvement in guitar music.
They moved in significant musical company, bringing the guitar to a
wide range of royal courts, concert societies and performer/com-
posers of other instruments. In this respect and many others, Sor and
Giuliani were worthy successors to their forgotten cultural antecedents like Milán, Narváez, Mudarra, Dowland, Corbetta,
Gaultier, Sanz and Weiss; it seems a pity that the nineteenth century
guitarists could not have been more aware of the parallels between
their efforts to propagate the virtues of guitar music and the struggles
of the great fretted instrumentalists of earlier generations.

Liberation from close acquaintance with the guitar's historical
development was a mixed blessing. Sor and his contemporaries were

thus compelled to make a fresh evaluation of technique and compositional substance. The new six stringed instrument severed its umbilical link with Baroque guitars and lutes and a novel type of guitar made its first appearance in the world, an exciting event in itself.

But the early nineteenth century guitarists were as a consequence working in shallow cultural soil. Their models for composition were those of other musical textures than the guitar, and particularly pianoforte and orchestral works. For this reason their example of writing extended sonatas and longer structures for the guitar was not followed up, until over a century later. Their pedagogic material proved of more immediate worth to their successors than the ambitious virtuoso music. Thus in a sense the example of Sor and Giuliani lay dormant until Segovia and the twentieth century composers once more revived the desire to create music of some architectural complexity.

The actual careers of these guitarists were however a brilliant burst of activity. Sor gained his early music education from the monastery of Montserrat (later celebrated in a guitar composition, the Castillos de España by Federico Moreno Torroba). Sor sang in the choir, learned to play his father's guitar (possibly a double strung five-course instrument) and studied violin, piano and harmony. Later he was commissioned in the Spanish army, and stationed near Barcelona.

While still a soldier he came under the patronage of the Duchess of Alba. Adolphe Ledhuy's biographical essay about Sor in the *Encyclopédie Pittoresque de la Musique*, tells how the Duchess of Alba 'took him under her protection and gave him all the affection of a mother . . . to aid his studies she had prepared for him in her establishment a work-room where he could consult Italian scores and practise the piano'. The Duchess was described by a French marquis, Fleurot de Langle, in ecstatic terms:

> The Duchess of Alba has not a hair on her head that does not stir desire. Nothing on earth is as lovely as she is; it is impossible to surpass her. When she walks down the street all the world is at the windows to look, and little children stop playing games to see her.

Legend has associated the Duchess with La Maja Desnuda and La Maja Vestida by Goya, who was said to be deeply in love with her. Thus in terms of the guitar the Duchess has a double significance: not only was she the patron of Sor, but Segovia's guitar has immortalised her in music in his superb playing of Granados' composition La Maja de Goya (arranged by Miguel Llobet), one of the finest Spanish works to be transcribed for the guitar. Her husband, the eleventh Marquis of Villafranca (Don José Alvarez de Toledo Osorio Perez de Guzman el Bueno), married her when she was thirteen, and took the title of the Duke of Alba to preserve the line and its fortune; he was reputed to be a great lover of music and throughout his life corresponded with Haydn.

Unfortunately for Sor, after this auspicious beginning, the Duchess died on 23 July 1802, when the guitarist was twenty-four years old. He worked for a while in administrative posts for the Duke of Medinaceli and lived in Andalucia. His sympathies with French ideals ultimately forced him to leave his country in 1813. From this time Sor's greater significance as a guitarist can be dated, though it should be stressed that his compositional output was by no means exclusively confined to the guitar but included operas, ballets, songs and symphonies. Ironically enough, all but Sor's guitar writings have been consigned to silence since his lifetime.

Sor travelled to England in 1815 and achieved considerable acclaim, staying there until 1823. His Op. 9 was published in London in 1821; the title-page records 'As Performed by the Author at the Nobilities' Concerts'. Of Sor's various recitals in the British capital his most renowned was possibly on 24 March 1817 when he played the third concert of the season for the Philharmonic Society, performing his 'Concertante for the guitar with violin, viola and 'cello'. In *Memoir of the Philharmonic Society*, George Hogarth writes:

> In a concertante for the Spanish guitar, composed and performed by M. Sor, a guitarist in great vogue at that time, he astonished the audience by his unrivalled execution.

Sor's eminence in London musical society increased and he became an Honorary Member at the founding of the Royal Academy of Music in 1822, a tribute both to his musicianship and to the amiability of his character.

At the age of forty-four Sor embarked on a journey to Moscow, possibly because of his love for Félicité Hullin, a ballerina. He travelled by way of Berlin and Warsaw (where he gave a concert on 22 October 1823), and arrived in Moscow in November 1823. In Russia these were the years of Tsar Alexander I, of whom Byron wrote:

> *The Coxcomb Czar*
> *The autocrat of waltzes and of war,*
> *With no objection to true liberty*
> *Except that it would make men free.*

Just a few years before, in 1812, Napoleon had begun his ill-fated invasion of Russia, only to be defeated by the Russian winter and Alexander's army. It was also the era of Pushkin, whose period of banishment in Siberia had been extended in the year that Sor visited Moscow.

Ledhuy gives a fairly full account of Sor's success in Russian aristocratic circles:

> In Moscow Sor was introduced rapidly into the most distinguished society. In a country where music is developed to a high degree of perfection, his talent was appreciated. His guitar produced the greatest effect. They were amazed to see him play with equal facility in all keys on an instrument with one string less than the Russian guitar. . . On one of his journeys to St Petersburg, Sor was summoned to the presence of the Tsar's mother, where the whole Imperial family was gathered. He was a great success. Several days later, he played for the Empress Elisabeth who gave him so many tokens of esteem that he believed his future was assured. But just as the artist was about to reach a position worthy of himself and his patroness, she died shortly after the Emperor. Sor composed a funeral march for military orchestra which was chosen by Emperor Nicholas and played at Alexander's funeral by the musicians of the Preobrazhensky regiment, the elite of the guards. Empress Alexandra desired to have this march arranged for piano, and this was the occasion to load the composer with gifts. At the time of Nicholas' Coronation, Sor returned to Moscow to help in the rehearsals of his ballet *Hercule et Omphale*.

As with the Duchess of Alba, Sor's hopes were thwarted by the premature death of a powerful patroness — Alexander's mother; but once again Sor's personality impressed women of power and influence. Sor seems to have possessed the gift of impressing a royal family of dubious attractiveness, and was presumably in Russia during the startling events of December 1825 when Nicholas I put down insurgents with a battery of artillery; this event was attended by the Preobrazhensky guard and other elite regiments who had previously performed Sor's funeral march. Sor had a talent for being in the places where central historical happenings occurred; his life was not that of the ivory tower.

Sor's link with the guitar in Russia provides some fascinating historical connections. He met the Russian guitarist M.T. Vyssotski, and in memory of this encounter wrote Souvenir de Russie, Op. 63 (his last composition). This piece was later transcribed for the Russian seven string guitar by Sikhra, with whom Makaroff, a famous Russian player, studied. Boris Perrot, who was a friend of Julian Bream, met Makaroff at his deathbed. Makaroff had known Napoleon Coste, one of Sor's pupils, though in his memoirs (pub-

lished in *Guitar Review*, 1947-48) he shows himself to be more
interested in the music of Giuliani than of Sor.

It seems probable that Sor's visit to Russia provided an impetus for
the guitar in that country far greater than that represented by
available resources. The Russian connection with the instrument has
endured to the twentieth century particularly in the work of Vladimir
Bobri, whose editorship of the *New York Guitar Review* and his
friendship with Segovia have proved a valuable stimulus to research
into the guitar's history.

On Sor's return to Paris in 1826 or 1827 many of his compositions
began to appear in print; during his absence in Russia his publisher
Antoine Meissonnier had published sixteen books of Sor's works.
However Sor eventually parted from Meissonnier and became his
own publisher; under his own steam he produced his famous
Méthode pour la Guitare, which appeared in 1830, and remains one
of the most fascinating tutors ever written for the guitar.

In his Method, Sor examines the basis of guitar technique as he
understands it. His discussion of the instrument, its makers and its
problems provides one of the finest examples of analysis in the guitar's
history. He states in his introduction that he speaks 'of that only
which my reflections and experience have made me establish to
regulate my own play . . . I have exalted no maxim into a principle, till
after a due consideration of the motives for so doing.' Thus he lays
down the empirical foundations of his system, formed from an
extensive study of musical theory as well as a strong conviction that
the guitar is worthy of more than being just a means of accompaniment.

He looks first at the type of instrument he prefers:

> The guitars to which I have always given the preference are those of
> Alonzo of Madrid, Pagés and Benediz of Cadiz, Joseph and Manuel
> Martinez of Malaga, or Rada, successor and scholar of the latter, and
> those of M. Lacote of Paris. I do not say that others do not exist; but
> never having tried them, I cannot decide on that of which I have no
> knowledge.

Next comes the vital question of how to sit with the guitar. Sor
stresses again how 'Having had no master, I have been obliged to
reason before raising any maxim into a fixed principle'. He argues
that just as a pianist will sit opposite the middle of the keyboard so the
twelfth fret of the guitar 'should be found opposite my body'. The
guitar should be supported underneath on the player's left side by a
table, and the left arm should not be too raised or 'the circulation of
the blood must be affected in the parts most distant from the body'.
Thus commonsense about the physical demand of tendons and

circulation makes him reject the French and Italian posture of sitting with the neck of the guitar too high.

Sor's right hand technique is also logical; most of the work is done by the thumb, index and middle fingers, with the anular or ring finger brought in to play chords. Unlike Carcassi, Sor does not suggest the archaic principle of anchoring the little finger on the soundboard.

His left hand position is directly in line with modern thinking on the subject. Instead of using the thumb on the sixth string, and bringing the thumb over the top of the instrument, he positions it behind the neck:

> I employed the thumb as it is used in the pianoforte, namely, as a pivot on which the whole hand changes its position, and which serves as a guide in returning to the position quitted. . . This experiment induced me to establish it as a principle to place the thumb always at half the width of the neck, facing the finger which answers to the second fret.

The action of striking the string with the right hand is 'to keep my fingers as little curved as possible' thus eschewing 'giving to my finger the form of a hook' which would cause the string to 'jar against the frets'. He established the best striking point along the string as being 'at one-tenth of the whole length of the string from the bridge', in which position Sor 'obtained a clear and lengthened tone without its being violent'. To produce louder sounds, Sor will 'touch it nearer the bridge than usual, and, in this case, I must exert a little more force in touching it'.

Sor mentions how the guitar imitates the sounds of other instruments such as horn, trumpet, oboe and flute. At this point he brings in a strong rebuke for those who play with nails:

> Never in my life have I heard a guitarist whose playing was supportable, if he played with nails. The nails can produce but very few gradations in the quality of the sound. . . .

Thus Sor retreats not only from modern technique, but also from the method of Aguado whose teacher instructed him to use nails at a time when 'A guitarist was then a stranger to all other music besides that for the guitar'.

Sor's technique was presumably equal to everything he wrote for the instrument. He has written a forceful explanation of his thinking about the guitar, laced with insight and a little venom. The book rests on his immense authority as an international virtuoso whose name, as he himself puts it 'Europe has kindly honoured'. It remains a vital exposition of essential ideas, caught mid-way between a scientific textbook and an artist's treatise.

Sor evolved his own patterns of understanding about the exigencies of guitar technique. Less than a century after Sor's Method was published, Andrés Segovia had completed his process of technical analysis; apart from the age-old and vexed argument over the use of nails, Sor and Segovia would not have come to blows over many of the matters discussed, especially when it came to Sor's twelfth and last basic principle for studying the guitar, 'To hold reasoning for a great deal and routine for nothing'.

His sixth principle 'Never to give work to the weakest fingers, whilst the strongest are doing nothing' would not have elicited enthusiasm; modern concepts of technique centre precisely around the development of weak fingers. However the fourth and fifth principles 'To consider fingering as an art' and 'Never to make an ostentation of difficulty' remain cornerstones of the guitarist's craft, let alone the first principle 'To regard the effect of the music more than the praise as to skill as a performer'.

The last years of Sor's life were spent in Paris, and he died on 10 July 1839. Guitarists have sanctified his memory ever since. His life is a fascinating mosaic of creativity, travel, concertising, success and failure; his many compositions not for the guitar have perished to memory, and his guitar works have become increasingly popular. To the guitar he gave a new sense of identity, and extended its techniques in physical and compositional terms. Sor brought the guitar into the musical mainstream of his day and through his work with Panormo took a close interest in the problems of guitar construction, (though the difficulties were not solved until the arrival of Torres and the greater string length).

> The tone of Giuliani was brought to the greatest possible perfection; in his hands the guitar became gifted with a power of expression at once, pure, thrilling and exquisite. He vocalized his adagios to a degree impossible to be imagined by those who never heard him — his melody in slow movements was no longer like the short unavoidable staccato of the pianoforte — requiring a profusion of harmony to cover the deficient sustension of the notes — but it was invested with a character, not only sustained and penetrating, yet of so earnest and pathetic a description as to make it appear in reality the natural characteristic of the instrument. *In a word he made the instrument sing.*

These remarks, written a year after the death of Giuliani, later published in *The Giulianiad*, denote the fervent admiration which his playing inspired. It was 'by the elastic touch of the fingers of the right hand (properly supported of course by the pressure of the left) that this, the *ne plus ultra* of tone in guitar playing, is to be attained. Without great attention to the disposition of the right hand, the slightest approach to this beauty cannot be effected'.

Even allowing for a surfeit of adulatory enthusiasm, no new thing in guitar writing, it is clear from this account that Giuliani's approach to the instrument was exceptional. The marvel of his tone was however 'secondary to the grand quality of expression'.

Giuliani's right hand technique, his tone and the quality of his legato seemed to the writer a kind of miracle quite different from the staccato necessities of pianoforte. (Traditionally guitar enthusiasts seem not to admire the keyboard and Segovia's oft-quoted comment that the piano is 'a rectangular monster that can be made to shout by digging into its teeth' continues the prejudice among guitarists.)

In the same article Felix Horetzky (1800-71), a Polish pupil of Giuliani, is quoted:

> 'Among the professors of the Spanish guitar, it is well known that the justly celebrated Mauro Giuliani, is not only the first and most distinguished performer thereon, but he must be considered as the inventor of a new method of playing by which he has demonstrated the abundance of harmony, and the beauty and power of which this agreeable instrument is capable.'

This issue of *The Giulianiad* also argues the relative claims to superiority of Sor and Giuliani, and commends Sor's Op. 7, C minor Largo; this writer, well ahead of his time, suggests the establishment of a college 'where pupils (on all instruments) should undergo suitable examinations, like surgeons, to prove that they are skilful, before they are permitted to practise'. This step would sort out those 'who profess, by their advertisements, to teach the guitar in "Six Lessons!" thus, by their fallacious assertions, infecting inexperienced minds with an idea that the guitar is only fit for an accompaniment'.

This early defender of the classical guitar was, it seems, very much in the position of later generations of committed guitarists, who thought it necessary to defend the instrument verbally against prejudice, misconception, poor teachers and widespread ignorance. Great players such as Sor or Giuliani might lay bare the immense potential of the guitar but at less august levels of music making than salon or recital room, the instrument was constantly abused, physically by bad players and verbally by its critics.

The amateur's defence of his beloved guitar from the early nineteenth century onwards possesses a familiar tone of voice, slightly raised, moderately aggressive, on the defensive and apparently expecting to be criticised bitterly for his beliefs. The guitar's progress between the Scylla and Charybdis of a lack of recognition in musical circles and the prejudice of the unmusical has not been entirely comfortable even in the twentieth century.

The eighteenth century doldrums had erased the earlier reverence towards the guitarists of Baroque courtly life, and the guitar's slow assumption of a classical identity was fraught with missionary zeal, plaintive letters and the strivings of minority cults. No such advocacy was necessary for the claims of keyboard, violin or even the harp; the guitar's associations were at that time (as they still can be) a mixture of humble strumming, fine accompaniments and virtuoso soloists. It was therefore totally appropriate that a magazine dedicated to Giuliani, one of the finest players of his age, should act as the forum for guitar propaganda and acclaim him for the magical 'new method' which would give the lie to the old misunderstandings about the guitar.

Giuliani is an especially interesting guitarist if only because of his associations with the musical power-house of nineteenth century Vienna, though there is of course much in his music to delight in. Born in Bisceglie, Italy in 1781, on the Adriatic coast of southern Italy, Giuliani's music appeals for its warmly lyrical characteristics and his national love of the textures and passion of the cantabile style of guitar composition. At the age of twenty-five Giuliani plunged into the turbulence of Viennese musical life.

In Vienna he came into contact with Beethoven, Moscheles and Hummel, among others, and his compositions were influenced by the virtuosity of these personalities. Hummel (1778-1837) had been a pupil of Haydn and Mozart, and studied with Clementi in London; he succeeded Haydn as Kapellmeister to Prince Esterhazy. Czerny wrote of his playing:

> Never before had I heard such novel and dazzling difficulties, such clarity and elegance in performance or such intimate and tender expression, or even such good taste in improvisation.

Hummel was a great authority as performer and pedagogue. His instruction books for keyboard systematised technique and dealt with all the problems of pianoforte. His stay in Vienna was between 1811 and 1816, and Giuliani appeared with Hummel and the violinist, Mayseder, in concert during 1815. Hummel even wrote compositions for the guitar, including some chamber music, though it is rarely, if ever, performed nowadays. However this was magnificent company for a guitarist and shows the respect which Hummel, one of his era's top virtuosi, must have felt for Giuliani's musicianly qualities.

Moscheles (1794-1870) became the teacher of Mendelssohn with whom he enjoyed a lifelong friendship. On good terms with Beethoven and a rival to Hummel, Moscheles was considered in his day to be a most eminent composer and performer. He was one of the first pianists to play Beethoven's sonatas in public. In 1814 a Grande Duo Concertante for guitar and piano was published at Modena; to Giuliani's guitar part, Moscheles added an elaborate piano accompaniment, the whole work extending to four movements. A later edition followed in Paris in 1828, the composition being dedicated to the Archduke Rudolph of Austria, (a patron of Beethoven, who dedicated several piano sonatas, the Piano Concerto No. 4, and the Archduke Trio, Op. 97 to Rudolph). In 1818, Giuliani with Moscheles and Mayseder gave a recital for the Archduchess of Parma.

It is said that Beethoven attended a concert by Giuliani in 1808, and there is an account of the guitarist dining with the great man. By 1810 however Beethoven was so deaf that conversations had to be written down and it seems probable that the small sounds of the guitar would thus have been less than fully audible to him.

Associations with the distinguished composers of the day did not, on this basis, resolve the guitar's problems in the long term. Yet, though Beethoven and Moscheles did not compose for the instrument, they did accept a guitarist as a worthy fellow musician, and the guitar was not unspoken for in the glorious years of Vienna.

Giuliani left Vienna in 1819 and spent the rest of his life in Italy. He died in 1829 in his forty-eighth year. The obituary in the *Giornale delle Due Sicilie* commented:

> The guitar was transformed in his hands into an instrument similar to the harp, sweetly soothing men's hearts.

Four years after his death *The Giulianiad* was founded in his honour and was published between 1833 and 1835, a unique monument to a remarkable personality of the guitar.

Dionisio Aguado (1784-1849) is in retrospect a lonely prophet of later concepts of guitar technique. His compositions are hardly ever performed in recitals, and his studies are not given the affection that students lavish on Sor, Giuliani and Carcassi. But alone among the nineteenth century players Aguado advocated the use of 'the nails', a technique later exploited by Segovia which was to bring the guitar out of the shadows into the brightest sunlight.

Aguado at the time, possibly overawed by the personality of Sor, seems to have had regrets about his use of nails. Sor in his *Méthode pour la Guitare* leaves no doubt about his feelings;

> It is necessary that the performance of Mr. Aguado should have so many excellent qualities as it possesses, to excuse his employment of

the nails; and he himself would have condemned the use of them if he had not attained such a degree of agility, nor found himself beyond the time of life in which we are able to contend against the bend of the fingers acquired by long habitude. His master played with the nails, and shone at a period when rapid passages alone were required of the guitar, when the only object in view was to dazzle and astonish . . . It was only after many years that we met again, and he then confessed to me that, if he were to begin again, he would play without using the nails.

Whether Aguado was just being tactful to Sor is not clear but in the last edition of the former's Method (*Escuela de Guitarra,* Madrid, 1843), he speaks of the matter in terms that might almost have come from a textbook by Segovia himself:

> I consider it preferable to play with the nails in order to obtain from the guitar strings a tone unlike that of any other instrument. To my mind the guitar has a character peculiar to itself; it is sweet, harmonious, melancholic: at times it becomes majestic, and although it does not admit of the grandeur of the harp or piano, it yields, on the other hand, a delicate grace . . . In order to produce these effects I prefer to play with the nails, because if properly used, the resulting tone is clear, metallic and sweet; it must be understood however that the strings are not struck with the nails only, because then the sound would not be very pleasant. The string is attacked first with the finger-tip, the fleshy part of it that faces the thumb, with the fingers somewhat stretched out (not so bent as for playing with the tip only) sliding over the string to the nail. The nails must not be too hard; they must be trimmed into an oval shape and barely over the surface of the flesh, for, if they are too long, they interfere with the dexterity by considerably delaying the action of the strings, and moreover make the touch less sure; in the right way they enable very fast runs to be executed with great clarity.

Of all the great players born in the nineteenth century, only Segovia pondered the full implications of these words, and from a similar concept, and nature's blessing on the formation of his fingers and nails, evolved a remarkable approach to guitar sonority. Playing with nails alone is likely to produce a thin timbre; the fingertip flesh creates a less brilliant sound. To use flesh and nail in partnership both brightens up the flesh tone and subdues the brittle sharpness of the nail.

Of the twentieth century players of significance, only Emilio Pujol has clung to the idea of using fingertips without nail. In his book on the problem, *El Dilema del Sonido en la Guitarra* (Ricordi, 1960), he expresses his views in terms that Sor would have approved:

> The sound produced with the nails strikes one's ear as if each note were a very small, sharp arrow piercing our sensibility. It is conical, pungent

and nasal, reminiscent of the lute and the harpsichord, with an odour of frankincense and a savour of ancient ballads . . . The tone of a string struck with the finger-tip possesses an intrinsic beauty, which affects the deepest feelings of our sensibility, just as air and light permeate space.

These ideas were derived to some extent from the example of Francisco Tárrega, with whom Pujol studied. The great twentieth century players have all however used their nails, following Segovia's example; Segovia himself incurred the displeasure of many of Tárrega's disciples in his early years by going against the master's dictates.

For Aguado and Sor there was an additional factor in the complex squabbles over use of nail or fingertip. Guitars in the early nineteenth century were rather smaller than those of the post-Torres era, and paradoxically, small guitars are not easy to hold satisfactorily. Nowadays even young children can often hold a full-size guitar more easily than a smaller one. Obviously the sitting position alters the right hand position and the angle of the fingers' attack on the strings.

Whereas most guitarists after Tárrega have a reasonably uniform sitting posture, involving the use of a footstool, the players of Sor's generation solved the problem of sitting with the guitar unilaterally, each to his own. Aguado, for example, invented a tripod with which to hold the instrument, and this clever contraption impressed even Fernando Sor who believed that the full effect of his Fantasie Elégiaque, Op. 59 could only be achieved by using the tripod:

> Without the excellent invention of my friend Aguado, I would never have dared to impose on the guitar so great a task as that of making it produce the effects required by the nature of this new piece. I would never have imagined that the guitar could produce at the same time different qualities of tone — of the treble, of the bass, and harmonic complement required in a piece of this character, and without great difficulty, being within the scope of the instrument.

Daring to impose musical demands on the guitar constitutes the essence of its progress, and 'different qualities of tone' represent the life-blood of the guitar. Thus the problem of posture with the instrument is vital. Even today, despite the standardisation mentioned above of the basic principles of holding the guitar, the sitting player and his general body language express infinitely important messages to his audience of involvement or detachment, mastery, intimacy, tension or relaxation; in the nineteenth century, until Tárrega and his larger build of guitar solved the problem, the situation was too experimental.

Matteo Carcassi, in his famous *Méthode complète pour la guitare*,

(Paris, c.1840), still very much in print and available in various editions, came quite close to a reasonable solution which must have helped the students of his time:

> In order steadily to hold the Guitar it is necessary to sit on a chair a little higher than those generally used and to place the left foot on a hassock of proportionate height to the chair on which one is sitting . . . the pupil has to place the Guitar in an oblique line of the left knee, as indicated in the preceding figure; such a position is preferable to all the others because it offers three points of support to the instrument, which is then well balanced without needing help from the hands to hold it; the other positions present the disadvantage they often cause stiffness.

This seems preferable to Sor's use of a table or even Aguado's tripod. But actually three points of contact will not be enough; the fourth point of contact which Carcassi used was to rest the little finger on the front of the guitar. This factor, mentioned in Chapter Nine in connection with the lute, was a fundamental physiological error, and a throw-back to centuries of lute practice. According to Carcassi's principles softer tone colours and sounds could be obtained by shifting the hand forward over the soundhole; this would itself have been a destabilising effect on right hand technique. Part of Sor's mastery may have been his willingness to relinquish the right hand's little finger from its prop position.

In traditional lute technique the positioning of the little finger on the soundboard would help to deaden the extraneous overtones of such a lightly constructed instrument. There may have been a further reason; it is difficult on the lute to provide a resting place for the arm, and the presence of part of the hand holding the lute in place would have helped to steady the posture. It is noticeable how many self-taught guitarists, folk-singers, and children, even today, almost as a subconscious prompting, drop the little finger onto the soundboard of the guitar; this is a very natural gesture to compensate for the weakness of undeveloped fingers.

On the Torres type of larger guitar, it was easier than on the lute or earlier types of guitar, to provide a suitable resting place for the right elbow, which acted then as a kind of fulcrum for the right arm. Once this had been realised, the right hand mechanism could become physically liberated and more dexterity in the movement of the right hand achieved. In fact one tendon goes from the little finger and the ring finger to the elbow, and to pin the little finger to the soundboard is to limit the possible movements of the right hand. The early nineteenth century guitarists were groping their way towards an understanding of the principles of holding the guitar.

They were possibly handicapped however by playing the smaller size of guitar, and by the fact that flesh techniques generally utilise the first and second joints of the right hand fingers. Nail techniques would not have been possible in the older style of anchoring the little finger, as such a position would inhibit the movement from the knuckle necessary to achieve good nail tone. Thus even Sor, despite his free right hand movements, preferred to cling to the older concepts of what constituted good tone, an argument that still occasionally makes its presence felt.

The contemporaries of Sor did not therefore adopt common technical lines of approach even with regard to the simple act of sitting down to play. What is fascinating however is that all the issues relative to guitar technique as practised by later players were implicitly or explicitly discussed in the Methods including such problems as guitar construction, types of string, hand positions, general postural difficulties, and the type of music appropriate to the guitar.

Ferdinando Carulli (1770-1841) has had his musical reputation salvaged by a remarkable Serenade for two guitars, after being pilloried by Segovia for his sterile lack of imagination. Carulli is a more significant figure in the early guitar movement than might at first be realised.

His *Méthode complète pour la guitare* (Paris, 1810) has been in print for most of the time since it first came out, and ran through five editions before being enlarged into an extended sixth edition. Carulli, again under the spell of men like Czerny and Clementi, systematised the principles of guitar technique with methodical if somewhat dull effectiveness. He also published a book entitled *L'Harmonie appliquée à la Guitare* (Paris, 1825), a historical precedent for several similar texts published in our own century.

Most of Carulli's life was spent in France, though he was originally a Neapolitan. He worked with Lacote to improve the guitar's structure. In 1810 he presented his son Gustave with a magnificent guitar now preserved in the Musée du Conservatoire Nationale de Musique in Paris. Its purfling and heavily ornate sound-hole reveal that the tradition of using the guitar as a piece of inlaid furniture was not entirely extinct, and the guitar seems to have only eleven frets. Carulli may have thought this was more than enough scope for a young beginner.

In the edition of *The Giulianiad* referred to earlier, Sor is quoted as follows:

> The manner of constructing the body of the instrument is almost everywhere understood extremely well, and most Neapolitan, German

and French guitars, leave in this respect, very little superiority to the
Spanish . . . and if I wanted an instrument I would procure it from
M. Joseph Martinez of Malaga, or from M. Lacote, a French maker,
the only person, who, besides his talents, has proved to me that he
possesses the quality of not being inflexible to reasoning.

The writer of the article, having established Lacote's significance as
a luthier, goes on to talk about these guitars:

> The superiority of Lacote's guitars consists in their symmetrical
> proportions, in the quality of the wood, in the mathematical exactness
> of the frets, neck and head, and in their general workmanship. A
> proper regard seems to be paid also to the thickness or rather thinness
> of the wood, and, above all, that the wood shall be well seasoned. The
> pains Lacote takes in superintending his manufactory has finally gained
> for him the reputation of being one of the first, if not the very first,
> maker in Europe. Add to this the inspection and examination which
> these instruments undergo by men such as Sor, Carulli &c before they
> are finally sent from his workshop.

Thus Carulli's influence in his age was quite pervasive, and he
receives an honourable mention in the same breath as Sor. As well as
composing his successful Method, he wrote over four hundred other
works for the guitar including concertos and ensemble music. His
material today, apart from the duo writing, is regarded as primarily
worthy for pedagogic purposes, but not for solo recitals. He thus
recruits his support from the amateur guitarists who may exercise
their hands on his writing, but do not give him their hearts.

Amateur players are usually fonder of another Italian, Matteo
Carcassi (1792-1853), a Florentine who like so many others eventually
gravitated to Paris, that perennial Mecca of artists. Carcassi emulated
Sor and Giuliani in the extent of his concertising, playing in London
in 1822 (his debut) and several times in later years, as well as touring
Germany, and giving many recitals in France.

Twenty-two years younger than Carulli, he continued the older
man's pedagogic interests in systematising guitar technique. His
Méthode complète pour la Guitare, Op. 59 takes the player through
all keys, and places the emphasis on a knowledge of chords,
arpeggios, scales, and a thorough exercising in all the basic guitar
devices. He established several principles worthy of the attention of
modern students, providing that the spirit and not the detailed text of
his advice is followed:

> In composing this Method it was not my intention to produce a
> scientific treatise; I have simply had in view to facilitate the study of the
> Guitar by adopting a system which in the most clear, simple and
> precise manner, might offer a thorough knowledge of all the resources

of this instrument . . . I took the greatest care to dispose on a progressive plan each lesson in order that a pupil totally ignorant of this instrument might learn by degrees to play from the first to last exercise without meeting any of those difficulties which through their aridity are too often the cause of his getting discouraged.

Independently of the fingering of the left hand of which I have extensively treated, the training of the right hand has always appeared to me one of the most essential points for succeeding in the acquisition of a steady and pleasing execution . . .

By the continual use I have made with my pupils of the rules on which this Method is based I can assert that any intelligent person who will attentively study this book from beginning to end, will acquire a perfect knowledge of the mechanism of the guitar.

I shall always esteem myself amply rewarded for my labour if I can obtain the certainty of having composed a useful work.

The little pieces contained in the first part of the Method are truly progressive and their simplicity and musicality may account for the continued popularity of the work over one and a half centuries. The second part consists of slurs, trills, scales in thirds, sixths, octaves and tenths, reminding one of violin tutors of the same era. The third part is recreational though arranged in progressive order of difficulty.

Carcassi is also remembered for his book of *Twenty-five Melodic and Progressive Studies* which illustrate his fluency and lyricism, and a certain sentimentality that might not have pleased Sor. The Carcassi studies are quite different from Sor's compositions and though less substantial in terms of suitable recital material do contain some excellent melodies, as well as involving the student in arpeggio patterns, tremolo technique, scale passages, slurs, etc. Wherever the guitar is played in the world Carcassi's studies seem to find their way, especially his popular Study in A, played sooner or later by every aspiring guitarist:

One year before the death of Carcassi, Francisco Tárrega was born. A tremendous gulf, as between new and old traditions, separates the two generations of guitarists. Carcassi was the last of Sor's contemporaries, those players born in the eighteenth century whose recitals and teaching gave the six string guitar its first impulses to creative life. Carcassi and Tárrega are divided not only by a subtle distinction in ability, but by the figure of Antonio de Torres Jurado (1817-92) whose establishment of the full-size modern classical guitar was to change its voice, its technique and its aspirations.

Without the genius of Torres, the guitar's destiny might have faltered irrevocably. Instead, as so often before, the Protean shape and size of the instrument evolved towards a more flexible and expressive artistic ideal, and in so doing began to leave the early nineteenth century guitar tradition isolated within the confines, sweet but restricted, of the Panormo and Lacote guitars on which players had lavished so much energy.

The guitar now entered its mature phase and though it had many years of struggle ahead, the instrument returned for its central development to the land of Milán and Narváez, Sanz and Sor, to complete the shaping of a further chapter in its complex history.

13. Interregnum

There are as many different sounds as there are fingers.

Chopin

In the first two decades of the nineteenth century many great composers, some of them the finest virtuosi of the age, were born including Berlioz (1803), Mendelssohn (1809), Chopin and Schumann (1810), Liszt (1811), and Verdi and Wagner (1813). Of these illustrious names only Berlioz showed any interest in the guitar and in his Treatise upon *Modern Instrumentation and Orchestration* (1856) he explains its stature as he saw it:

> The guitar is an instrument suited for accompanying the voice and for figuring in a few unnoisy compositions, as also for executing singly pieces more or less complicated in several parts, which possess a true charm when performed by really good players . . . It is almost impossible to write well for the guitar without being a player on the instrument. The majority of composers who employ it, are, however, far from knowing its powers; and therefore they frequently assign it things to play, of excessive difficulty, of little sonorousness, and little effect . . . In the usual position of the right hand, the little finger resting upon the body of the instrument, the thumb is used for playing the three lower strings . . . One can hardly, I repeat, without playing the guitar write for it pieces in several parts, containing various passages, and introducing all the resources of the instrument. In order to form an idea of what the best performers are able to produce in this way, the compositions of such celebrated guitar-players as Zanni de Ferranti, Huerta, Sor, &c., should be studied . . . Since the introduction of the pianoforte into all houses where the least taste for music exists, the guitar has dropped into somewhat rare cultivation excepting in Spain and Italy.
>
> Some performers have studied it, and still study it, as a solo instrument; in such a way as to derive effects from it, no less original than delightful . . . Nevertheless its melancholy and dreamy character might more frequently be made available; it has a real charm of its own, and there would be no impossibility in writing for it so that this should be made manifest.

Berlioz was a true aficionado of the guitar but his Treatise is not a glowing testimonial to the instrument's stature in the mid-nineteenth century. Today only the scholars of guitar history can recall the likes of Ferranti (1802-1878) or Huerta (1804-1875) elevated by Berlioz as 'celebrated guitar-players'.

Admittedly Ferranti received a framed tribute from Paganini himself, certifying his prowess as 'one of the greatest guitarists I have ever heard'. Huerta, a Spanish player, toured the United States, Cuba and Martinique, as well as Europe, and in 1827 gave a concert with none other than Moscheles. He also has a further claim to fame in that he married one of the beautiful daughters of the guitar maker Louis Panormo, and was praised for his skill by Victor Hugo.

The French critic Fétis praised Huerta in the *Revue Musicale* of 1830 as a player who 'raised the guitar to the same sublime height as Paganini did with the violin'. Huerta travelled as far as Egypt and the Holy Land to give recitals, played in many European courts, and was a friend of Rossini. But virtuosity without a corresponding gift for composing in the ages before recording, is a transient effect, and the small collection of works he left behind is not a lasting memorial.

Another teacher of this epoch was José Broca (1805-1882), a guitarist and composer whose works are still in print though not played in the concert hall. His significance seems to lie primarily in the fact that he taught the guitar to Felipe Pedrell (1841-1922), one of the great pioneers and enthusiasts of Spanish national music, whose work was described by Falla as 'the cornerstone of the arch upon which modern music rests'. Broca also taught Esteve Joseph Ferrer (1835-1916), a guitarist who gave recitals in Spain and France and became professor of guitar at Barcelona. Thus the influence of the obscure players of the nineteenth century flows into the twentieth century, and in the case of Pedrell, with great consequences for the health and vitality of modern Spanish culture.

Two guitarists born in the same year are Johann Kaspar Mertz (1806-1856) and Napoleon Coste, a Frenchman (1806-1883). Their paths crossed in 1856 when they entered for a prize for the best guitar composition, offered by Nikolai Makaroff in Brussels. Mertz won with his Op. 65, Concerto for solo guitar, and Coste came second with his Op. 27, 28, 29 and 30 being submitted. Mertz died before he could collect the reward.

Coste was a pupil of Sor in Paris, perhaps his most remembered disciple, for his studies are still used by guitarists and display many imaginative and novel concepts. In 1828 he performed a duo concert with an Italian player Luigi Sagrini when they offered, among other pieces, Giuliani's Variazioni Concertanti, Op. 130, still a popular work among recording artists. Coste's virtuoso career was terminated by a broken right arm, perhaps during the 1850's. His contribution to the preservation of the guitar heritage of Sor and Giuliani is certainly a significant one, even though his own compositions are hardly ever performed in the concert hall.

A pupil of Giuliani was the Polish guitarist Bobrowicz (1805-c.1860), who was acclaimed in 1833 after a concert (given by Clara Wieck) as the Chopin of guitarists, a strange compliment which in later years was also accorded to Francisco Tárrega. Another Polish player was Felix Horetzky (1800-1871), previously quoted for his connection with *The Giulianiad*, who gave recitals throughout Europe, including appearances in Vienna, London and Edinburgh; while in Scotland he gave lessons to Stanislaus Sczepanowski (1814-1852), another Pole who later studied with Sor in Paris, before beginning a concert career that extended as far as St. Petersburg, including recitals in Madrid (1842), London, Berlin, Cracow and Bucharest, amongst others.

Another guitarist of the period who achieved considerable fame was Giulio Regondi (c.1822-1872), who played as an infant prodigy at many of the European courts, being acclaimed this time as 'the Paganini of the guitar'. Regondi appeared with Moscheles in 1836, and toured Europe in the grand progress characteristic of so many distinguished performers of this epoch; Regondi's route taking in Prague, Vienna, Paris and London, where his premature death of cancer robbed the guitar of a prominent virtuoso.

The Spanish guitar tradition, as if preparing for the appearance of Tárrega, was preserved after Sor and Aguado by José Viñas (1823-1888) and Julián Arcas (1832-1882); Viñas toured Europe in his early twenties and several of his compositions are still in print (at least one has been recorded by Maria Luisa Anido, a pupil of Llobet). The majority of his works rest in peaceful silence however.

Arcas is of greater importance in that his compositions were an influence on Tárrega who played them in his concerts. His Fantasia sobre la Jota Aragonesa, still popular with guitarists, is often erroneously attributed to Tárrega though it is not in his style or idiom. Arcas visited England in 1862 and played to the royal family at the Brighton Pavilion. He played a Torres guitar and was on good terms with that luthier. Tárrega, at the age of ten, met Arcas after one of his recitals and impressed the older maestro considerably.

Mention should also be made of Antonio Cano (1811-1897), many of whose compositions are still published. He became professor of guitar at the National Conservatoire, Madrid, in 1868, and wrote a successful *Grand Method for Guitar* (Madrid, 1852) which ran to

several editions. He was at some time an associate of Aguado and is
often credited with an arrangement of Estudio Brillante in A by
Alard, a piece frequently played by twentieth century guitarists in a
version by Tárrega.

A representative of the guitar in England was Madame Pratten
(1821-1895), born in Mulheim, Germany, the daughter of Ferdinand
Pelzer (1801-1860) who had helped in the publication of *The
Giulianiad*. She settled in London, wrote three methods for the
guitar and many other compositions, and took part in concerts. In
1871 she played Giuliani's Third Guitar Concerto accompanied on
the piano by a niece of Giuliani.

What is one to make of these scattered and obscure names which flit
like ghosts across footnotes or odd pages of guitar history? Their
music has not attracted twentieth century players and pieces like
Arcas' Jota demonstrate a sterile exhibitionism which may have been
all too characteristic of the guitar's musical role at this time.

It is difficult to evaluate these virtuosi, who were acclaimed in their
day and whose travels propagated the guitar in many countries. If
however the published works of Broca, Viñas, Arcas, Pratten,
Mertz, and even Coste, represent the usual recital material then it can
not be claimed as a very worthwhile epoch in the guitar's development.

In the age of Chopin, Liszt and Schumann, the guitar needed a
stronger soil than this. The instrument seems to have relied on
dazzling but shallow effects of dexterity and brightness. The players
kept the guitar alive by their efforts, but they were less inspired as
composers. It was from this comparative slough of despond that
Francisco Tárrega would attempt to lift the guitar.

PART THREE

THE GOLDEN AGE

14. The Torres Guitar

There is sweet music here that softer falls
Than petals from blown roses on the grass . . .

Tennyson: *Song of the Lotus Eaters*

Before dealing in detail with the life and work of Francisco Tárrega, who laid down so many of the basic principles governing guitar technique and repertoire accepted in the twentieth century, it is appropriate to examine the work of Antonio de Torres Jurado (1817-1892). Torres was one of the most inventive luthiers in the guitar's history and, in a sense, created the modern guitar as we now know it. His instruments displaced the Panormo and Lacote type of guitar and established themselves as prototypes for all subsequent guitar makers of distinction.

Torres first met Tárrega in 1869 when the latter was seventeen. A wealthy businessman, Antonio Cánesa Mendayas, picked up the information that the phenomenal success of Arcas was mainly due to his possession of a Torres guitar. It was decided that Tárrega should have such a guitar put into his hands.

Cánesa and Tárrega visited Torres in Seville. At first Tárrega was shown one of the more ordinary guitars in the shop, but when he began playing, Torres was so impressed by the young man's skill that he brought out one of his finest instruments. This was a maple wood guitar with a spruce tapa or front, cedar neck, and ebony fingerboard, and presumably superior to any instrument Tárrega had ever seen before except perhaps that played by Arcas in a concert he had attended. Cánesa purchased the guitar for him and Tárrega played it for many years.

Torres thought deeply about the problems of guitar construction. He established the string length of his instrument at sixty-five centimetres, compared with the Panormo and Lacote guitars of between sixty-two and sixty-three centimetres. (Later makers often increased the string length to sixty-six or sixty-seven centimetres.)

The larger size of the Torres guitar moved the instrument forward into a realm of greater dynamic and tonal possibilities, attributes which Tárrega's compositions exploit admirably. This extension in the size of the guitar was a crucial step in its development.

Distance between frets became proportionately greater and therefore much of the music written by Sor and his contemporaries for performance on the smaller size guitar became rather more difficult except for those with big hands. (The same sort of problem has occurred in the history of the pianoforte where the keys are individually a little wider than those on spinets, virginals, clavichord, or harpsichord, thus favouring the wide stretch of a player such as Liszt or Rachmaninoff.) The Torres string length soon became the accepted ideal and there has been no regression to the more convenient but less powerful smaller models of the pre-Torres era. The advantages of his innovation outweighed the obvious disadvantages, though in future, concert artists would have to be born with the right size hands if they were to achieve total mastery of the complete repertoire.

It is worth noting that many of the early seventeenth century's five-course guitars had been constructed with the Torres-like string length of sixty-five centimetres or more. Stradivarius made a guitar about 1688 of seventy-four centimetres whilst a Tielke guitar in the Victoria and Albert Museum, London, is seventy-two and a half centimetres in string length. Torres thus had excellent precedents for his decision to make guitars of a certain size and was not creating large instruments such as the world had never seen or heard before; he was however bidding adieu to the smaller guitars he must have known as a young man.

Torres developed a theory that only the front of the guitar, the table or tapa, really affected guitar tone to any significant extent. The choice of wood for the tapa becomes the determining factor for the resonance and clarity of the guitar's sound. The timber selected must have grown at the correct rate of development in ideal circumstances relating to altitude and temperature. The grain of the wood must neither be too coarse, as with timber that grows too quickly, or too fine — it must be just right. The construction of a fine instrument can only be as good as the timber selected.

The front of the guitar, made from spruce and sometimes cedar, is constructed from a piece of quarter sawn timber. A plank of about eight millimetres in thickness, is sawn into pieces of four millimetres to provide two matching halves for the front of the guitar. These two pieces are carefully planed and shaped to form the tapa of the instrument.

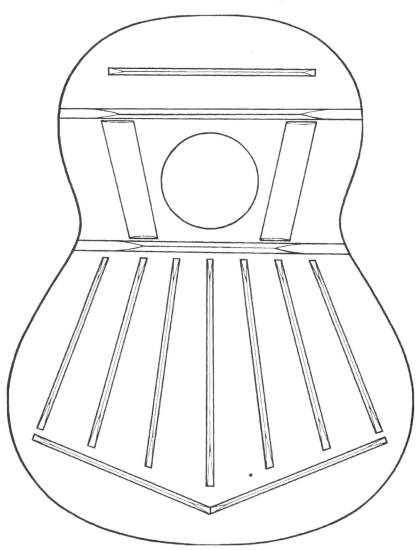

a. Antonio de Torres Jurado (1817-92)

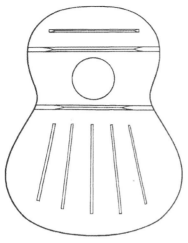

b. Joseph Panormo (1767-1837)

c. Domingo Esteso (1882-193?

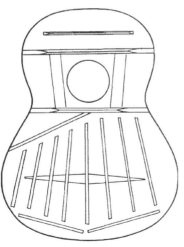

d. Ignacio Fleta (1898-1978)

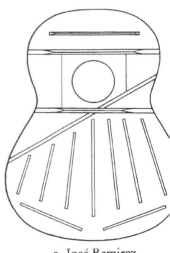

e. José Ramirez

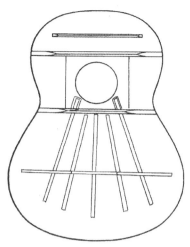

f. Robert Bouchet

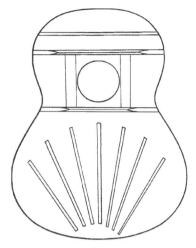

g. José Yacopi

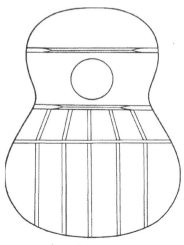

h. Vicente Tatay

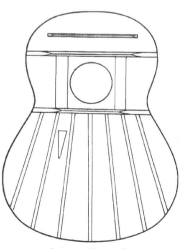

i. Juan Estruch

To enable the front of the guitar to achieve its fullest potential as a vibrating diaphragm for the instrument's resonance, Torres evolved a system of bracing the tapa with his own distinctive type of fan-strutting. Previous guitars through the ages had used struts under the front to strengthen the wood against the pull of the strings. Torres devised a new method of fan-strutting to create clarity and balance across all six strings and a new concept of guitar tone.

After Torres had shown the way, other luthiers followed, developing their own ideas about bracing the tapa but designing instruments very much along his lines in terms of measurements and ideals. Torres is thus the father of the classical guitar as we know it, and Tárrega's advocacy of his type of instrument did much to banish the smaller guitars favoured by the early nineteenth century. The guitar had now achieved a new identity and the work of Torres sealed the fate of the beautiful but limited voice of the instruments made by Panormo, Lacote, Martínez and Pagés.

11a. *Two Ramirez Guitars:* two concert guitars from the workshop of José Ramirez of Madrid, both dated 1977.

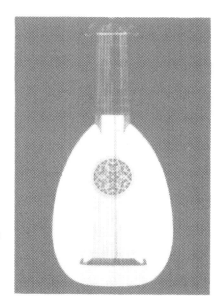

11b. *A Dolmetsch Lute:* a concert Renaissance lute (ten course) in the collection of the City of Leeds College of Music.

12a. *Ramirez Bridge.*

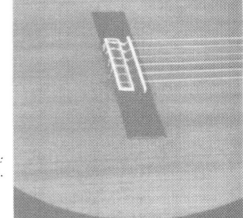

12b. *Ramirez Bridge:*
side view.

13a. *Rosette of a Dolmetsch Lute:* this shows a design of complexity and beauty.

13b. *Rosette of a Ramirez Guitar:* the rosette of a guitar is a reminder of the Arabic influence in Spanish culture.

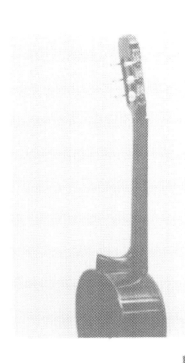

14a. *Machine-heads of a Ramirez Guitar:* its appeal is in the classical symmetry of form and line. The 'Spanish heel' at the base of the neck is an essential aspect of the structure.

14b. *Peg-box of a Dolmetsch Lute:* another distinguishing characteristic of the lute's identity.

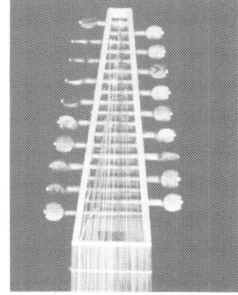

15. The Poet of the Guitar: Francisco Tárrega (1852-1909)

. . . La guitarra cuando Tárrega la pulsa, es algo más que el instrumento, es un ser vivo que vibra al compás del sentimiento del músico . . .

(Report of Tárrega's recital at Vall de Uxo,
19 November 1904)

The life of Francisco Tárrega was by no means as spectacular as that of great players like Sor or Giuliani. The three fold activities of giving recitals, composing and teaching were similar to those of Sor's contemporaries but Tárrega's life, despite various concert tours abroad, was rooted in his native Spain.

He was born at Villarreal, Valencia on 21 November 1852. As a boy he studied piano with Eugenio Ruiz, and learned a little about the guitar from Manuel Gonzalez, a blind guitarist. In 1862 Tárrega attended a concert given by Julian Arcas, who played a Torres guitar; the boy was introduced to Arcas and also played for him. Some years later, as has been previously related, occurred the historic meeting between Torres and Tárrega.

After military service, Tárrega entered the Real Conservatorio, Madrid, about 1874, where he studied piano and harmony. He played the guitar throughout his time as a student and performed a recital at the Conservatorio. At this period of his life he may have begun his lifelong task of transcribing music for the guitar from other instruments, a task for which his pianistic abilities eminently qualified him.

In 1879 a visit to Alicante enabled him to meet Arcas once more, as well as a pupil of Arcas who later helped him to arrange recitals in the area. He also met his future wife, Maria.

By 1880 Tárrega was already being acclaimed as 'the Sarasate of the guitar'. His repertoire at the time is said to have included works by Sor, Aguado, Arcas, Viñas and Cano, as well as some of his own transcriptions.

In March, 1881, Tárrega went to France where he played a number of recitals in both Lyons and Paris, including a performance in the presence of Queen Isabel II, Princess Mathilde and Baron Rothschild. In the Odéon Théâtre, Paris, Tárrega performed at a concert to commemorate the death of Calderon, presided over by none other than Victor Hugo, who was greatly pleased with Tárrega's playing. By May however, Tárrega was depressed, and a visit to England did not help to cheer him up, where he found the English stiffness, the language, the climate and the fog quite unbearable.

He returned to Spain after a short while and married Maria. His marriage provided Tárrega with several children, some of whom died tragically in their infancy.

In 1884 Tárrega gave a concert in collaboration with Albéniz in Barcelona, a city in which Tárrega later took up residence in 1888. In Barcelona, Tárrega's friends included Granados and Malats, as well as Albéniz and other leading Spanish musicians.

Tárrega continued to give recitals throughout his life, receiving glowing reports from critics wherever he played. He performed in Perpignan, Cadiz, Palma de Mallorca, Cannes, Nice, Monte Carlo, Paris, Granada, Rome, Naples, Milan, etc. His programmes included his own compositions as well as transcriptions from Chopin, Mozart, Schubert, Mendelssohn, Verdi, Albéniz (including *Granada*) and Gottschalk. Thus the pattern of Segovia's recitals was in the tradition established by Tárrega in which a mixture of compositions for the guitar and appropriate transcriptions provided contrast and seriousness.

Several of Tárrega's transcriptions, including that of Chopin's Nocturne Op. 9, No. 2; Op. 32, No. 1; and Beethoven's 'Moonlight' Sonata (first movement), as well as other arrangements of Beethoven, Wagner, Rubinstein and Berlioz, now seem somewhat grotesque in the context of the guitar. However, apart from these obviously unsuitable adaptations, it is to Tárrega's credit that he realised the guitar need not be confined to the limits of its contemporary horizons. His arrangements of the music of Albéniz are particularly successful in terms of the guitar and won the composer's approval; they may have also given aspiring writers for the guitar new ideas of the instrument's latent capabilities.

Francisco Tárrega died in 1909, the year of Segovia's professional debut at the age of sixteen in Granada. It is to be regretted that Segovia and Tárrega never met, but appropriate that in the year of his death, his great successor should have begun the work which consolidated and fulfilled Tárrega's vision of the guitar as a noble and beautiful instrument.

Twentieth century recitalists perform comparatively few of Tárrega's compositions in the concert hall. He is near enough to us in time for his significance to exceed that of his written works alone. Tárrega's influence has come down to us through such pupils as Emilio Pujol, and Miguel Llobet (1878-1938) whom Segovia described as 'a great artist' and from whose transcriptions have come many familiar repertoire pieces.

Tárrega developed new principles of guitar technique and in his recitals and compositions exploited the rich sonorous potential of the Torres guitar. Whereas the early nineteenth century masters had been hypnotised by the grandeur of sonatas and extended sets of variations in the style of Mozart and Beethoven, Tárrega was more fascinated by the evocative singing voice of the guitar working within miniature musical structures. Thus he wrote no sonatas or fantasias and created no large-scale compositions.

He was interested in Chopin's stylish cantabile on the keyboard, especially as Tárrega himself had a thorough training in pianoforte, but his compositions produced mazurkas and preludes, not concertos, ballades or sonatas.

Tárrega's allegiance to Chopin's cantabile did not hinder his awareness of himself as a Spanish composer. Whereas Sor, Aguado and Giuliani were drawn towards European musical circles outside Spain and Italy, Tárrega represents the Spanish guitar at its most nationalistic, a factor which ensures his popularity among amateurs and some recitalists, but not among many of the critics.

The most famous of Tárrega's compositions reveals his desire to shape the guitar's voice into evocations of Iberia. Recuerdos de la Alhambra is a superb example of Tárrega's wistful creation of atmosphere. It is no more than a thin sliver of delightful melody, tastefully harmonised and calling forth a world of imagination, slender but memorable. By exploiting the 'tremolo' technique, the guitarist's only device by which an unbroken, legato melodic line can be simulated, Tárrega demonstrates the old adage, 'the song of the piano is a discourse, the song of the harp is an elegy, but the song of the guitar is a song'.

Recuerdos de la Alhambra is a composition that could only be written once. With the honourable exception of Agustín Barrios, most composers since Tárrega who have attempted to write tremolo studies, have been rewarded for their efforts with feeble echoes of Tárrega's little masterpiece. His name will always be linked with Recuerdos, and the composition was performed by Segovia from his early concerts onwards as a brilliant demonstration of the guitar's natural singing voice.

Capricho Arabe is another of Tárrega's works with a Spanish scenario. A melodic line is placed over a simple accompaniment to evoke Moorish Andalucia. As with Recuerdos de la Alhambra, Tárrega's use of higher positions up the neck of the guitar and tonal effects achieved by precisely indicated fingerings gives the piece a very different atmosphere from anything written by Sor or Giuliani. This is guitar writing, *sui generis*, not to be imagined on any other instrument.

Both Recuerdos de la Alhambra and Capricho Arabe are totally idiomatic works, expressing a Spanish imaginative romanticism through the guitar. Tárrega's strength as well as his limitations lie in the fact that he is always the complete guitarist, bringing the technical requirements to perform his music up to a high level and integrating the music with the needs and indigenous nature of the guitar.

Some of the well-known Tárrega mazurkas, such as Adelita, Marieta and Mazurka in G, are examples of the best guitar compositions for amateur playing ever conceived. Along with Lagrima, one of the most popular items for less skilled players, these tiny gems of the repertoire show Tárrega's empathy with his pupils and his rapport with their enjoyment of the guitar. He rejoiced in naming compositions after his friends and disciples, and captured their character within the framework of a few bars, whether melancholy or sprightly.

His approach to the guitar, like that of Sanz, sets the imagination to work. Titles such as Las Dos Hermanitas, Sueño, La Cartagenera, Alborada, Pavana, Danza Mora and Danza Odalisca, in themselves convey the essence of his approach to music; his work is unpretentious and very human, and yet, despite its popularity, spontaneous and inventive. It inhabits the world of the salon and the private room, and not so much the grand concert hall, but it possesses great charm even where it verges towards sweetness and an excess of sentiment.

Tárrega's analysis of technical problems brought about, in the tradition of Sor and his contemporaries, the composition of many studies. This included sometimes the shaping of the melodies of Bach and other composers into the form of exercises. However Tárrega's estudios frequently fall midway between virtuoso musicianship and the pedagogic requirements of his students with the result that his efforts in this area have not won acclaim in the recital hall, with two major exceptions. Segovia's playing of Tárrega's Sonatina on a Theme of J.D. Alard and Recuerdos de la Alhambra, also a kind of study, have become familiar to international audiences as examples of the estudio de concierto genre.

The little exercises and studies of Tárrega lack the earnest conviction of those of Sor, Giuliani and Aguado. Few guitarists nowadays seem to work long hours on Tárrega's technical medicine, though his longer works are the everyday diet of many aficionados.

Guitarists sometimes tend to be ambivalent in their attitude to Tárrega. He reminds many of their first headlong passion for the guitar, and the self-restricting romanticism of his music, with the overexposure in the concert hall of a few choice works, has meant that his inclusion in a recital is not always intellectually respectable. Some even treat the whole issue of Tárrega with considerable disdain. But his music has been recorded by Segovia, Bream, Diaz, Yepes and Williams, and the few fragile flowers of his imagination continue to bloom in the heat of many guitarists' enthusiasm.

His thinking was even more helpful to the twentieth century recitalist's need to extend the repertoire through transcriptions. Tárrega was the first to transcribe works for the guitar from other instruments with serious intent since the vihuelistas, and much of his output in this respect provided a foundation for Segovia's repertoire. The latter's playing of Haydn, Mendelssohn, Beethoven, Chopin, Grieg, Malats, Schumann, Albéniz and Bach, can often be traced back to Tárrega's original transcriptions. It was Tárrega's 'star pupil' Llobet who introduced Segovia to such perennial glories of the

Segovian canon as Granados' Danzas Españolas, Nos. 5 and 10, La Maja de Goya, the Catalan Folk Songs and Albéniz' Torre Bermeja, and other such pieces.

Tárrega's great labour for the instrument springs into its true perspective through the historical hindsight afforded us by Segovia's career. Tárrega's developments by themselves did not sponsor a revolutionary reassessment of the guitar's powers, though most of the ingredients were there in his playing and thinking.

Pictures of Tárrega reveal the progress that had been made in technical matters since the days of Sor. The left foot is supported by a footstool (banishing Sor's use of a supporting table or Aguado's tripod) and the player appears in a comfortable, natural posture, playing his Torres guitar. The right hand has eased the little finger off the soundboard and the left hand controls its barrés. The right hand is at right angles to the strings, and Tárrega is often credited with the application of apoyando or rest-stroke, that right hand technique of striking through a string and coming to rest on the string beneath; this method of playing the string creates a firm and pleasant tone.

Unfortunately Tárrega did not develop the use of the flesh and nail technique advanced by both Aguado and Segovia. The latter, in his autobiography, mentions the undisguised hostility of Tárrega's disciples to any who used their nails. But apart from this omission, Tárrega laid the basis of modern techniques, and Segovia, who never met Tárrega, gained great benefit from the older master's example, transcriptions and original works.

Tárrega's contribution to the guitar is a rich source of inspiration. He exploited the tone colours of the Torres guitar, cultivated the Spanish impressionistic qualities of the instrument, transcribed prolifically and played many concerts which validated his claims for the guitar's expressiveness. He laid the foundations of a School of Tárrega, whose disciples, though often bigoted and blinkered, and less talented than their maestro, at least gave the young Segovia something to react against in creative terms. Tárrega's finest students, Llobet and Pujol, continued the great work that their mentor had initiated.

16. Andrés Segovia: Origins of Greatness

Fair seed-time had my soul, and I grew up
Fostered alike by beauty and by fear.

Wordsworth: *The Prelude*

Andrés Segovia was born in Linares, Andalucia on 18 February 1893. The story of his life and career is related in his autobiography, chapters of which were first published in the New York *Guitar Review* in 1947, and (with added material) in book form in 1976.* As has often been remarked, Segovia became a legend in his own lifetime, raising the guitar to the level of a serious recital instrument, establishing a repertoire, and passing on the flame of inspiration to the great players who continued his example.

Unlike some great artists who have written autobiographies, Segovia's book is written in a spirit of dignified reticence. His art as a guitarist speaks for him louder than his words, eloquent though his language and utterances may be. Over the turmoil of his early struggles to acquire technical and interpretative mastery and then to advance his career in its initial stages, many fine veils are drawn. The process of elevating the guitar to its present respected stature in the world of music was not without anguish and set-backs, despite the immense success Segovia's art ultimately achieved.

The most difficult part of Segovia's long journey was perhaps the identification of the guitar's worth in the hostile environment which faced the instrument in the early twentieth century, despite Tárrega's efforts and in the Spanish guitar's own country.

From his early childhood Segovia was attracted to the sound of the guitar which in Andalucia must have been a fundamental aspect of daily life. But its very familiarity among the people brought about the guitar's lack of musical reputation. Serious young musicians were diverted from the crudities of the guitar towards the magnificent

---

* *Andrés Segovia: an autobiography of the years 1893-1920:* Macmillan, New York 1976; Marion Boyars, London, 1978.

pantheon of piano, violin and 'cello, with their established repertoire and prospects of employment as performer or teacher. The guitar found its advocates among gypsies and amateurs.

Occasionally a hint of something better would trickle through the barrier of prejudice against the guitar. Segovia, at the age of about twelve, heard Gabriel Ruiz de Almodóvar play a prelude by Tárrega, and his response was dramatic:

> I felt like crying, laughing, even like kissing the hands of a man who could draw such beautiful sounds from the guitar.

Segovia felt disgust for the flamenco and folk music he had been trying to learn, the inevitable starting point for aspiring players. Later an amateur guitarist in Córdoba gave Segovia some more works by Tárrega and other composers. His heroes at that time were Sor, Giuliani and Tárrega who offered some indication that composers and players had toiled to bring the guitar's voice into creative reality.

But even the more artistic examples of guitar music were not sufficient to satisfy Segovia for long. Throughout his career he has found it necessary to stress that he never met Tárrega, thus indicating that more than this composer's offering was necessary to the destiny of the guitar. Tárrega, in Segovia's mature estimation, was subject to various limitations and in effect 'the scope of his noble work did not equal the intensity of his devotion'.

Tárrega played mainly in private, not in public, and performed to guitarists who lacked the finer points of discrimination.

> Consequently he could not achieve significant changes in the general feeling about the artistic value of our neglected instrument.

Moreover Segovia believed that Tárrega's followers were mediocre, with the exception of Miguel Llobet. Segovia maintained a precise balance between admiration for Tárrega's inner vision of the guitar's capabilities and concern that Tárrega's work had not been able to achieve what was really needed. To Manuel Ramirez, the esteemed guitar-maker from whom Segovia received his first worthwhile instrument, Segovia mentioned how Tárrega 'created the soul of the guitar' and vowed to walk 'in the steps of the sainted Francisco'. He could walk in the steps, but he would need to walk further than that to change people's concept of the guitar, and this he knew.

In the quarters where help for the guitar might have been expected, Segovia encountered hostility and that desire to corral the instrument within a coterie which often both preserves and threatens the artistic well-being of the classical guitar. The religious zeal and enthusiasm of Tárrega's disciples kept alive the master's message. But it was time to spread the word, not keep it locked up in monastic isolation. Moreover the tradition needed drastic modification, and the conservative timidity of Tárrega's pupils was in direct contrast to the boldness with which the maestro himself turned over hallowed concepts of the guitar's role.

Daniel Fortea, a pupil of Tárrega and a mediocre composer of trifles, refused to allow Segovia to see the manuscripts of his teacher's unpublished transcriptions. Fortea's rudeness to the man destined to become the world's foremost guitarist produced a fruitful reaction; Segovia vowed to rescue the guitar from its small-minded enthusiasts by eventually, when the time was ripe, approaching leading composers and asking them to write for the guitar. Thus the bigotry of the Tárrega clan achieved by accident a breakthrough in the guitar's history:

> I had to free the guitar from such jailers by creating a repertoire open to all.

Segovia's concert debut at the Ateneo, Madrid, naturally provoked an antagonistic reaction from the supporters of Tárrega, one of whom remarked, 'worst of all . . . he plucks the strings with his nails'. In Valencia too, a stronghold of the disciples of Tárrega, Segovia discovered that however well he played, the guitar aficionados withheld approval, again mainly because Segovia's flesh and nail technique went against Tárrega's edicts. In Segovia's autobiography the insults to his feelings are not forgotten though they may be understated; their effect was to strengthen his resolve to move beyond the circles of influence of these people.

Even Miguel Llobet, the best player among those who studied with Tárrega, played, in Segovia's opinion, with rasping, metallic tones, 'lacking in roundness, volume and resilience'. Llobet shared Tárrega's belief that the guitar was not intended for large concert halls, an article of faith which ran contrary to Andrés Segovia's deepest ambitions.

However, as has been mentioned, Segovia celebrated his friendship with Llobet by playing many of his arrangements, perhaps the greatest possible tribute to some of the finest fruit of Tárrega's tradition.

17. Guitarists and their Repertoire: the Spanish Harvest

Listening to the persuasive voice of the guitar, I said to myself, 'How is it possible that such a beautiful instrument has not serious music composed for it?' My friends came to my rescue by helping me to find the kind of music that I was looking for.

Andrés Segovia

Segovia's career gathered increasing momentum after his first visit to South America in 1920. A short time before leaving Spain to embark on this eventful tour, Segovia found that his repertoire contained scarcely enough material for two recitals. This would include the various pieces by Sor, Giuliani and Aguado, the selected concert items by Tárrega, transcriptions of music by Bach, Beethoven, Schumann, Handel, Mozart, Mendelssohn, Debussy, etc., and some of Llobet's arrangements. But even before the trip to South America, Segovia began his work of persuading composers to write for the guitar, the first time in the instrument's history that this had been attempted.

Federico Moreno Torroba (b. 1891) was introduced to Segovia by a violinist in the Spanish National Symphony Orchestra. Torroba had studied at the Conservatoire in Madrid under Conrado del Campo and was making a reputation as a composer for his zarzuelas and choral works with their strongly Spanish flavour. He was the ideal personality to begin the task of creating a suitable repertoire that Segovia could use in international recitals.

His first offering was the third movement of the Suite Castellana, a Danza in E major. This composition was not apparently completely to Segovia's liking for he never recorded it, but Danza initiated a fertile flow from Torroba's pen. In 1926 Fandanguillo and Arada, the first and second movements of Suite Castellana, were published by

Schott in the new Segovia Guitar Archives series, the most significant publishing venture for the instrument that the world had seen.

Under Segovia's editorship, several more evergreens of the recital hall were added to the repertoire by Torroba. These included the famous Sonatina in A (Ricordi Americana S.A.E.C., 1953) recorded by many great players in the fullness of time, as well as Nocturno (Schott, 1926), Burgalesa, Preludio and Serenata Burlesca, (Schott, 1928) and Pièces Caractéristiques (Schott, 1931).

Torroba's tribute to the spirit of his native city, Madrid, a lively and witty work entitled Madroños, did not appear in print until 1953, though written several years before. Other popular Torroba pieces were those in his suite Castillos de España (Editorial Cadencia, Madrid, 1973) which included compositions such as Romance de los Pinos appropriately renamed Montemayor to fit in with the theme of castles.

Departing from the Segovian repertoire, Torroba has composed a flamenco concerto in four movements (Concierto en Flamenco) in collaboration with Sabicas and Concierto de Castille, recorded by Renata Tarragó, as well as many less significant solo works, a guitar quartet and a Concerto for two guitars.

Torroba's guitar music suited Segovia's artistic temperament perfectly, and the composer has been rewarded by frequent performances in recitals and recordings, thus achieving international fame in a way that his orchestral compositions could not accomplish for him. The guitar has returned his compliment to its voice by establishing Torroba's name as one of the most popular Spanish composers for the instrument. Segovia recorded this music as soon as the 78 rpm 10 inch discs were available to him, and has often re-recorded pieces such as Fandanguillo, Arada and Burgalesa and movements from the Sonatina in A.

The compositions of Torroba are undemanding on the listener, very rhythmic, concise, with imaginative titles, and closely linked with the dances of Spanish folk music though without being too dependent on flamenco motifs. Torroba was above all, like Tárrega, a lyrical composer and his melodies, whilst not consisting of too many notes, are deeply idiomatic on the guitar. As with Tárrega, and unlike Sor and Giuliani, it is impossible to imagine Torroba's guitar music played on any other instrument. However, his work is not easy for the guitar and frequently requires true virtuosity under its smooth and unruffled surface.

Of course most of his music was composed explicitly for Segovia, who shaped the works with his individual rhythmic fluidity characteristic of his approach to the guitar. Segovia never plays in terms of the metronome, and out of his hands, with his close personal identification with the music, Torroba's work loses some of its magic. The simplicity of the composer is both appealing and limiting. Stylistic mannerisms recur throughout his work and the Torroban voice relies on subtle shifts of accent to impart the fullest degree of life to its lilting sweetness.

For this reason Torroba's music fell from favour among many recitalists in the 1970's, though in the twenty years before this, his work was an integral part of the aspirant's repertoire. John Williams performed the Sonatina at his London debut, and both Williams and Bream recorded this and other blooms from Torroba's garden during the early years of their careers.

The most severe of Torroba's limitations, looking at his work as a whole, is the reliance on a small range of key signatures, mainly E, E minor, A, G and an occasional D. Burgalesa, one of the most attractive slow atmospheric pieces written for the guitar, is however in the key of F sharp major, a real departure from the restrictions of usual guitar keys. His Sonatina in A, though full of charm and elegance, flounders in the manner of Giuliani and fails to transcend the dominating open string keys of the guitar (E, A and D, with D tuning on the sixth string). Thus the Sonatina appears as a somewhat conservative work in a miniature cast, delightful but not profound.

Yet Torroba was a true pioneer of the guitar, breaking into new and exciting territory. The precedents available to him were comparatively few, and his work was influenced most by hearing Segovia perform the works of Tárrega, Sor and Giuliani. His imaginative and evocative titles suggest a particular debt to Tárrega.

He was one of the first composers after the early nineteenth century guitarists to attempt the writing of a respectable Sonatina, thus endeavouring to give Segovia those extended musical works available to pianists and violinists. As his minor works are played individually or in small groups in recitals, Torroba's lack of adventurous modulation is not always noticeable. But in the extended works such as the Pièces Caractéristiques or Castillos de España, a certain monotony can jade the lyricism of the total structure. Torroba tried to master the more sustained forms but he will be chiefly remembered for the ability with which he could conjure up atmosphere and colour in shorter compositions.

Torroba represents Spanish romanticism of the twentieth century with all its virtues and limitations. To his credit he returned to the guitar again and again to create pieces which will always be associated with Segovia's art. His wistful cameos are a sweet extension of Tárrega's Spanish guitar and a worthy opening to the new chapter in the history of the instrument which began when Segovia first persuaded him to compose for it.

In 1920 Manuel de Falla composed one of the most significant twentieth century works for the guitar, Homenaje, Pour le Tombeau de Claude Debussy. Though Falla's biographer, Jaime Pahissa, writes a detailed account of how Llobet 'had repeatedly asked Falla to write a work for the guitar, and Falla finally agreed', Segovia claims that the genesis of the work was prompted by Torroba's success with Danza in E major. In this way both Llobet and Segovia contributed to Manuel de Falla's wish to write for the guitar.

Falla and Segovia were good friends, and in 1932 they travelled together in the company of Dr. José Segura, a professor of Granada University, from Geneva to Venice. In 1924, at his vital Paris debut, Segovia played before an audience which included many leading composers including Falla and Roussel.

Regrettably Manuel de Falla did not write more for the guitar, though he intended to compose a piece entitled La Tertulia. Various of his orchestral works arranged for guitar including Danza del Molinero (Farruca) from *El Sombrero de Tres Picos* (*Three-Cornered Hat*), and El Círculo Mágico, Romance del Pescador and Canción del Fuego Fatuo from *El Amor Brujo* (*Love the Magician*); The Fisherman's Tale and Song of the Will-o'-the-Wisp were arranged by Pujol, whilst the Miller's Dance, in various transcriptions, became one of the most popular virtuoso showpieces, though never played by Segovia. Emilio Pujol also arranged Spanish Dance No. 1, from *La Vida Breve* (Max Eschig, Paris, 1957) for two guitars, a work recorded by all the great duos and a firm favourite with audiences.

A few other works have also been transcribed. The Dance of the Corregidor (*The Three-Cornered Hat*), the Seven Popular Spanish Songs (arranged for voice and guitar), and the famous Homenaje (arranged for the piano from the guitar score, one of the few original guitar compositions to be honoured in this way). Thus Falla's voice is not absent from the guitar even though he only composed one work directly for the instrument.

Manuel de Falla was not a prolific composer and like so many great musicians had more to think about than the guitar's repertoire, though for aficionados this remains a tragic omission from a man who perhaps was so supremely suited to write for Segovia. Most of Falla's music is rooted in the harmonic and rhythmic patterns of Spanish folk culture, and the throbbing pulse of flamenco is felt throughout his orchestral writing. A Guitar Concerto from his pen would have been a great prize, and infinitely preferable from the guitarist's point of view to the Harpsichord Concerto which is more rarely performed.

This failure to compose for guitar was not perhaps altogether accidental. Between Falla and the Spanish national instrument was a certain distance which he preferred to overcome by imitating the guitar with the orchestra, rather than by treating the guitar in terms of its habitual national characteristics. As Falla himself wrote in connection with *The Three-Cornered Hat:*

> My intention has been to evoke by means of the instrumentation in particular passages, certain guitaristic values.

He saw the guitar as 'The instrument most complete and richest in its harmonic and polyphonic possibilities' and in 1903 wrote an article for the Austrian Guitar Review on the instrument's musical significance.

These promising symptoms of interest in the guitar were not fulfilled directly by Falla. His vocation was to the higher call of Spanish nationalist music which needed a greater horizon than the guitar could offer him. Born in Cadiz in 1876, he came during his formative years under the magical spell of Felipe Pedrell's fervent enthusiasm for creating music of a truly Spanish nature, founded on the previously despised strength of folk traditions. As Falla himself wrote:

> Our music must be based on the natural music of our people, on the dances and songs that do not always show close kinship . . . It has occasionally been asserted that we have no traditions. We have, it is true, no written traditions, but in our dance and our rhythm we possess the strongest traditions that none can obliterate.

This creed was surely taken up on the guitar's behalf by composers such as Torroba, Turina and Rodrigo, who gave to the instrument the distillation of centuries of flamenco art. Falla, after studying for seven years in Paris in the musical circle of Debussy, Dukas, Ravel, Satie, Schmitt and Roussel, eventually returned from his educational exile and, quite appropriately, settled in Granada near the Alhambra, a living symbol of the Spanish heritage. From his music and life so many Iberian artists drew their inspiration, and his gift to the guitar is implicit in everything he wrote and not just in those pieces arranged specially for it.

He died in 1946. David Ewen in *The World of Twentieth Century Music* (London, 1968) summed up Falla's work exquisitely:

> No major composer in the twentieth century produced as little as Manuel de Falla . . . But most of what he has written are master-pieces — fastidious in workmanship, rich in poetic beauty, evocative of

the colourful personality of Spain.

Joaquín Turina (1882-1949) followed Torroba and Falla into the ranks
of those leading Spanish composers who applied their talents to the
guitar. Having presented Segovia with a remarkable Sevillana
(Fantasia), one of the most evocative recreations of a flamenco
dance to reach the more austere classical instrument, Turina's
reputation among guitarists was enhanced by his Fandanguillo
(Schott, 1926). This much played perennial of the repertoire exploits
many aspects of the guitar's tonal colours, including devices such as
pizzicato, tambura, cantando, rasgueado, fast scale passages and
delicate arpeggios, all fused in an episodic structure in which the
gentle theme constantly returns:

Turina's music combines vigour with refinement as it probes the
essence of Spanish rhythms without losing an inward reflectiveness.
Later compositions of Turina have sometimes been criticised as an
effort to explore the vein of expressiveness laid bare in Fandanguillo,
with little stylistic development. This has some truth in it, but no
composer should be censured for knowing what he does best, and
Turina's popularity in the concert hall has not been extinguished,
though in the 1970's guitarists played his work less than in the twenty
years previous.

Turina's Hommage à Tárrega (Schott, 1935) included two more
flamenco-inspired dances, a Garrotin and Soleares. The latter did not
preserve the strict rhythmic pattern of the flamenco originals, and the
themes are from Turina's own imagination, not from the world of
flamenco itself. But it captured an impression of Andalucian vivacity
and the spirit of the dance and quickly established itself as a standard
work. Another composition in similar style, Ráfaga (Schott, 1930), a
title meaning 'storm', was yet one more delightful miniature in
Iberian style. All three of these pieces owe much to the energy and
vigour of folk culture, but it is difficult to see immediately why
Tárrega should be honoured in connection with Garrotin and
Soleares; one explanation could be in the light delicacy of Turina's

palette, like Tárrega's an exercise in water-colour textures, not the greater mastery of an oil painting. In both composers the sway of melodic lyricism is more noticeable than a reliance on cruder rhythmic pulses; only in Sevillana does Turina achieve some of the earthy richness of Spanish music.

Like Torroba, Turina attempted an extended structure with his Sonata (Schott, 1932). This appeared very rarely, if at all, in Segovia's programmes, though of course dedicated to him. Only Narciso Yepes among the great guitarists has espoused this work for recording and concert purposes. Its overall effect is more verbose than Fandanguillo, and is often considered exhibitionist rather than substantial.

Like a fastidious perfectionist, Turina wrote comparatively few guitar compositions, in a handful of works producing a voice characteristic of himself alone, yet gathering up the Spanish folk idioms and transforming them to a dignified classical mode of utterance. In recitals Fandanguillo and Sevillana are especially sure in their effect, evoking the intimacy and inwardness of the Spanish soul and not the bravura wrongly imagined as the predominant feature of Andalucian music.

True flamenco is a melancholy, introspective art and even its exuberance is tinged with tragic meaning and expresses the dark side of the temperament of southern Spain. Turina's minor keys suggest the deep duende but the emotion is contained within a framework of Apollonian restraint, totally appropriate to Segovia's presentation of his country's music.

Turina, like Falla, spent several years in Paris, the Mecca of all Spanish composers, and was influenced among others by César Franck. He came from Seville, knew Albéniz, and studied piano at the Schola Cantorum in Paris with Moszkowski (1854-1925). Turina also studied with José Trago, the teacher of Manuel de Falla, and throughout his life was in awe of the great Debussy, though the French composer's influence is not at all noticeable in Turina's guitar music.

Segovia repaid his debt to Turina handsomely. One of his first recordings is a 78 rpm 12 inch disc with Fandanguillo on one side and Recuerdos de la Alhambra on the other; Segovia played Fandanguillo and Sevillana throughout his career, as well as occasional renderings of Ráfaga and Hommage à Tárrega.

Turina demonstrates that quality not quantity establishes reputations. He seems never to have been tempted to write a Guitar Concerto or to include the instrument in a string ensemble. But the simple strength of his solo works continues to evoke sympathetic responses in the hearts of guitarists and audiences alike. Like Torroba, he is one of the most significant Spanish composers to rally to Segovia's banner and provide the guitar with quiet but fervent intensities.

18. The Twentieth Century Guitar: Problems and Dilemmas

Spanish music is like certain of our Spanish wines; it quickly gets into your head and makes you tired.

Albéniz

Felipe Pedrell (1841-1922) had provided much of the enthusiasm and inspiration for the leading Spanish composers of the late nineteenth and early twentieth centuries. Falla himself said:

> The cornerstone of the arch upon which modern Spanish music rests is the work of the musicologist, Felipe Pedrell.

Pedrell's researches covered the folk songs of gypsies and beggars as well as the glories of Renaissance Spain and the music of Cabezón and Victoria.

In *Por Nuestra Música* (Barcelona, 1891) Pedrell put forward his ideas on how the essential Spanish spirit should be re-created in Spanish opera by going further than the exterior forms of language. His quest for a culture that was deeply representative of Spain's own soul, and his pride in his country's art, contrasted with the tendency for nineteenth century Spanish musicians to despise Iberian music and to look to the rest of Europe for artistic salvation. Fernando Sor was an example, for our purposes, of how the spectacular presence of great European composers drove his art from the rhythms and structures of his own country into a refined imitation of the harmonies of Mozart and Beethoven.

Pedrell wished to release Spanish musical energies by creating an awareness of historic achievements and the continuity of powerful traditional folk elements. He influenced Albéniz and Granados, as well as Falla, Turina, Torroba and Rodrigo.

Segovia's early career coincided with the fervour of this new Spanish musical renaissance. Pedrell had been aware of the guitar's importance in Spain, and said of Tárrega:

> He gave the music of his instrument . . . wonderful breadth . . . and
> the art stirred the spirit of the composer, opening up to his inspiration,
> vast horizons.

Carlos Pedrell, (1878-1941), Felipe's nephew, wrote some guitar
compositions for Segovia, thereby establishing a link between the
great musicologist and the new art of the guitar. Segovia's music
epitomised an essential part of the nationalistic discoveries, for his
recitals brought together many periods of the Spanish guitar from
Luys Milán's epoch onwards. Thus Turina, Torroba, Falla and
Rodrigo found in Segovia a truly distinctive Andalucian identity,
able to give utterance on an international stage to the validity of
Iberia's rich cultural heritage.

These composers, as we have seen, did not frequently choose the
guitar for the burden of their song. In Turina's Mujeres Españolas
(1917) the piano is given the task of portraying a lady of immense
beauty; she is musically described by means of an Andalucian melody,
and this theme is accompanied by chordal patterns which imitate a
guitar. Falla's Noches en los Jardínes de España (1915) contains no
actual guitars but throughout the instrument's textures are evoked.
His Harpsichord Concerto (1926), written for Landowska, also
suggests, in its first movement, the patterns of flamenco guitar.

Though imitation may be a genuine tribute, this kind of homage
took its strength from the music of the guitar, traditional or otherwise, but did not offer the instrument much in return. The guitar's
repertoire certainly expanded, but at the same time Spanish
composers owed their highest allegiance to the claims of orchestral
composition. At least now the composers could look to a supreme,
uncompromising, virtuoso performer, perhaps the ultimate player
after centuries of one tradition or another. Yet composers found
themselves able only to provide a limited number of pieces for
Segovia to play.

For this dilemma there must have been a good reason. Part of the
composer's problem lay in the fact that his orchestral scores imitated
the flamenco guitar. To transfer such dances to the classical guitar
would become a redundant art after a while; a guitar in the concert
hall would be reduced to imitating guitars in the hands of the
flamencos, just as Albéniz' piano music is an exercise in the evocation
of the guitar. Therefore composers would find it easier and more
convenient to use an orchestra to convey the dimensions of Spanish
culture, producing an effect of the largest guitar in the world.

Thus the Andalucian flamenco tradition, with its colossal energy
and spontaneous excitement, dominated the rhythmic and tonal
consciousness of so many composers, but at the same time weakened

their impulse to write for Segovia's guitar. This strange irony of
guitar history occurred during the 1920's in Segovia's efforts to
establish a repertoire. His countrymen found themselves unable to
do much with the classical guitar except to mirror the passions of the
people's guitar, which Segovia had learned to despise as a boy in
Granada. There was a distinct limit to the number of fandanguillos,
sevillanas, soleares, garrotins, etc., which could be placed in
Segovia's hands. Before long, audiences might prefer to hear the real
thing on the flamenco guitar, rather than witnessing a gentle tribute,
from Segovia and his composers, to a still vibrant art.

   To some extent this did happen. The flamenco guitar eventually
left the caves of Granada and (after many adventures) appeared
in the world's concert halls in solo recitals. Next to the full-
blooded flamenco of Montoya, Sabicas and Ricardo, playing real
soleares, the more restrained urgings of Torroba and Turina could
possibly appear charming but academic. It is significant in this
respect that Falla's Homenaje looks away from Spain towards France
and, while quoting Debussy's Soirée dans Grenade, does not imitate
the flamenco guitar but assumes a voice characteristically its own;
Homenaje is thus a stronger, more individual work than most of the
output for guitar of Torroba and Turina with their mimetic anguish.

   Perhaps it is a minor law of music that if you imitate another
instrument, eventually that instrument will re-appear. Albéniz
imitated the guitar in his piano writing and Segovia's work has
restored Asturias (Leyenda), Granada, Sevilla, Torre Bermeja,
Tango, Zambra Granadina and Capricho Catalan to the source of the
composer's inspiration. Other players have coaxed Cádiz, Córdoba,
Rumores de la Caleta and similar pieces onto the guitar.

   Similarly, repeated concert performances of music for lute, viheula,
Baroque guitar and even harpsichord, all reasonably transcribed for
classical guitar, have led many back to the original instruments. It
follows that these echoes of flamenco, performed often enough,
will initiate a pilgrimage to the place of its birth, and this has indeed
happened with a rise in the popularity of 'flamenco puro', the
Spanish music of the guitar played without commercialised
exhibitionism and with respect for the traditions which engendered
such music.

   Faced by this predicament Segovia advanced several steps further. If
the Spanish composers, though essential, could not provide the
guitar with the same richness as their orchestral compositions, the
instrument would have to break out of the Iberian prison. By bringing
in foreign composers, the guitar would then be delivered from the
claustrophobic embrace of implicit gypsies, nostalgic nights in

mythical gardens and the mystical spell of a Granada that existed only in the imagination.

The leading Spanish composers were aware of the limits of Iberian music, even when they were conscious of its vitality. In *Musicians and Mummers* (Cassell, London, 1925), the autobiography of Herman Klein, Albéniz is quoted concerning Tomás Breton's Spanish opera *Dolores*:

> Dolores is literally the most Spanish opera that has ever been written. Breton embodies the musical genius of the people; they love him because he gives them the tunes and the dances that they adore. It is what you would call the 'crude raw material'; but that makes no difference, no more than the familiarity of the plot. Dolores was produced at Madrid only a few months ago and the habitués of the Zarzuela Theatre there went crazy over it — mind, the very same public that you cannot induce to listen to Bizet's *Carmen* because it is not genuinely Spanish, only a French imitation. You ask me which I prefer? I don't hesitate to answer — Bizet; only don't tell anyone I said so.
>
> You see, *cher ami*, I never utilise the 'raw material' in its crude state myself. You have only to listen to *Pepita* to perceive that. What I like is to *suggest* our national rhythms, and infuse the spirit of national melodies into my music. That suffices. Spanish music is like certain of our Spanish wines: it quickly gets into your head and makes you tired.

It is for the reasons that Albéniz puts forward that his own music is so popular among guitarists and their audiences, though even among the former a slow awareness is beginning of the magnificence of his work in its original setting for piano, a splendour that cannot be fully realised on the six strings of the guitar. Albéniz as transcribed by Tárrega and Segovia, has certainly proved more durable than Torroba and Turina, but it remains a pity that he did not write directly for the guitar.

Later Joaquín Rodrigo unleashed new energies in guitar writing, and his music will be looked at in a later chapter in more detail. Rodrigo solved the problem of the classical guitar's surfeit of refinement by combining it with an orchestra capable of both imitating the guitar and enlarging its resonances. Amazingly his most successful composition, Concierto de Aranjuez, did not become part of Segovia's repertoire. Yet here was a magnificent expression of Spanishness, fusing utter vitality with the classical guitar's own natural sweetness.

Segovia's insight in persuading non-Spanish guitarist composers to write for the instrument was a crucial step in liberating the guitar from its dependence on Iberian harmonies and the school of Tárrega.

Through the simple act of looking outwards, first to South America and then to Europe, the guitar became truly international, and its pure Spanish origins were transcended and enriched by an infusion of new blood.

19. Sounds from South America

sol,
yo quiero
mirate
con los viejos
ojos de América.

Pablo Neruda: *Odas Elementales*

Manuel Ponce (1886-1948) became one of the first non-Spanish composers to write for Segovia, bringing to the guitar the accents of Mexican folk music and the qualities of a sophisticated musical intelligence. He attempted to create for the instrument more extended compositions such as sonatas and variations, wrote one of the finest Guitar Concertos and even composed for guitar and harpsichord. His large output gave Segovia ample opportunity to perform a widely varied selection. Ponce composed more than eighty works for guitar from the time of his first meeting with Segovia in Mexico in 1923. Of his contribution to the twentieth century repertoire Segovia wrote:

> Anyone who loves the instrument . . . must reverence the memory of Ponce. He lifted the guitar from the low artistic state in which it had lain. Along with Turina, Falla, Manen, Castelnuovo-Tedesco, Tansman, Villa-Lobos, Torroba, etc., but with a more abundant yield than all of them put together, he undertook the crusade to liberate the beautiful prisoner. Thanks to him — as to the others I have named — the guitar was saved from the music written exclusively by guitarists!

Ponce wrote a superb Sonata Mexicana as one of his first big works in the 1920's, a four movement sonata evoking imaginative Mexican themes. Segovia gave Ponce four descriptive titles for this work; I Bailecito del Rebozo (Dance of the Scarf), II Lo Que Suene el Ahuehuete (Dream of the ahuehuete, a Mexican tree), III Intermedio Tapatio, (Interlude of native tap-dancing), IV Ritmos y Cantos Aztecas, (Aztec rhythms and melodies). Thus Sonata 1, as it was first called, grew from the germ of an idea by Segovia, an auspicious beginning to Ponce's association with the instrument.

In 1928 Thème Varié et Finale, Sonata III, Tres Canciónes Populares Mexicanas and Preludio were published in Schott's Guitar Archives Series. Sonata Clásica (Hommage à Fernando Sor) and Sonata Romántica (Hommage à Schubert) came into print the following year; guitar composing of this period seems to be somewhat too indebted to the concept of paying homage to great musicians, as if to give the instrument access to wider traditions. Ponce's pastiche of Sor in Sonata Clásica has proved a less popular work; though recorded by Segovia — the notion of composing in the style of an earlier guitarist being a process of self-destruction — the sonata is neither as good as genuine Sor nor the authentic voice of Manuel Ponce.

The first half of Segovia's recitals often included the notorious Suite, allegedly written by Sylvius Leopold Weiss, but actually a Ponce original (see Chapter Eight). Ponce's love of imitation is found elsewhere in his composing as in his Suite en Estilo Antiguo for orchestra (with Prelude, Canon, Pavane and Fughetta) where the theme of the Fughetta is taken from a Bach fugue in E major. He also delighted in writing Prelude and Fugue structures for piano on themes taken from Bach and Handel.

In 1930 his immensely popular Twelve Preludes were published, miniatures owing much to Tárrega (rather than Chopin) and appropriate vehicles for both Segovian tone-colour and pedagogic development of students. These works displayed a true sense of the guitar's charm. They were followed by a massive blockbuster, Twenty Variations on 'Folia de España' and Fugue (Schott, 1932).

This extended composition includes every possible guitar technique used by traditional composers such as the development of chordal textures, arpeggios, monody, fugue, harmonics, tremolo, sustained legato, etc. Some players have considered this to be the finest work for the instrument, equivalent to the weightier items of a piano recital. To many virtuosi it presented an Everest that had to be conquered; Segovia recorded the piece on 78's and both John Williams* and Julian Bream featured it in recitals during the 1960's. Max Harrison of the London *Times* described the composition as 'an interminable work of which guitarists are unaccountably fond'.

It is a work which appeals more to the player than the listener, though this could apply to quite a lot of modern guitar compositions. Falla heard Segovia practising the Variations and Fugue and was

---

* Williams himself recorded variations on 'Folia de España' and Fugue in April 1978.

apparently deeply impressed; whether Segovia's enthusiasm or Ponce's music appealed more strongly is not revealed in the account of this episode.

Sonatina Meridional (Schott, 1939), often referred to by Segovia as Canción y Paisaje and sometimes thus only performed by him to the extent of the first movement, and a remarkable Valse (Schott, 1937) with a curious drone bass and lyrical middle section, have taken their place as standard perennials of guitar recitals.

But it was Ponce's Concierto del Sur, for guitar and orchestra, premiered in Montevideo in October, 1941, by Segovia which has established the composer's reputation as a formidable talent among twentieth century writers for the instrument. Ponce first considered the idea of a Guitar Concerto in 1926, but was inhibited by a fear that the tiny orchestra which is the guitar would not match well with such a powerful partner. As Segovia remarked:

> We feared that the tenuous and expressive sound of the guitar would be swallowed up by the orchestra or that its delicate and poetic timbres would fade before the sonorous mass, like small lanterns of the night before the invasion of day.

The completion of Mario Castelnuovo-Tedesco's Guitar Concerto in D, convinced Ponce of the viability of such a project, especially as he conducted the orchestra in Mexico when Segovia played Castelnuovo-Tedesco's concerto there. Thus a certain natural reticence robbed Manuel Ponce of being the first to write such a work for guitar and orchestra. The brilliance and beauty of his Concierto del Sur would, however, be sufficient in themselves to establish him as one of the most persuasive of all composers ever lured into the guitar's spell.

In 1929 Manuel Ponce took over the Chair of Musical Folklore at the University of Mexico. His pupil, Carlos Chavez (1899-1978) said of him:

> The historical significance of Manuel Ponce in relation to Mexican music is enormous . . . At the beginning of our century the Mexican composers scarcely ventured beyond the limits of 'salon music'. It was at this time that Manuel Ponce undertook to compose in the large forms, achieving such magnificent results as his Piano Concerto and his Trio for Piano, Violin and Cello. These two monumental works were the foundation stones of a higher Mexican musical expression . . . It was he who created a real consciousness of the richness of Mexican folk music.

Thus, as with Falla and Turina, it was orchestral and ensemble music which integrated the richest threads of Ponce's native folkloric traditions. His guitar writing frequently refers explicitly to Mexican

culture in title and style. Yet Ponce developed in composing for
Segovia, on occasion, a more esoteric approach than that adopted by
his Spanish contemporaries. He was after all deeply influenced by
Europe, having studied in Bologna with Enrico Bossi and in Berlin
with Martin Krause, about 1906. Twenty years later, at the age of
forty, Ponce studied with Paul Dukas in Paris. The latent strength of
Mexican folk material intermingled with the vital twentieth century
mainstream of musical thinking. This blend of contemporary
experimentation and classical European structures, juxtaposed with
the earthier reliance on Mexican rhythms, can be seen in much of
Ponce's guitar composition in almost paradoxical splendour.

Ponce wrote for Segovia's guitar, and thus secured for the maestro
a vivid extension of musical possibilities. But like the Spanish
composers, Ponce found it difficult to transmute the vigour of
Mexican folk guitars into the melodic langour and rich nostalgia of
Segovia's style. His guitar works are thus less close to his native
culture than similar efforts of other South American composers like
Villa-Lobos, Lauro and Barrios. Ponce's orchestral writing was more
appropriate for the burden of his nation's characteristic identity. The
indigenous refinement of Segovia is some distance from the ebullient
roughness of the popular Mexican guitar traditions.

Ponce resolved the dilemma in his own way. Mexican, Brazilian
and Venezuelan music all rely on more melodic material than Spanish
flamenco, with its strict compás and limited stock of thematic
substance. Segovia was superbly equipped to convey Ponce's lyrical
gift, though the throbbing rhythms of Mexico are less evident in the
composer's art, being subordinated to the inevitable refinement that
occurs when a classical musical intelligence confronts a native
culture. Ponce exploited his country's love of song and at the same
time steered the guitar into deeper waters, seeking within the
instrument's capabilities as he understood them, to achieve
structures of a European magnitude and breadth.

This new, thoughtful and scrupulous eclecticism in the guitar's
repertoire was an element later composers could develop further.
Ponce's efforts were not, in the long term, entirely durable.
Guitarists love his music, which they find technically taxing and
aesthetically satisfying, but audiences receive less from Ponce's
Sonatas and Variations than the guitarist's involvement in the music
merits, and his work is sometimes included more as an intellectual
stiffening than for its overwhelming appeal.

Ponce has the ability to please players and baffle audiences,
especially where, as in Sonata III, the intellectual and the folkloric
elements co-exist without being totally synthesised. His music

suffers also from its unusual attribute of rarely displaying flamboyant virtuosity in the manner of Villa-Lobos or Lauro, and yet presents the player with many demanding challenges. Its overall effect is that of a civilised sensibility seldom resorting to the promptings of a peasant vulgarity or pagan savageness; in the wrong hands this music can even appear slightly anaemic, lacking the red corpuscles of the Spanish or Brazilian pulse.

For these reasons Manuel Ponce's most successful writing for guitar is when it appears at its most direct as in the Twelve Preludes, Tres Canciónes Mexicanes, Sonata Mexicana, Sonatina Meridional and, a transcription from piano, Scherzino Mexicano (arr. Manuel Lopez Ramos, Peer International Corporation, 1967). Guitarists will continue to rejoice in his longer works as evidence that the guitar can possess stamina as well as charm. It is to Ponce's everlasting credit that he was prepared to be prolific with the time spent on his guitar composing, sometimes achieving less than his ambitions suggested, yet opening up the guitar's horizons in an amazing way. In the end, and in many different ways, Ponce enriched the instrument's history immeasurably and raised it to new, unprecedented levels. As Segovia remarked:

> From the time that I first became acquainted with Ponce in Mexico in 1923 . . . he composed more than eighty works for the guitar; large or small, they are all of them, pure and beautiful . . .

Heitor Villa-Lobos (1887-1959) played and composed for the guitar many years before first meeting Andrés Segovia. Some of his guitar works have been lost or remain unpublished. An official Brazilian publication, *Villa-Lobos — Uma Interpretação* by Andrade Muricy, lists the following guitar compositions:

1899   Mazurka in D
1900   Panqueca
1904   Valsa Concêrto No. 2
1908-12 Suite Popular Brasileira (Eschig, 1955), Mazurka Chôro, Schottish Chôro, Valse Chôro, Gavotta Chôro, Chorinho
1909   Fantasia
1909-12 Eight Works:
           1. Paraguaio, 2. Brasil, 3. Chorar, 4. Saudade, 5. Paranaguá, 6. Cabeçudo, 7. Rio de Janeiro, 8. Padre Pedro
1910   Canção Brasileira
          Two Valses (A minor, C sharp minor) from Chopin

	Dobrado Pitoresco
	Quadrilha
	Tarantela
	Prelude (F sharp minor, from Chopin)
1917	Sexteto Místico (for flute, clarinet, saxophone, harp, celeste, guitar)
1920	Choros No. 1 (Arthur Napoleaso, Rio de Janeiro, 1962)
1929	Twelves Studies (Eschig, 1952)
1940	Six Preludes, Nos. 3 & 4, first performed 12/11/43 by Abel Carlevaro. No. 6 is lost. Nos. 1-5 (Eschig, 1954)
1951	Concerto for Guitar
	Allegro preciso — Andantino e Andante — Allegro non troppo (Eschig, 1955)

(The text stipulates that the first performance was given 2/6/59 by the Houston Symphony Society, with Andrés Segovia as soloist, an assertion that is difficult to verify.)

This list, though only a small part of Villa-Lobos' amazing output of over two thousand compositions, is further reduced by the fact that only a few of these items are published at all. The extant guitar works are therefore the Suite Popular Brasileira, Sexteto Místico, Choros No. 1, Twelve Studies, Five Preludes, the Guitar Concerto and one or two transcriptions for two guitars or voice and guitar. His immense reputation in the guitar world thus rests squarely on a remarkably limited number of works.

Villa-Lobos and Segovia first met in 1924, a historic encounter which encouraged the composer to write Twelve Studies dedicated to the maestro of the guitar. In return Segovia's preface to the Twelve Studies comments:

> Villa-Lobos has made a gift to the guitar's history of the fruits of his talent as vigorous and wise as that of Scarlatti and Chopin.

The Studies were apparently composed in Paris in 1929, and were published in 1953 by Eschig. Though Segovia invokes the name of Scarlatti, it was surely Chopin from whom Villa-Lobos took his cue. Chopin's two sets of Etudes Op. 10 and Op. 25, written between 1828 and 1836 are perhaps the finest fusion of technical virtuosity and musical insight ever achieved in the history of any solo instrument. John Ogdon has written of Chopin's Etudes:

> They enshrine the sound of the piano and so unified are their form and content that it would be almost impossible to imagine them

transcribed for any other instrument.

Villa-Lobos, with characteristic ambition was thus reaching for a glittering prize — the emulation of the keyboard repertoire in terms of the guitar. Since the days of Sor, as we have seen, composers for the guitar hankered after the larger musical structures of pianoforte. Unfortunately the usual device of performing an entire set of Chopin's Etudes was not adhered to by guitarists when confronted by the challenges Villa-Lobos had prepared for them. Segovia set the trend by playing only a few of the Studies (usually Nos. 1, 7 and 8), thus implying that he disliked some of the others and did not regard them as an integrated structure in twelve parts.

The first complete performance of the set was given by Turibio Santos in Rio de Janeiro in 1963 at the invitation of the Villa-Lobos Museum; his recording of the Twelve Studies appeared in 1969. Narciso Yepes did not play more than eight of the Studies at one time in a concert but issued a recording of the whole set in 1971 on an album that included the Five Preludes.

In 1978 Julian Bream offered his performance of all twelve at the Wigmore Hall, London. The critic of *The Times*, London, Max Harrison commented:

> Villa-Lobos' Etudes are usually scattered miscellaneously through programmes of the conventional sort and, considering how central to the repertoire that cycle of a dozen substantial movements is, one is surprised at how rarely they are played together.
>
> However there is considerable internal and external evidence to show that that is what the composer intended, and certainly Mr Bream's performance justified the procedure once and for all.
>
> At least initially the Etudes are less overtly poetic than Villa-Lobos' later Preludes. Yet they follow a fully coherent progression as they journey from the material for arpeggio practice found in the Bachian No. 1 through, say, the rhapsodic No. 8 to the ambitious concert pieces that make up the final Etudes.
>
> There is plenty of Brazilian local colour on the way, some of it rather Frenchified, for Villa-Lobos composed the works in Paris during 1929, but here didacticism and fantasy meet.

Julian Bream's recording of the Twelve Studies duly followed later in the same year, another significant milestone in the guitar's history.

To perform the Twelve Studies in their entirety demands a supreme guitarist capable of imposing his mastery, technical and interpretative, over the entire structure; he must also prevent the better-known concert favourites from dominating the earlier technical studies and unbalancing the sequence. Villa-Lobos lacked Chopin's architectonic sense in the use of keys, though in this respect he was more inventive than many composers for guitar. The keys for each study are as follows:

> No. 1, E minor; No. 2, A major; No. 3, D major; No. 4, G major; No. 5, C major; [*So far this is a good use of contrast*] No. 6, E minor; No. 7, E major; No. 8, C sharp minor; No. 9, F sharp minor; No. 10, B minor; No. 11, E minor; No. 12, A minor.

Thus there is an E major/E minor preponderance among the fine studies from No. 6 onwards, especially when one considers the guitar's tendency to drift towards E major when in the key of A major, C sharp minor, A minor, and even G major. In the C major Etude, apparently a good key for this sequence, the composition gravitates towards E minor as an ostinato bass creates happy ambiguity. No. 12 in A minor uses a pedal E for its middle section which does not help in terms of tonal contrast to balance against the strongly E minor associations of No. 11. The tyranny of the guitar's tuning is particularly powerful in the works of Villa-Lobos, especially as he rarely employs the scordatura used with good effect by Castelnuovo-Tedesco, Ponce and even Tansman.

Taken individually the Studies constitute some of the most remarkable pieces ever imagined for the instrument. As a set they can only be played very occasionally and then necessarily by a guitarist of outstanding personality and ability.

The Preludes written by Villa-Lobos were given a partial debut in Montevideo in 1943 when Abel Carlevaro, an Uruguayan guitarist, played the first performance of Nos. 3 and 4. Segovia, pursuing his usual mysterious process of selectivity, recorded only Nos. 1 and 3. In the late fifties Julian Bream became the first to record all five Preludes as a set, following this with another recording in 1972. He chose to play them in this order, revealing again a structural dilemma which might or might not have been smoothed away if the missing sixth Prelude was ever found:

> No. 1, E minor; No. 5, D; No. 3, A minor; No. 4, E minor; No. 2, E.

Taken as separate pieces each of the Preludes is an exquisite jewel of the repertoire. Played as a set the A/B/A form in Nos. 1, 2, and 4, (No. 3 is A/B/A/B and No. 5 A/B/C/A), and the restricted deployment of keys, tend to stifle the spontaneity. Familiarity has too often bred contempt with the Preludes, and too many performances have jaded their quintessential freshness.

The characteristics of Villa-Lobos' guitar music are a remarkable combination of sweetness and strength, either of which during an inferior performance could be stressed at the other's expense. A rendering of the entire set is magical when the public is unaccustomed to the work of Villa-Lobos. But the Preludes were not intended for the chronic repetition to which guitarists in their zeal have subjected these marvellous miniatures. They have assumed the unhappy status of Chopin's E flat Nocturne, Beethoven's Für Elise and Bach's 'Jesu, Joy of Man's Desiring', as those great moments of inspiration which now, through frequent exposure, have been robbed of their original beauty and expire in a surfeit of rich sweetness and harmonic predictability. A further problem is that the Preludes appear technically easy on the page compared with some of the more weighty modern offerings, thus enticing ill-equipped players into dangerous territory. The recitals and recordings of the masters show that the Preludes have difficulties appropriate to themselves and, like the piano works of Chopin, any simplicity is a delusive façade.

For some time the Suite Popular Brasileira was quite neglected but the frequent exposure of the Preludes and certain of the Studies made it necessary for guitarists to explore other possibilities in Villa-Lobos' music. This suite is a fascinating mixture of Brazilian and European idioms, and the titles (Mazurka-Chôro, Schottisch-Chôro, Valsa-Chôro, Gavotta-Chôro and Chorinho) show how the composer's imagination was working. Melodies, of an undemanding nature are blended with the rhythm of the choros to create a pleasant hybrid.

Villa-Lobos raised the Choros to a musical form of considerable significance. Originally the Choros was a street ensemble of players of popular songs but Villa-Lobos saw it as one of the authentic voices of his country 'in which the various aspects of Brazilian music, Indian and popular, achieve their synthesis'.

To demonstrate his facility in this new structure Villa-Lobos wrote fourteen Choros, beginning with Choros No. 1 for solo guitar. This little piece became another perennial standard among recitalists, especially as an ever ready encore. Amateurs particularly adore this composition and love to attempt to play it, sometimes with dire results.

Villa-Lobos' other Choros reveal greater intellectual scope and a rich variety of instrumental textures. No. 2 is for flute and clarinet, No. 3 is for several wind instruments and male chorus, No. 4 is for brass, No. 5 a piano solo named Alma Brasileira. The later Choros are for a large orchestra often needing the addition of specific Brazilian percussion instruments.

The Guitar Concerto was completed in 1951, originally taking shape as a Fantasia Concertante for guitar and small orchestra. Segovia asked Villa-Lobos to add a cadenza between the second and third movements and the piece was thus elevated to the dignity of becoming a Concerto in the full sense. It languished unplayed for a while until Julian Bream broadcast the work on the BBC in 1957.

Concerning the Guitar Concerto critical opinion varies. In*Records and Recording* of February, 1972, John W. Duarte remarks:

> In truth the thematic material is a bit ramshackle, recalling that of some of the Studies and Preludes and owing much to fingerboard patterning rather than purely musical thought ... As a whole the effect of the Concerto is kaleidoscopic rather than organic and it lacks the charm and strong character of its rivals by Rodrigo and Castelnuovo-Tedesco; strangely, on the big occasion, Villa-Lobos' powers of memorable invention seem to lack their usual grasp.

This rather severe judgement on the Guitar Concerto is echoed in a general comment on Villa-Lobos' work by Sidney Finkelstein in *Composer and Nation: The Folk Heritage in Music* (London, 1960):

> Nevertheless lack of formal discipline remains Villa-Lobos' great limitation. This does not mean academic discipline. The missing element is better called psychological discipline. His music does not coalesce into a genuine human portrait seen in depth. We feel in it the presence of the Brazilian people, bringing together rich currents, ethnic and musical of Africa, Europe and Brazilian Indian. We do not get much inkling from the music of how the people live, or of what they are thinking ...

These two criticisms express a genuine reservation about Villa-Lobos' work that applies to some extent to his guitar music. His monument is in his music and the great exuberance and panache of his guitar works are there for all to experience in their full, life-enriching vitality. At the same time his contribution to the guitar represents, strangely enough, when considering its evergreen popularity, an opportunity lost as well as a repertoire gained. The handful of his surviving guitar pieces is small enough and we would have liked more. In particular a greater assault on those eclectic elements visible elsewhere in his work might have proved fruitful in the context of the instrument. Villa-Lobos, above all other twentieth century composers for the guitar, possessed the spark of genius capable of realising how far the instrument could be stretched technically and musically without stultifying its soul.

He gave the guitar a new sense of sonorous brilliance. The world has responded to the man's overflowing personality, the awareness of sheer living projected through his creative powers. Guitarists owe him a great debt, and in return Heitor Villa-Lobos' fame has been well served by an unrivalled adoration on the part of players and audiences for the man and his music.

20. Two Europeans

Everywhere and for ever I shall be with you,
For everywhere I left a piece of my soul.

Mickiewicz

The friendship of Mario Castelnuovo-Tedesco (1895-1968) with Andrés Segovia restored the lyrical Italian tradition to the guitar; a tradition which can be traced back through Giuliani, Carcassi and Carulli, to the gentle Baroque five-course instrument of Corbetta and Roncalli. Castelnuovo-Tedesco's Florentine upbringing produced in him a desire for composing music directly related to the contours of the voice. He was particularly fascinated by Shakespeare's songs and wrote two operas, *The Merchant of Venice* (1956) and *All's Well that Ends Well* (1958). His essential ideals were stated in the following terms:

> . . . to write good music without prejudices of any kind . . . I do not believe in theories. I have never believed in modernism, or in neoclassicism or in any other *isms*. I believe that music is a form of language capable of progress and renewal.

With this composer the guitar was liberated from its role as a vibrant mirror of folk vitality, and could assume another identity as the creator of intimate worlds of sensibility, imagination, romance, and sometimes the realm of the sentimental.

His early guitar works reveal how much his approach was synthesised with the needs of Segovia. He began in the 1930's to master the instrument as an expressive medium, and the titles selected are usually indicative of his colourful approach to guitar problems.

His first composition for guitar was in 1932, Variazioni (attraverso i secoli), the direct result of his meeting with Segovia at the International Festival in Venice that year. These Variations represent styles through the centuries, including a chaconne and a fox-trot. They have proved less popular among guitarists than his next work, Sonata in D (Omaggio a Boccherini), Op. 77, (Schott, 1935). This is one of the largest sonatas for guitar, with four contrasting movements and technical demands on the player which cover the entire fingerboard. The texture is noticeably denser, more resonant than that of the Spanish composers, and the two slower movements, with their superb use of scordatura, are warm examples of Italianate romanticism, reminding us of the many pieces for guitar and string quartet that Boccherini composed.

Castelnuovo-Tedesco did not produce any more sonatas for guitar though in all he composed nearly one hundred pieces. His Capriccio Diabolico (Omaggio a Paganini) Op. 85, like the Sonata in D, was occasioned by Segovia's remark to the composer concerning the love of the guitar shared by Boccherini and Paganini. Capriccio Diabolico implicitly acknowledges Segovia as the guitar's great virtuoso in the tradition of instrumentalists who developed new possibilities in their art sufficiently to revolutionise the world's concept. Unfortunately Capriccio Diabolico (written in 1935 and published in 1939 by Ricordi) did not find favour with later guitarists to any extent. Its forceful bravura style, alternating with lush rubato and rich tone-colours, seemed appropriate only in the hands of Segovia.

Tarentella, Op. 87a, (written in 1935 and published in 1939 by Ricordi), was another vehicle for Segovia's use, though this piece attracted more players. Castelnuovo-Tedesco employs many of his characteristic devices such as repeated basses, block chords, sinuous rubato passages, brilliant scale sections reminiscent of fiddle playing, and so on. Both this and Capriccio Diabolico were recorded by Segovia and represent, with the Sonata in D, the second wave of guitar compositions after the triumphs of acquiring a repertoire in the 1920's. Thus, once composers were attracted to the instrument rapid developments occurred. From the 1920's onwards things never stood still and the speedy evolution of available music contributed unprecedented colour and variety to the recitalist's potential palette.

Of these developments the writing of a Guitar Concerto in D, Op. 99 in 1939 was one of the most exciting. This was the first significant attempt to place the guitar in an orchestral context since the concertos of Giuliani, and it is fitting that an Italian should have won the earliest laurels in the twentieth century concerto arena.

The vocabulary of the three movements is traditional even if the break-through in terms of the guitar was inventive and new. The Guitar Concerto in D has proved popular ever since its premiere in Montevideo in 1939, though it had to wait until July 1949 for its first recording. Of particular interest in the work are the expressive cadenzas which offer the soloist ample opportunity to impress the audience with the guitar's innate lyricism.

The Concerto opens with full orchestral tutti into which the guitar edges politely with little splashes of fourths and fifths, until embarking on a tremolo solo reminiscent of Capriccio Diabolico. A later solo passage in flowing arpeggios recalls the last movement of the Sonata in D. A particularly delightful touch is the guitar's conversation with the 'cello shortly before the recapitulation, an imaginative use of instrumental textures.

The second movement, sometimes called 'Farewell to the Tuscan Countryside', is true Castelnuovo-Tedesco, poignant, lyrical and wistful, and a fine example of his ability to create a gentle but evocative atmosphere in his music. The last movement is vivid and fast with an attractive deployment of thematic material.

In terms of the critics and the opinion of players, this Concerto appears to have been demoted since its appearance, outflanked by Rodrigo, Villa-Lobos and Ponce. The Concerto's appeal, quite separate from its value as a novel expressive use of guitar, is very much that of a slender miniature rather than a profound or moving work. It has charm but less depth and makes for a pleasant brief experience, not a disturbing crisis of anguish. The Concerto in D is a Segovian showcase, like many of Castelnuovo-Tedesco's guitar works, a tribute emanating from heart-felt admiration.

In 1950 Castelnuovo-Tedesco again opened up new territory for the twentieth century guitar with a magnificent Guitar Quintet, Op. 143. This work is a subtle synthesis of plucked and bowed sonorities, the guitar being perfectly integrated throughout with its string quartet cousins rather than being cast in the role of concerto prima donna. The composer exploits the full range of tone colour available to this combination, each instrument being asked to demonstrate passages of considerable brilliance. A variety of moods, tempi, melodic material, and textures give the four movements of the work a strong structural integrity. Despite the sweet pathos of the slow movement, the overall feeling is of optimism, leading forward to the exuberant Finale, an exciting musical discourse between all five instruments in which each has an equal contribution.

In the same year his Fantasia for Guitar and Piano shows his ability to blend instruments with imaginative expressiveness. The Debussy-like opening evoking the atmosphere of a dream, broadens out to suggest fiestas, trumpets, drums and crowds. The final section of this two-movement piece, employs a theme similar to that used later in *Platero y Yo* — a Primavera motif denoting joy on waking one morning in spring.

Castelnuovo-Tedesco broke away from his habitual practice of writing for Segovia by composing a number of pieces based on the names of certain personalities connected with the guitar such as Alirio Diaz, Siegfried Behrend, Manuel Lopez Ramos, Laurindo Almeida and Segovia himself, amongst several others. These works have perhaps appeared too much of a personal greeting card to merit espousal for concert purposes, though the composer pursued this custom of writing such items from 1954 until 1967.

Of greater interest have been the twenty-eight pieces accompanying passages narrated from *Platero y Yo* by Juan Ramón Jiménez, winner of the Nobel Prize for Literature in 1956. The inspiration of the pieces was discovered in a long series of episodes, written by Jiménez in prose of a romantic nature, about the life and death of Platero, a donkey, from the viewpoint of Platero's owner.

Castelnuovo-Tedesco intended his music in *Platero y Yo* to fuse the spoken word with descriptive music. Segovia, however, recorded ten of the episodes without a narrator, thus setting a precedent for recitalists. The music does depend to a large extent on the promptings of Jiménez' original words but Segovia's advocacy of the work represents his tribute to a composer who did so much for the guitar. For several years *Platero y Yo* was available only in manuscript, jealously guarded by a few privileged guitarists. It was eventually published by Berben in 1972: (such was the spell of Juan Ramón Jiménez on composers that in the same year another *Platero y Yo* Suite, this time by Eduardo Sainz de la Maza, appeared, though this work was less dependent on the meaning of the original words and used broader descriptive sections).

Apart from solo pieces, Castelnuovo-Tedesco achieved other flights of imagination which he applied in an unprecedented way to the needs of the guitar. His contribution to the art of the guitar duo is unrivalled and his 24 Preludes and Fugues for two guitars (1962), Sonatina Canonica (Eschig, 1961), Fuga Elegiaca (1967, dedicated to the memory of Ida Presti) and Concerto for two Guitars and Orchestra, Op. 201 (1962), represent the finest flowers of his cultivation of this neglected field.

Other works in his amazingly diverse output include a Second Guitar Concerto, Op. 160 (1953), two song cycles with guitar accompaniment, a Sonatina for Flute and Guitar, Op. 205 and Twenty-Four Capriccios de Goya, Op. 195, a large-scale series of compositions which have not found favour with players. His *Appunti(Notebooks)* in three volumes, a kind of student's *Gradus ad Parnassum*, were published by Edition Suvini Zerboni, and constitute his final offering to the guitar.

His endeavours on behalf of the instrument thus stretch from 1932 until his death in 1968, most of his guitar compositions in terms of quantity being written after 1950 when the pace quickened. He was a rare example of a composer who pursued the task of writing for the guitar to the limits of his ability. Surprisingly his work has often been neglected except for the Concerto in D, the Sonata, *Platero y Yo*, and Tarentella. In recitals the multiplicity of his composing has been displaced by less traditionally minded composers or by the Spanish and South American personalities of the guitar.

Among the great players only Segovia, and to a lesser extent Alirio Diaz, have consistently advocated his music, with the exception of the perennial Concerto in D. The impressionistic lyricism of his work and his close association with Segovia have paradoxically tended to limit his appeal. Yet even if not overplayed, his solo compositions still form a significant part of the recitalist's awareness, and his Sonata in D remains as one of the outstanding virtuoso peaks in the history of the guitar. It seems entirely likely that guitarists will ultimately return to a new evaluation of Castelnuovo-Tedesco for there are still many pieces among his compositions which have not yet been fully appreciated.

Most of those who composed for Segovia were intent on achieving a sense of national identity in their guitar writing, especially if they were Spanish, Mexican or Brazilian. Alexander Tansman (b.1897) brought to the instrument the strong musical culture of Poland, reconciling modern harmonies with melodic and rhythmic energies of his nation's music. Just as Tárrega had been enviously impressed by the sensitive strength of the Mazurka, so Segovia found a reliable musical companionship in the Polish dances created by Tansman.

Like Chopin, Tansman lived in exile in Paris for many years, and it was there that he met Segovia. His first work for guitar was an extended Mazurka written in 1925 (Schott, 1928). Its varied textures, ranging from melody with pedal bass, to repeated arpeggio patterns, reveal a composer of adaptable demeanour whose native idioms could fit quite naturally to the necessary restraints of the guitar.

His busy musical life as pianist, conductor and composer, and his production of symphonies and other large orchestral works including piano concertos, seem to have prevented Tansman from writing again for guitar until 1951. In that year his Cavatina, dedicated to Segovia, was awarded first prize at the Academia Chigiana's international composers competition. This was published by Schott in 1952, and nine years later a concluding movement to the Suite, Danza Pomposa, was published separately; this was added to the Suite at Segovia's suggestion and returns the work to the Polish mainstream of inspiration. The other sections, Preludio, Sarabande,

Barcarole and Scherzino, though Polish in their use of rhythm and harmony, by name belong to the usual European traditions of the suite form.

In the mid-fifties Tansman achieved a finer registration of Polish feeling in three dances, Canzonetta, Alla Polacca and Berceuse d'Orient, which immediately found their way into Segovia's concert repertoire. They later became encapsulated in another suite entitled 'In Modo Polonico' (Eschig, 1968) where the Canzonetta was called Reverie and Berceuse d'Orient assumed the Polish title of Kolysanka No. 1. The movements of this Suite were Entrée, Gaillarde, Kujawiak, Tempo de Polonaise, Kolysanka No. 1, Reverie, Alla Polacca, Kolysanka No. 2 and Oberek. Concerning 'In Modo Polonico', Tansman wrote:

> I have been fascinated by the musical personality of Andrés Segovia ever since the first time I came into contact with his art, and I am proud of being one of the first young composers (at that time) to write a work for him. Our collaboration has never ceased . . . This Suite is inspired by the old courtly dances of Poland. Some of them (the Gaillarde and the Branle) exist under other names throughout Europe; other dances are typically Polish (the Polonaise and the Mazurka) . . . the suite has been dealt with in the language which appears to me the most appropriate for a work based on national and traditional forms: that is to say, I have avoided all stylisation and that wilful modernisation which, if applied to the pure line of melody, to the popular style of harmony, and to its rhythmic principles, can only result in artificiality and hybridism.

Thus Tansman attempts to unite the old and the new, the dances of the past with a sense of modernity, and the rhythms of Poland with the Spanish accents of Segovia's guitar. The synthesis is a fascinating one and the composer succeeds in producing several finely etched miniatures which have proved most popular among recitalists.

In its entirety the suite is too prolonged and fails to sustain excitement and interest throughout. Over half of the nine movements are in either D major or D minor, and the vivid originality of each dance prevents an overall coherence. Tansman's Cavatina was a more successful larger structure that achieved formal integration of theme and key; Segovia's recording of 'In Modo Polonico' even includes the early Mazurka of 1925, an indication that the later suite is more like a fabricated necklace than a truly organic unit.

Despite this reservation, Tansman's Polish voice brings a spontaneous freshness into the guitar repertoire, augmenting its romance associations with a breath of Eastern Europe. Like Polish vodka, his music is best when not imbibed to excess. It cannot be said

that Tansman radically metamorphosed the guitarist's concepts of
the instrument but he did provide the repertoire with several works
of enduring charm and proved the guitar's potential as an international musical medium.

21. Segovia and the Critics

'Tis with our judgements as our watches, none
Go just alike, yet each believes his own.

Pope

As we have seen, the travels of Andrés Segovia induced several nationalities to write for the guitar. Many of these composers could make use of the precedents established by Torroba, Falla and Turina, as a starting point for their own creative activity. New idioms and concepts of possible techniques began to enrich Segovia's recitals.

Each composer brought new sounds within range of the guitar. Many kinds of musical structures appeared, from the tiny cancion to extended variation sequences and sonatas of a magnitude not previously attempted since the works of Fernando Sor. Experiments with textures and modulations expanded the potential capacities of the repertoire away from merely impressionistic descriptions in sound, characteristic of Tárrega and other Spanish composers, towards ambitious attempts to place the guitar on a parity with other solo instruments.

The composers were rewarded by Segovia's loyal advocacy of their work. The chosen few were elevated almost to the level of saints of the guitar as their creations rapidly became the staple fodder of recitalists. Their compositions were published, recorded and closely studied by aspirants to guitar fame, following Segovia's example.

Equally impressive was the list of composers who did *not* enter Segovia's magic circle and become bewitched by his playing. Among the generation of composers born during the last two decades of the nineteenth century, the most distinguished names are conspicuously absent. These were the contemporaries of Manuel Ponce and Heitor Villa-Lobos. To mention but a few, they include Stravinsky (1882-1971), Berg (1885-1935), Rachmaninoff (1873-1943), Prokofiev (1891-1953), Bartok (1881-1945) and Ravel (1875-1937). They were not drawn to the solo guitar, to its lasting impoverishment.

Among others, Arnold Schoenberg (1874-1951) incorporated the guitar into his output, viz. the Serenade of 1923, writing for it in the bass clef. His pupil Ernst Krenek (b. 1900) later wrote a suite for guitar. Darius Milhaud (1892-1974) wrote one work, Segoviana (1957), but this was never performed by its dedicatee. Albert Roussel (1869-1937) also wrote a piece named Segovia, and this was premiered in Madrid in 1925. Francis Poulenc (1899-1963) composed one miniature, a Sarabande, dedicated to Ida Presti.

Segovia's devotees among composers (with the possible exception of Villa-Lobos) were not among the greatest musicians of their age, and their music has its limitations. Segovia often had to clutch at straws, to persuade, encourage and cajole, and sometimes to play inferior works in the hope that better material might emerge. The establishing of his repertoire was not an easy matter, and he was grateful for any help, even if some of his available sources were not representative of all that was finest in twentieth century music.

The post-1920 compositions, which made up the Segovian contribution to the instrument's new identity, emanate therefore from a select group of personalities. On the work of about half a dozen such composers the foundations of the modern guitar were established. The rest of a recital programme consisted for Segovia of transcriptions from other periods from Milan onwards, and the guitar works of Sor and Tárrega, with pieces from Albéniz and Granados.

Critics have often returned to the theme of how impoverished the guitar repertoire actually is. In *The Times*, London, 1963, the music critic rounds off a complimentary review of Segovia with the words:

> Yet in spite of all these surface beauties and the frisson of hearing an instrument perfectly played, would it be heretical to suggest to guitar fanciers that a whole evening of guitar music hardly adds up to a satisfying concert?

The implicit mockery of 'guitar fanciers' and the stigma of 'surface beauties' reveal how the critic's reaction perhaps contradicts the essential experience given by the concert itself; on this occasion Segovia played Torroba, Ponce, Granados and Albéniz, in the second half of the recital; all tickets in the spacious Royal Festival Hall were sold, and presumably nobody asked for their money to be returned. Perhaps however the critic has instinctively understood the nature of a Segovia recital; the music played, though living and vital in Segovia's hands, might not otherwise be so impressive. The magnificence of the player transcends the music played, a recurrent idea throughout the guitar's history.

If a definition of 'great' music is a work which could never imaginably receive the ideal or ultimate performance in which the fullest possible justice was rendered to its demands (one thinks here of Beethoven's Hammerklavier Sonata or Bach's Chaconne), then Segovia's contemporary pieces were never great for on numerous occasions he may have given them a rendering, in recital or on record, which will never be surpassed. These pieces were written for him, conceived interpretatively in close collaboration with the composer, and performed many times. Segovia's playing must surely have attained the composers' vision of their work. This is possibly a flaw in much of the Segovian canon, that his personality and mastery has exceeded, in the fullness of time, the original challenge contained in the works dedicated to him. The public have invariably gone to concerts to hear and see Andrés Segovia, and what he has played in the recital has been both predictable and of secondary significance to them.

In the 1960's, Stephen Walsh, again writing in *The Times*, commented:

> . . . certainly it is a matter for regret that the guitar has even now not established itself as a strong intellectual medium. . . . But Segovia's magic is to draw his listeners into a web of silence and for this only the insubstantial and elusive will suffice.

A little while after this, another critic in *The Daily Telegraph* of London added his voice to the chorus of those torn between admiration of the maestro's charisma, skill and musicianship and mild condemnation of the slender material out of which the web of enchantment is woven:

> . . . and though one could admire Segovia's unfailing skill and finesse, though even here one could become absorbed by the withdrawn, almost self-communing nature of his playing, it seemed a pity that his time should be spent on such undistinguished material.

If Segovia's repertoire is so undistinguished that it is inferior to the potential power of his artistry, then several questions arise. Is it the guitar itself that is limited, or do we possess in the twentieth century the instrument of yet another miniature tradition, attracting a coterie who flock to the magnetic personality of the great player? The coterie is, of course, bigger than the bands of aficionados who followed the work of Milán, Corbetta and de Visée, or Sor, Giuliani and Tárrega, because of the means of communication in the modern world. But is the guitar, despite the great numbers who go to concerts and buy records, still an oddity in the musical world, having little contact with the wider horizons of music?

The answers to these questions involve areas of musical history and social developments. The critics nowadays tend to listen and to write about recital experiences in mechanical terms of evaluation. The atmosphere of the concert, the player's presence, the living moment of creative flow between performer and public — all these are rarely mentioned in modern criticism. The critic invariably assumes that the public go to concerts to *hear* music, and the quality of the composition is all that matters. Hence the great disparities between one's experience of attending a concert and the reviews which appear the next day in the papers.

People do not attend concert halls just to hear music. They attend, even in a large theatre, a precious human ritual of togetherness where music takes place. All the senses are involved at a concert; seeing the artist or orchestra, hearing the noises that the crowd makes, tasting the coffee or whisky in the interval, and then there are the tactile sensations, not always pleasant, of sitting quite still in the process of paying attention to what the performer is achieving.

With a loud orchestra or a grand piano the illusion can be sustained that the sole object of being present is to hear music, the volume being loud enough to overcome most of the other sense impressions. The guitar recital however, more than most live performances, stresses the humanity of both player and public. Though the critic may possibly be above the common run of men, the mass of people gathered together experience a sense of excitement, of the primeval spirit of music making.

Music originated in small groups, where contact between player and audience was vital. This two-way communion is still present in flamenco juergas, in Indian villages, in the Arab market-place and even in the salons of Europe. Gradually, halls in Europe suitable for performances have grown bigger. The nineteenth century enlarged the orchestra, and the Wagnerian proportions increased the alienation of the audience from the spontaneous intimacy characterising the music of previous centuries.

Tárrega and Llobet had not wanted the guitar to be removed from its private setting to big impersonal contexts. Segovia wished to reach the largest possible audience and yet keep a great deal of the guitar's communicative and personal flair.

Segovia knew that the guitar is indeed elusive and insubstantial, a slender thread of poetry. A guitar recital is an exercise in echoes and tiny associative sounds, small tapestries of resonances, areas of minutely distinctive colourings, intimacies vouchsafed to a sympathetic audience in a still, small voice. In the noisiest century of all time, the guitar's gentle insignificance attracted many followers. It

15. *Andrés Segovia.* Courtesy of Ibbs & Tillett Ltd.

hardly set out to provide them with a big experience of epic dimensions. It spoke directly in terms of melancholic nostalgia and with a singular kind of poignancy. Thin wisps of sound transported the listeners away from the traffic-laden city outside, whether New York, Paris, London or Rio de Janeiro, back to the world of Segovia's youth and the guitar's hidden past. Segovia's demeanour and musical style reminded audiences of the quiet backwaters of Andalucia, of the sound of half-heard guitars wafted from shaded balconies.

Bernard Gavoty, in his book *Andrés Segovia* has attempted to describe the romantic appeal of a guitar recital by the maestro:

> Where Segovia leaves the tale the music takes it up, leading us in a dream to a place which human words cannot attain. What adjectives can ever bring Granada before us? But let those wise fingers be employed on the six taut strings; they will call up the chirping of the grasshopper, wing-shells rubbing together, the rasping saw of the cricket, the toad's golden blisters, the nocturnal fairyland of the slumbering gardens — and Granada, like a rose in the night, rises, swaying under the silvery moon.

Composers, players and critics later reacted quite stongly against this Watteau-like charm, preferring a grittier intellectualism to soft images of grasshoppers, toads and the moon of Granada. The art of Segovia was deliberately distinct from the prolonged assault of a piano or violin recital with their self-confident extrovert dynamic range and the established pedigrees of their composers. For Segovia the distant murmurs of guitar sound constitute the instrument's attractiveness:

> A humorist once said to me, 'The piano is a rectangular monster whose teeth you scrape to make it howl, and string instruments only make a noise when you flog them. The guitar alone responds to persuasion.'

(from Bernard Gavoty's Andrés Segovia, Geneva, 1955)

Segovia thus admired the repertoire of other solo instruments but not the forceful means by which the sounds were elicited. He disliked the wrong kind of vigour. *The Observer* of London in May, 1970, made an interesting observation about his character:

> Segovia is supremely civilised. He drinks only the purest wines, reads only the rarest literature . . . At 15 Segovia gave his first concert in Granada to an audience composed mainly of the sceptical and the curious. 'They could not conceive that the Spanish guitar was for anything but flamenco. I have spent a lifetime trying to redeem the guitar from flamenco. The guitar is the purest and most total instrument. You play just one simple phrase, not a symphony or a concerto, and it satisfies.'

Some years later, in an interview published in the New York *Guitar Review* of 1977, Segovia explained his attitude towards flamenco:

> I love the flamenco, but the *true* flamenco — not the flamenco heard these days. The flamenco guitarist of today has removed his attention from the ideals of yesterday, when this noble art was prized for a depth of emotion which could be produced by a certain simplicity of approach. Today's guitarists are more theatrical, they want to show their technique, to dazzle the public with pyrotechnics. And so they not only insert chords not belonging to the true flamenco, but they also emphasise the rapid scale passages, tremolos, and so forth. The result is not to my taste.

Segovia's art is therefore aimed at a natural musicality. The guitar in his hands is not intended to be exhibitionist or startling. The appeal is in his concept of a true expressiveness which evokes but makes no undue display. The flashy shallowness of much guitar performance is eschewed and any such players are cast, artistically, into outer darkness. A fine description of the elusive style of Segovia was given in *The Daily Telegraph* by Peter Stadlen:

> He tunes inaudibly and all but invisibly. When he does seem to be tuning the piece has in fact started, and it is up to us to adjust to a small tone. Yet one never longed for a smaller hall, such is the lure of his deceptively take-it-or-leave-it interpretations.
>
> They are made up of an infinite variety of touch and nuance applied with tantalising unpredictability. There is no telling whether the next note will be hit dead centre or glissandoed up to, whether the next phrase will contain a vibrato and where, whether a run will sound silvery or hollow.
>
> Almost invariably it is after the event, not until a given episode has been concluded, that one comprehends what he had been aiming at. Thus, unlike the familiar extrovert type of guitar virtuoso, this noble artist leaves one exhausted, not emotionally, but whether or not one realises it, intellectually.

Thus at least one critic has come to the point of realising how in music soul and mind are indivisible more often than not. Segovia's guitar demands from us an attentiveness which must be of the intellect; the majesty of his art invariably addresses our sensibilities. His music has always asked for a total response from audiences and they have for six decades been willing to surrender to his request with no spirit of resistance. It is not the kind of art with which one would normally associate the workings of the intellect (the art of music which puzzles the ear), but hearing him play has always been a complete experience of a rare kind.

The life and work of Segovia were not only a perfect ideal for later guitarists to follow, thus building a firm foundation for the guitar's future development, but also an achievement of a unique kind in itself. Even if a thousand players had not continued his work, the greatness of Segovia would still stand as a monument to the powerful working out of the guitar's expressive destiny and a watershed in the instrument's multiple traditions.

22. Two Spaniards

Allow me to say with pride that the guitar by being deeply Spanish is becoming universal. Spain took the guitar because the Spaniard has so rich an individuality that he is a society in himself, and the guitar by her rich polyphonies and tone colours is an orchestra in itself.

Andrés Segovia

By some ironic turn of fate, the supreme work for the guitar to emerge from Spain in the twentieth century, the Concierto de Aranjuez by Joaquín Rodrigo (b. 1902), is not dedicated to Segovia. According to Vicente Vayá Pla in his biography of the composer (*Joaquín Rodrigo, Su Vida y Su Obra*, Madrid, 1977), the Spanish Civil War, Segovia's sojourn in South America and the troubled European situation, made it totally impossible for Rodrigo to offer Segovia the premiere of this work.

The two musicians had first met in 1929 in Paris, and some time after this Segovia made a request that the composer should write a work for guitar and orchestra. The blow of losing the foremost concerto of the age seems to have hit Segovia particularly hard for he never played the Concierto de Aranjuez, a tragic loss for all admirers of the guitar. Rodrigo's Fantasia para un Gentilhombre (1954), uniting Gaspar Sanz' themes with a tribute to Segovia restored the connection between these two leading personalities of the guitar's history, though it is a less charismatic work than the Aranjuez Concerto.

Rodrigo dedicated Tres Piezas Españolas to Segovia, whose playing of the Fandango, one of the most technically difficult solos ever conceived for guitar, gives an indication of how magnificently he would have dealt with the Concierto de Aranjuez. Segovia also recorded Zarabanda Lejana, originally written for piano (1926).

Joaquín Rodrigo wrote nearly twenty titles for solo guitar between 1926 and 1976, as well as four brilliant Concertos, and an outstanding

Tonadilla for two guitars (written in 1960 and published in 1964 by Ricordi). Rodrigo did not feel obliged to dedicate most of his compositions to Segovia, and his dedicatees include Villa-Lobos, the vihuela of Luys Milán, the Presti-Lagoya Duo, Narciso Yepes, Regino Sainz de la Maza (Concierto de Aranjuez), Alirio Diaz, Nicolas Alfonso and Ernesto Bitetti.

Part of this lack of close collaboration between Segovia and Rodrigo was certainly due to the former's wide-ranging international travels during which he did not return to Madrid as frequently as was necessary to sustain a creative relationship. Perhaps also Rodrigo felt ties of loyalty to his own circle of guitarists in Spain, players in the direct line from Tárrega, whose relationship with Segovia does not always seem to have been one of unqualified adoration of his achievements. The complex dynasties of the guitar were in any event beginning to widen and coalesce, as eager young talents jostled to enter the lists.

Whatever the facts might be about differences of opinion among the guitar's leading figures during the thirties, the fact that Segovia never performed the Concierto de Aranjuez allowed new reputations to be made without the inevitable processes of comparison. The first to make a real reputation with the Concerto was Narciso Yepes, whose early recording of the work established him as an international guitarist of formidable powers.

The Concerto set new standards in technical demands and was the most successful use of the guitar to re-create in serious terms the effervescent vitality, moodiness and pathos of Spanish culture. Rodrigo, having caught diphtheria at the age of three, steadily lost his sight till the day came when he could no longer distinguish between light and dark. This personal tragedy did not prevent him from fulfilling his artistic ambitions. He studied with Paul Dukas in Paris, and was a friend of Falla. His remarkable character and his unique musical gifts enabled him to transcend the handicap of blindness just as his great predecessor, Cabezón, had also allowed no obstacles to impede his creativity though he too was without sight from early infancy.

In one respect Rodrigo's composing for the guitar may have been advantageously influenced by not being able to see the struggles of the guitarist's fingers. Only the sound of the music impressed him, and like the late sonatas of Beethoven, Rodrigo's Concierto de Aranjuez revolutionised all known principles of technique appropriate to the instrument.

Rodrigo was never inhibited by the usual limitations of the guitar in his composing. Once he imagined a sound it had to be played. In each movement of the Concierto de Aranjuez scale passages are introduced of a speed and fluency that could be equally effective in terms of a flute. The third movement offers the guitarist the opportunity to display many brilliant techniques including arpeggios, contrapuntal playing, rasgueados, tremolo, and harp-like sweeps across the strings, as well as dazzling runs across the length and range of the fingerboard.

The second movement, perhaps the most beautiful composition in the whole of the guitar's history, demands from the player a new approach to the instrument. Here fluidity, clarity, apparent ease and effortless mastery are at a premium. The guitar becomes disembodied from its technical problems, and rises musically triumphant in glorious liberation to heights of cantabile freedom hitherto only realised in violin or vocal music.

Rodrigo has made the following remarks about the Concierto de Aranjuez:

> Throughout the veins of Spanish music, a profound rhythmic beat seems to be diffused by a strange, phantasmagoric, colossal and multiform instrument — an instrument idealised in the fiery imaginations of Albéniz, Granados, Falla and Turina. It is an imaginary instrument which might be said to possess the wings of the harp, the heart of the grand piano, and the soul of the guitar.
>
> This 'soul' was made apparent for the first time in the homage paid by Manuel de Falla in his elegy 'Pour le tombeau de Claude Debussy'. The guitar, an instrument steeped in popular tradition, has now gone beyond the music of the people. By virtue of the sensitive innovations of Francisco Tárrega, its technique has been prodigiously expanded ... The Aranjuez Concerto is meant to sound like the hidden breeze that stirs the tree tops in the parks, and it should be only as strong as a butterfly, and as dainty as a veronica.

Rodrigo's other concertos, including Fantasia para un Gentilhombre, have charm, elegance, and virtuosity, but never achieved the charismatic spell of his first Concerto. The Fantasia para un Gentilhombre gains its strength from the music of Sanz, but this leaves the imaginative powers of Rodrigo little scope except by way of selection and clever orchestration. His characteristic flourishes have spirit but not the depth of national feeling which informed the Aranjuez Concerto.

His Concierto Madrigal (originally composed for the Presti-Lagoya duo) for two guitars is a picturesque work, composed along similar lines to the Fantasia with ten separate movements, Fanfarre, Madrigal, Entrada, 'Pastorcito, tu que vienes, pastorcito, tu que vas', Girardilla, Pastoral, Fandango, Arieta, Zapateado and Caccia a la

Española. The Concierto Madrigal is based on a Renaissance madrigal 'Felices ojos mios', thus, like Tansman, bringing together the antique roots of Spanish song and the guitar.

Concierto Andaluz for four guitars is a lively three movement work (Tiempo de Bolero, Adagio, and Allegretto), whose last movement would not be out of place as theme music for a western film. Both these concertos, written 1966 and 1967 respectively, proved ideal for the talents of the remarkable Romero family, who have recorded both works whilst Angel Romero has also recorded the Concierto de Aranjuez on two occasions.

Like other composers for guitar of the twentieth century, Rodrigo has written extended solo works, including Sonata Giocosa (1960, Chester), dedicated to Renata Tarragó, who after Yepes made the second recording of Concierto de Aranjuez in 1959-60, and Sonata a la Española (Eschig, 1969), dedicated to Ernesto Bitetti, and recorded in part (the last two movements Adagio and Bolero) by Luise Walker.

One of the most popular solo pieces by Rodrigo, apart from the Fandango mentioned earlier, is En los Trigales (In the Wheatfields), a frequently performed sultry evocation of the sounds of harvest.

Thus Rodrigo turned to the guitar in a more vigorous way than Turina, Torroba or Falla, and carried the energies and thrust of Andalucian flamenco idioms into the territory of classical players. His music incarnates the twentieth century soul of Spanish culture, and his art does not enfeeble the guitar by merely imitating traditional rhythms or refining them out of existence. Rodrigo's compositions have an earthy virility. Despite the small number of works for the guitar from his pen, his right to be considered the foremost Spanish composer of the twentieth century for the guitar is unassailable and the Concierto de Aranjuez alone would have established such a reputation. Rodrigo is indeed a supreme creative force in the history of the instrument, a composer whose claims on the attention of guitarists constitute a challenge and an opportunity.

The work of Emilio Pujol (b. 1886) has already been mentioned in connection with his revival of vihuela music and his friendship with Tárrega and Rodrigo. In the early decades of the century Pujol toured South America and Europe, giving guitar recitals, both solo and with his wife as the Cuervas-Pujol Duo.

In 1934 the first volume of his guitar method, *Escuela Razonada de la Guitarra,* appeared, followed by three more parts in 1952, 1954 and 1971. This massive work, perhaps the finest tutor in the guitar's history, contained a complete analysis of all technical aspects, dealt with in great detail. It is a work of tremendous nobility, achieving on the pedagogic side what Segovia had achieved as a player; the *Escuela Razonada de la Guitarra* will remain as one of the few great works of the guitar's literature and no player should be without it. With this life's work Pujol deserves his reputation as perhaps the most eminent teacher of the twentieth century.

He wrote well over a hundred original compositions, including imaginative and picturesque studies such as El Abejorro (The Bumble-bee) sketched out in *Escuela Razonada* and published by Eschig in 1955, Paisaje, a Tárrega-like tremolo study on a theme by the master himself and Three Spanish Pieces (Eschig, 1926), including a difficult Guajira recorded by Ida Presti while still in her teens. His Homenaje a Tárrega was published in 1954 in the Segovia Archives Series (Schott), though no account has been found of Segovia's performance of this work.

Pujol's transcriptions of music for two guitars such as Goyescas: Intermezzo by Granados, Córdoba by Albéniz, and *La Vida Breve:* Spanish Dance No. 1, by Falla, have enriched the duo repertoire and proved immensely popular in both recitals and recordings.

His biography of Francisco Tárrega (published in 1960 in a limited edition) is one of the few great books about leading historic figures of the guitar. *El Dilema del Sonido en la Guitarra* (Ricordi Americana S.A.E.C., 1934, republished 1960) is one of the few texts that discusses the question of guitar tone and how it is achieved. Pujol's own biography was written by Juan Riera (Lerida, 1974).

Pujol represents a fervent link between the world of Tárrega and twentieth century Spanish tradition. No evaluation of guitar history would be complete without paying tribute to the enduring nature of his achievement as recitalist, teacher, scholar, musicologist and guardian of the instrument's heritage and culture.

23. The Continuing Tradition

The world's great age begins anew,
The golden years return . . .

Shelley

Andrés Segovia was well into his fifties before a new generation of outstanding virtuosi entered the international arena. Alirio Diaz (b. 1923), Ida Presti (1924-1967), Narciso Yepes (b. 1927), Julian Bream (b. 1933) and John Williams (b. 1941) were Segovia's heirs to the technical and interpretative riches he had achieved in his great endeavour and to the legacy of a repertoire created for him.

Throughout the early twentieth century there had been many fine players of distinction who toured internationally, though historically they were dwarfed by the massive prestige of Segovia.

Apart from the phenomenal career of Agustín Barrios (1885-1944), who will be considered in more detail later, the late nineteenth century produced Miguel Llobet (1878-1937), Emilio Pujol (b. 1886) and Regino Sainz de la Maza (b. 1897), among those who gave recitals throughout the world and left an indelible imprint on guitar history. (Sainz de la Maza's recording of the Concierto de Aranjuez was issued in 1968 when the guitarist was seventy-one; he made a London debut the previous year.)

The first two decades of this century bred a good crop of guitarists though none of them was destined to receive the supreme accolade given to the players who came after them. These included Maria Luisa Anido (b. 1907) of Argentina, a pupil of Llobet; Julio Martínez-Oyanguren (b. 1905) of Uruguay; Karl Scheit (b. 1909) and Luise Walker (b. 1910, and another Llobet student) of Austria, José de Azpiazu (b. 1912) and Vicente Gomez (b. 1911) from Spain, Laurindo Almeida (b. 1917) of Brazil, and Rey de la Torre (b. 1917) from Cuba.

Each of these personalities achieved a niche in twentieth century guitar history. Scheit and Azpiazu became renowned among players as editors and arrangers, and like Luise Walker, took up teaching professorships at leading conservatoires of Europe. Julio Martínez-Oyanguren (b. 1905) of Uruguay; Karl Scheit (b. 1909) and Luise with an orchestra and the first to appear in a moving picture (Sainz de la Maza is said to be the first player to provide background music for a film, in his case a Spanish production entitled *Goyescas*). Vicente Gomez, though not really a classical player being more interested in flamenco, also achieved fame in the forties when he appeared in a Hollywood film *Blood and Sand*, where, in the elegant company of Tyrone Power and Rita Hayworth, a rendering of Romance de Amor delighted the film-going public.

Laurindo Almeida became the most well-known guitarist of those born in this century before the end of the first World War. In the fifties he became a prolific recording artist of the classical guitar repertoire in a period when such records, apart from Segovia's, were quite scarce. His albums of Albéniz, Granados, Turina, Falla, Torroba, Barrios, Ponce etc. have been eclipsed by the later recordings of greater players, but in the 1950's provided an alternative to Segovia's virtual monopoly of the guitar on disc.

Almeida's immense versatility and his Brazilian intimacy with the guitar, enabled him to establish a reputation as a player of both jazz and the popular music of his country, as well as a composer and arranger for film scores. He was guitarist for several years in the Stan Kenton band.

Laurindo Almeida is not regarded with an unqualified admiration by many devotees of classical guitar. Yet his contribution to the instrument has been wide-ranging. He has written many delightful miniatures for solo guitar, as well as a really worthwhile *Guitar Tutor* (Belwyn Mills, 1957), and has persuaded many Brazilian composers to create works for him. Though his interpretative and technical gifts in the classical sphere are now often considered fallible, Almeida succeeded in extracting from the guitar a characteristic timbre entirely his own and instantly recognisable. He is one of the few players who has combined success in the world of jazz and popular music with ability in the classical repertoire, though in the process the latter may have suffered more.

A more orthodox player of real brilliance was José Rey de la Torre whose available recordings show a more scrupulous awareness than Almeida could lay claim to. A student of Llobet, he established an enviable reputation as a fine recitalist, but was unable to consolidate his success on an international scale. He was perhaps the most virtuoso of all Llobet's pupils.

Many of the talented players born in the pre-1918 era were unable on technical or philosophical grounds to move the guitar forward into wider musical spheres. Segovia found it necessary to combat and transcend the limitations of those who followed Tárrega's teaching, and he was not impressed by the rather rasping and metallic tone of Llobet or his overall technical ability. Guitarists who found themselves trapped in an adoration of Tárrega were thus destined to be limited to comparative mediocrity as artists.

Artistic failure for a guitarist is often represented by a dignified retreat into the conservatoire, the pursuit of musicology and pedagogy, the devotion to transcription and editing as a way of life and not, as in the case of the great players, as a means to the greater end of personal performance. Thus no great player able to challenge Segovia's omnipotence entered the battle until almost half a century after Segovia's professional debut in Granada in 1909.

A new breed of hardy international virtuosos, comparable to the great pianists and violinists of their generation, and determined to emulate and perhaps surpass the maestro's example, did eventually emerge. It would be necessary, just as Segovia had rejected much of Tárrega's approach and yet had accepted the fruits of repertoire and tradition before going on to evolve his own developments, for these newcomers to achieve the same kind of relationship to Segovia's authority. They would have to learn from his example and yet not be overwhelmed by the feeling that his achievement was insuperable.

Segovia had proved that the guitar could be taken out of the coterie into the sunlight of international acclaim, that the fragile and carefully guarded traditions could be enriched by a new repertoire and an appeal to composers of many nationalities. A guitarist might achieve the renown won by Kreisler, Paderewski or Casals, and the sky was the limit. The path to the summit was tortuous and hard, but it was possible to ascend. Young guitarists were given new heart by the great man's example.

Technical progress on the instrument was, for the aspirant to supreme honours, usually directly related to Segovian principles. Even more important was the existence of material in which the necessary techniques were deployed. Possession of a copy of Segovia's transcription of the Chaconne and other works by Bach, of compositions by Turina, Ponce and Castelnuovo-Tedesco, indeed of any publications in Schott's Guitar Archives series, was sufficient to indicate a possible horizon towards which the ship could be steered. The original inspiration of Segovia — the works of Sor, Aguado, Giuliani and Tárrega — were also readily available as a guide to the hazards to be circumnavigated.

Thus Julian Bream at the age of thirteen could in about 1947 present a programme to the Cheltenham Guitar Circle which included Segovia's arrangements of a sonata by Scarlatti and Bach's Courante from the Third 'Cello Suite, as well as his editions of Ponce's Sonata Clásica and Turina's Fandanguillo. At a similar age John Williams performed Segovia's edition of Sor's Op. 9, Variations on a Theme by Mozart, on a television programme for children on 2 January 1954. These two young players, destined for the highest honours, could cut their teeth on a repertoire of proven validity.

In the post-war era, Segovia's technique and prestige was a formative influence on so many guitarists of potential greatness. Alirio Diaz of Venezuela first encountered Segovia in 1945, and later moved to Europe to study with the maestro at Siena in northern Italy, where Segovia established a summer school. John Williams, too, made the annual pilgrimage to Siena. Julian Bream met Segovia in 1947, having been introduced to him by Dr. Boris Perott, the President of the Philharmonic Society of Guitarists.

None of these younger players failed to achieve his own individual development. Slavish imitation of Segovia's stylistic mannerisms was never a guiding principle. Each guitarist produced his own sound and was moulded by a unique musical environment. Segovia's influence extended as far as the creation of a finer awareness of tone quality, a legacy of many excellent compositions, and the stimulus of an illuminating presence.

As with all powerful father-figures, the new sons of Segovia's traditions sometimes found it psychologically necessary to assert themselves against the dominant ideal. Each player would secure his own area of territory as far as repertoire was concerned, impress another generation of composers to begin writing for the guitar, and each guitarist would extend the tradition in his own idiosyncratic way. It is axiomatic that greatness as an instrumentalist means a sublime change in the guitar's role. The great players Diaz, Yepes, Presti, Bream and Williams, all alter our concept of the instrument's possibilities, continuing the work that Segovia had begun.

Alirio Diaz, for example, was soon acknowledged as the greatest player (with the possible exception of Agustin Barrios) to emerge from South America. Equally at ease in all periods of the repertoire, his recitals usually include a selection of Venezuelan pieces, some of them by Antonio Lauro (b. 1917), one of the leading composers among Diaz' countrymen. The titles of these works, such as Angostura, El Marabino, El Niño, Carora, Flores Negras, El Diablo Suelto, etc., reflect the lively imagination which inspires music in close contact with folkloric traditions.

Diaz plays in a style quite distinct from that of Segovia. The dominant feature of his playing is of a brilliant headlong progress rather than the sensuous deployment of rubato and rich tonal resonances. The continuity of Diaz' playing is so full of momentum and spontaneity that it sometimes appears almost casual. Bach's Chaconne, Rodrigo's immensely difficult Invocation and Dance (dedicated to Diaz), and large works such as Castelnuovo-Tedesco's Sonata in D (Homage to Boccherini), as well as the intricate studies of Villa-Lobos or Barrios, are flung off with such apparent nonchalance and ease that Diaz could well be acclaimed as the Horowitz of the guitar.

He later studied in Madrid with Regino Sainz de la Maza, a connection which enabled him to incorporate in his recitals the Spanish-flavoured compositions of both Regino and his brother Eduardo, and to claim this corner of the repertoire as very much his own. Works such as Bolero, Zapateado, Habanera, Petenera, Rondeña, El Vito and many others, continue the line of cultural heritage linking Arcas, Tárrega, Turina and Torroba, in the exercise of the Iberian fantasy. Thus Diaz is the ideal player, technically and temperamentally, to unite in his performances folk vitalities with the refinement of the modern classical guitar.

A more controversial guitarist than Diaz is Narciso Yepes (b. 1927, Lorca, Spain). The best account of his early life and musical development is given by the Spanish writer José Maria Gironella, in a book dedicated to Yepes entitled *Todos Somos Fugitivos* (Barcelona, 1974). This relates how Yepes began to play the guitar at an early age, and later studied in Valencia with Rafael Balaguer and the composer Vicente Asencio (b. 1903).

Yepes often tells the story of how Asencio believed the guitar to be an inadequate instrument because of its lack of brilliance in scale passages. It is true that guitarists often cannot perform scales with the rapidity of pianists or violinists. Yepes applied himself to the problem and by the velocity of his playing proved to Asencio that players were at fault, not the guitar itself.

The Director of the Spanish National Orchestra, Ataúlfo Argenta, persuaded Yepes to go to Madrid and he gave a debut there in 1947. Later Yepes toured Europe and studied interpretation with Enesco and Gieseking. In 1952 he created the music for the French film *Jeux Interdits*, another movie which featured the folk song Romance de Amor.

Narciso Yepes made his first recordings in the 1950's and since 1967 has recorded for Deutsche Grammophon a long series of albums covering many areas of the repertoire including the Villa-

16. *Alirio Diaz*. Courtesy of Basil Douglas Ltd.

Lobos Studies and Preludes, the complete lute works of Bach (played on both Baroque lute and guitar), Sor studies, concertos by several composers including those dedicated to Yepes, and Spanish music.

Yepes has been associated with the Concierto de Aranjuez since his early recording of it, and his frequent international tours have made him one of the greatest box-office attractions among modern players. For audiences he possesses a charismatic appeal which has increased over the years.

His advocacy of Spanish music, and his success in attracting modern composers to write for him, such as Salvador Bacarisse (1898-1963), Mauricio Ohana (b. 1914), Bruno Maderna (1920-1973), Antonio Ruiz-Pipo (b. 1933), Leonardo Balada and others, establish Yepes as the most significant Spanish player after Segovia.

Yet in most respects Yepes remains a player least influenced by Segovia. He has consistently performed the perennials of the Segovian editions, by Turina, Torroba and Falla, as well as many of the familiar warhorses such as Sor, Giuliani, Tárrega and his own transcriptions of Albéniz and Granados. But Yepes brings to his interpretations a manner that is entirely his own and has preferred to shape his own artistic destiny.

This sharp sense of individuality which Yepes achieves is particularly noticeable in his use of a ten string guitar for all his recitals and recordings since the mid-sixties. The adoption of this instrument has offended the purists and fascinated the curious public. The ten string guitar combines the advantages of a normal guitar with the bass resonances of a Baroque lute, thus allowing Yepes to play the lute suites of Bach and Weiss with an enhanced authenticity. The extra strings also impart a specific resonance to the entire instrument even when only the top strings are used, and this sound is clearly to Yepes' liking. Composers have begun to write works specially for this hybrid guitar.

Ida Presti (1924-1967) was an infant prodigy of the guitar, appearing in public for the first time at the age of eight. In her teens and early twenties she gave many solo recitals, and made a few recordings, but her wider fame was established by her duo appearances with Alexandre Lagoya (b. 1929), her husband.

The amazing vibrant poignancy of her playing is a unique sound in the annals of guitar history, and she revealed what the guitar could achieve in terms of duet playing. In the Presti-Lagoya Duo two guitars seem animated by one spirit in a creative fusion of identities.

There are other significant guitar duos that have shaped the instrument's destiny, including that of Sor and Aguado, Llobet and Maria Luisa Anido, leading to some superb transcriptions, Evangelos

17. *Narciso Yepes.* Courtesy of Deutsche Grammophon.

and Liza, (the Athenian Guitar Duo), the Pomponio-Zarate Duo, the Dorigny-Ito Duo, Sergio and Eduardo Abreu, and also the establishment of a creative togetherness of the guitars of Julian Bream and John Williams.

The Presti-Lagoya Duo will however remain as the great epitome of what two guitars can achieve in terms of musical expressiveness. Fortunately, despite Presti's tragic death, their music will live on in their many recordings.

In the late nineteenth century the famous violinist, Juan Manén, declared that 'An Englishman playing the guitar is a kind of blasphemy.' This perhaps could apply to bad players of any nationality. What Manén could not have foreseen was the emergence of two great guitarists from England and the establishment of enviable reputations by many outstanding English performers.

Julian Bream (b. 1933) was the first British guitarist to receive international acclaim. From the outset his personality and musicianship marked him out as a man destined for great achievments. As early as the mid-fifties works were dedicated to him, including a Suite for Guitar by Stephen Dodgson and a Nocturne by R. Smith Brindle, intimations of the creative currents his playing would stimulate among English composers.

By 1956 Bream had commenced his recording career, initiating new approaches to the problems of putting the guitar and lute on record. Thereafter he produced albums at the rate of one or more a year, each issue bringing about new orientations in guitarists' thinking about the content of recital programmes.

His own concerts were a balanced selection of Baroque, Bach, nineteenth century, Spanish and contemporary music, and his performances and early records laid down a challenging alternative to the interpretations and musical concepts of Segovia. Bream entered the maestro's territory with his own readings of Frescobaldi, Scarlatti, Bach, Torroba, Turina, Falla and Villa-Lobos.

As well as meeting the twentieth century traditions head on, and absorbing them in masterly fashion, Bream made his own distinctive extension of the guitar's heritage. In 1961 he recorded Malcolm Arnold's Guitar Concerto, dedicated to him, following the success of Lennox Berkeley's Sonatina Op. 51, (written in 1958 and recorded 1960).

Benjamin Britten, England's leading composer, wrote Nocturnal in 1963, a *tour de force* that signified how Bream's persuasiveness was achieving in the sixties a similar feat to Segovia's constant wooing of composers four decades earlier. Like Ponce's Variations on 'Folia

18. *Julian Bream*. Courtesy of Harold Holt Ltd.

de España' and Fugue, Britten's Nocturnal, by choosing the variation form, achieved an intensity the guitar was well able to sustain. The umbilical relationship of the Nocturnal to Bream's devotion to the work of Dowland showed how profoundly Benjamin Britten had contemplated his creation. The relevance of selecting 'Come, heavy sleep', No. 20 in Dowland's *First Book of Songs or Ayres of Four Parts* (1597), as the basis for the variations was an appropriate testimonial for the regard England's greatest living composer felt for Bream.

The Nocturnal set a new standard for guitarists in both interpretative and technical aspects, just as Segovia's arrangement of the Chaconne had given players an Everest to attempt. For several years no other recitalist dared to include the Nocturnal in a concert programme, though eventually this particular dyke did break. The work also set new problems for guitar audiences, not always esteemed for intellectual stamina. Bream prepared his public for an assault on the higher levels of the musical sensibility, just as he had previously persuaded them to the unprecedented venture of accepting the delights of Dowland's lute music for a whole evening.

Bream had included fairly esoteric works such as Reginald Smith Brindle's El Polifemo de Oro (1956), Frank Martin's Quatre Pièces Brèves (1933), Hans Werner Henze's Drei Tentos (1958) and Roberto Gerhard's Fantasia (1957), in his recitals throughout his career, but took care to balance them with Spanish and South American offerings.

Steadily the ground was prepared for giving the guitar, through English composers writing for Bream, a respectable basis for more intellectual types of musical expressiveness. A record entitled *Julian Bream '70's* launched a decade of guitar students into a frenzied admiration of its compositions. These included William Walton's Five Bagatelles (1971), an Elegy by Alan Rawsthorne (1905-71), and Lennox Berkeley's Theme and Variations (1970), as well as a new Guitar Concerto by Richard Rodney Bennett (1970). The Concerto had been preceded by five Impromptus (1968), which though not recorded at this time, found an honourable place in many of Bream's recitals. Fantasy, Op. 107 by Malcolm Arnold, Paseo Op. 61 (1971) by Peter Racine Fricker, and Five for Guitar Op. 61 (1974) by Humphrey Searle, followed by a Guitar Concerto Op. 88 from the newly knighted Sir Lennox Berkeley concluded a particularly fruitful harvest from the English composers.

A titanic work was created by Hans Werner Henze who, searching for the 'unexplored spaces and depths' of the guitar, wrote an extended composition entitled Royal Winter Music (1977). This celebrated the characters from various Shakespearean plays, including Gloucester; Romeo and Juliet; Ariel; Ophelia; Audrey, William and Touchstone (from *As You Like It*); and finally Oberon. It is true to say that nothing quite like this composition had ever been conceived previously for the guitar, and it is set out in terms equivalent to the Hammerklavier Sonata of Beethoven as far as magnitude and ambition are concerned, and difficulty of execution.

Bream's recitals and records tended to bring about a new orthodoxy in the guitar repertoire, just as decades before, Segovia's band of composers laid down the basis of a player's programme. In the seventies young players of many nationalities took Bream as their mentor, imitating his selection from the contemporary composers, but unlike him, often lacking the insight and humanity necessary to project this music. Endless performances of Bennett's Impromptus, Walton's Bagatelles and even Britten's Nocturnal ousted the former dependence on the staple diet of Torroba, Turina and Villa-Lobos, creating in its wake crises in the guitar's history as many audiences wearied of those who took the new intellectualism for the only virtue.

What always impresses the public and critics about Bream's playing is his empathy with all kinds of music. His intensity and concentration absorbs all styles and all periods. From his hands the audience will accept any musical expression, yielding to his powers of persuasive shaping. His control of tone colour, quite different from Segovia, has brought a new sound into the world. But it is the clarity of his phrasing, the magnetic charisma of his personality, and the endless soulful depths of his music which make him perhaps the greatest successor and heir to Segovia's laurels.

Just as the early nineteenth century aficionados were likely to discuss the relative merits of Sor and Giuliani, in the same way players of our own time take particular pleasure in seemingly endless arguments about Julian Bream and John Williams. Such disputations, whether conducted verbally or in the often acrimonious pages of guitar journals, are usually more of a guide to the psychology and pre-judices of those taking part rather than a serious debate about objective musical values. Traditionally, as we see in many historical texts relating to lute, vihuela, or guitar, fretted instrumentalists delight in strong opinions and deep feelings, and their identification with particular players is extraordinarily intense.

There is no need to become too subjective or biased about either Bream or Williams. They exist individually as two equally bright stars in the firmament of the guitar, representing different approaches by reason of their personal history, character, physique and interests. They have each recognised the other's greatness as guitarists and in tribute to this recognition have given duo concerts together. Whatever competition may once have existed between them has now been surrendered in a mutual assumption of separate identity as musicians and in a powerful flood of reciprocal admiration.

Both players were child prodigies, and as such neither has lacked acknowledgement of his potential ability. The only question was of the use each would make of that ability and what kind of player would emerge. Bream had to move away from the strong tidal pull of Segovia's influence and become his own true self. Williams not only did not wish to be an inferior imitation of Segovia; in his formative years he had to face the challenge of Bream's vision of the guitar.

By the time Williams left the Royal College of Music in 1959, Bream was already launched on a successful international career of recitals and recordings. Even for Williams, equipped with prodigious musical gifts and Segovia's blessing, it was a formidable challenge to face. The eight years' seniority of Bream had enabled him to build up a large following and a unique situation was developing, for Britain had not previously possessed two guitarists of such outstanding ability.

Undaunted, John Williams gave his historic Wigmore Hall debut on 6 November 1958 and followed this triumph with two records, issued early in 1959. His playing was both intensely lyrical and technically perfect, though it was the latter which astonished the pundits more. The tributes which flowed in often neglected to notice the shaping spirit of musical intelligence for which the superbly honed technique was no more than a means to an end. Williams was the least exhibitionist of all musicians and his mastery of the instrument scarcely ever lent itself to extrovert display.

In this he was a true disciple of Segovia. His playing demeanour was that of restraint, control and order, an Apollonian contrast to the almost Dionysiac intensity of Bream's performing posture. Together they represented the Jekyll and Hyde contrasts of the guitar's own personality, one signifying a classical forbearance, the other the romantic soul. Over the next twenty years, their musical identities complete, Williams, a seemingly more remote concert artist, discarded the traditional formal recital attire and wore colourful guru shirts, whilst Bream, prince of spontaneity, preserved decorum in white tie and tails.

If either guitarist had donned swimming trunks to give performances it would scarcely have mattered as their strong and

19. *John Williams.* Courtesy of Harold Holt Ltd.

complex individuality transcended the conventions of external attire. Williams at one point even dispensed with the usual fixed recital programme, announcing each item from the stage in a bid to draw the audience further towards the musical experience and thus leaving his options open to choose and shape his concerts according to the urge of artistic instinct.

In the early sixties Williams conquered the capitals of the world in sustained tours to Europe, Russia, the Far East, Australia and the U.S.A., though later he grew tired of the rootless peripatetic progress expected of a concert artist. His recordings poured from the presses in a torrent of creativity with albums covering the whole available repertoire with special reference to Spanish music, J.S. Bach, Scarlatti, and Guitar Concertos (including those written for him by Stephen Dodgson and André Previn, as well as Concertos by Rodrigo, Giuliani, Castelnuovo-Tedesco, Vivaldi, Arnold, Villa-Lobos, Ponce, Leo Brouwer etc.).

To the dismay of purists he experimented with the electric guitar and issued several albums of sonorities and ensemble arrangements quite remote from the ordinary preoccupations of classical players. But these activities co-existed with making further magnificent contributions to the classical guitar's accepted repertoire. Williams' protean versatility explored many avenues and if some of his discoveries took him down cul-de-sacs, nothing was lost in the process.

His early training under his father's tutelage, his own genius for the guitar temperamentally, intellectually and physically, and a lifetime of obvious self-discipline in musical matters, left him in possession of the greatest guitar technique ever known. There was certainly nothing in the history of the repertoire that he could not master with consummate skill, and the celebrated peaks of the recitalist's art, Bach's Chaconne, the Fourth Lute Suite, Rodrigo's Concierto de Aranjuez and Fandango, the entire range of the difficult compositions of Agustín Barrios, and transcriptions such as the Valses Poeticos of Granados, were subdued in his hands until no trace of difficulty was apparent.

Such virtuosity was already familiar to those who frequented piano recitals and experienced the power of the great violinists and 'cellists. For the guitar audiences it was something totally staggering and unexpected. Williams is the embodiment of a great classical artist, a player through whom music speaks without being distorted by the impress of the performer's personality. Audiences and critics, unaccustomed to the concept of artistic objectivity when applied to the guitar, and misled by Williams' body language during recitals, believed him to be less than fully involved in the music. Time will reveal the full stature of John Williams as a great musician who drew the guitar closer to the orbit of the ulterior impersonality of art, untainted by whim, mood, or individual weakness. T.S. Eliot, commenting on the sensibility of a poet in 'Tradition and the Individual Talent', puts the classic attribute of true creativity into words:

> What happens is a continual surrender of himself as he is at the moment to something which is more valuable. The progress of an artist is a continual self-sacrifice, a continual extinction of personality.

24. The Mysterious Box

I have heard an old guitar maestro say, 'The duende *is not in the throat; the* duende *surges up from the soles of the feet'. Which means that it is not a matter of ability, but of real live form; of blood; of ancient culture; of creative action'.*

Lorca: *Theory and Function of the Duende*

One of the most remarkable occurrences in recent years has been the discovery of the music of Agustín Barrios (1885-1944). This Paraguayan virtuoso of the guitar was scarcely known until John Williams initiated a revival of enthusiasm for Barrios and eventually issued a record of some of the composer's finest work.

Laurindo Almeida and Alirio Díaz had both recorded various pieces by Barrios, and the latter had been a consistent advocate of the famous Danza Paraguaya. But neither player delved into the substance of this music with the same intensity as Williams.

It was found that Barrios pursued a remarkable concert career from 1910 until his death in 1944. He had composed over three hundred works, of which at least a hundred survive, and between 1915 and 1926 made many records on 78's both of his own work and the traditional repertoire of Bach, Sor and Tárrega.

An image emerged of a kind of primeval Liszt of the guitar world, a flamboyant artist, frequently dressed as an Indian, whose large hands and inward genius gave him a unique capacity as player and composer. His technically difficult works reached out to encompass a universe of imagination and innocence. Titles such as La Catedral, Sueño en la Floresta (Dream in the Dell), Maxixé and Una Limosna por el Amor de Dios (also known as Ultima Canción as it was composed shortly before his death), took the listener into a demi-Eden of the guitar, inspired by John Williams' amazing advocacy of compositions requiring a sublime virtuosity, and by the freshness of the Barrios approach.

Though some critics protested that Barrios was no more than a virtuoso miniaturist, the composer would not be cut down to the size they ordained for him. The compositions of Barrios were a full-blooded expression of the indigenous guitar of South America, lacking the sophistication of Villa-Lobos and none the worse for that. His naiveté was an essential part of the appeal.

New vistas of guitar possibility opened up before the eyes of eager performers. The repertoire, loaded down in the sixties with a surfeit of intellectualism, was now restored to its roots. Barrios used the guitar as only a great player could, unaware that technical limitations existed and intent on projecting the full powers of his unbridled imaginative faculty. The exuberance in his music suddenly achieved for the guitar what Dylan Thomas had for poetry — the infusion of colour, dark forces and complete disdain for academic subtleties.

His studies, preludes, waltzes and dances (including cuecas, choros, estilos, zambas, maxixes and tangos) restored the flow of blood to the body after the beginning of an unhealthy concentration on matters of the head alone. The tremendous authority of John Williams, himself a player of many finely intellectual compositions, was placed firmly behind Barrios' music in an effective demonstration of fervour. The Paraguayan jungle had rescued the instrument from the groves of Academe, snatching the repertoire from the monopoly of college graduates. The bitter complaints from those locked in the unloving embrace of atonal dissonance could be discounted on the principle that any player who criticised Barrios was therefore quite incapable of playing his music, a fact that was possibly true.

In his 'Dedication to the Guitar' Barrios revealed the depths of his fantasy, a true soliloquy in the tradition of the guitar's romantic origins:

> Tupa, the Supreme Spirit and protector of my race, found me one day in the middle of a verdant copse wrapt in admiration whilst contemplating nature. And said to me, 'Take this mysterious box and reveal its secrets.' And locking up in it all the singing birds, left it in my hands. Obeying the orders of Tupa I took the box and placing it close to my chest, I embraced it and spent many moons at the side of a spring. And one night Jacy, painted in liquid crystal, feeling the sadness of my Indian soul, gave me six silver rays of light so that with them I could unmask the secrets of the box. And the miracle occurred: from the depths of the mysterious box there emerged a marvellous symphony of all the virgin voices of our America.

As Shakespeare expressed it, 'This is the very ecstasy of love', an identification of personality with the voice of the guitar that could only have come from an extraordinary and gifted player. It reminds one of Segovia's remark, 'I have been captured for life by the guitar . . . Faithful only to the guitar'.

It is said that Barrios and Segovia did actually meet in 1921 and 1944. They would have had much to tell each other. Both lived unreservedly the life of the artist, unmasking the mysteries of the box as in a sacred mission. When faced with the extremity of death, Barrios even used the guitar as a form of prayer, thereby creating one of the most poignant songs of the guitar.

His 'Gran Tremolo', Una Limosna por el Amor de Dios, encompasses the tradition of Tárrega as well as the passion of Barrios. It takes us back to Lorca's poem 'La Guitarra'.

> *Empieza el llanto*
> *de la guitarra.*
> *Es inútil callarla.*
> *Es imposible*
> *callarla . . .*
> *Llora por cosas*
> *lejanas . . .*
> *Oh, guitarra!*
> *Corazón malherido*
> *por cinco espadas.*

(The lament of the guitar begins. It is useless to silence it. It is impossible to silence it . . . It sobs for distant things . . . Oh, guitar, heart wounded by five swords.)

25. New Horizons

*Everything is the sum of the past and nothing is
comprehensible except through its history.*

Teilhard de Chardin

The future of the guitar is assured.

Andrés Segovia

The digging of archeological sites brings the realities of the past to
living awareness before it is too late. Soon, perhaps building on the
same foundations, cathedrals, skyscrapers or supermarkets may be
erected and the evidence of historic cultures is then obliterated. The
evaluation of guitar traditions presents problems which are not dis-
similar.

It is certainly easier to assess past glories than to come to terms
adequately with the rapidly emerging developments of contemporary music. Guitarists are engaged, like other instrumentalists,
in a complex process of sifting through the legacy of acceptable
repertoire whilst helping to develop the guitar's future artistic
aspirations.

In the shifting currents of debate, often confused by prejudice,
national temperament, musical research, fashionable opinion and the
general flux of modern art forms, the guitar is caught frequently
between Scylla and Charybdis in a difficult voyage of self-ex-
ploration. The rapid ascent of the instrument's fortunes as it moved
from the street to the court, from parlour to salon and from Spanish
verandah to the concert hall, makes a realistic appraisal of its achievements somewhat hazardous. The volatile popularity of the guitar
over several centuries also gives cause for uncertainty about its
future.

In effect the classical guitar still finds itself in a dilemma. Over a
period of time many remarkable personalities have dedicated their
loyalties to it, either as players, composers, luthiers or teachers. It

now struggles to consolidate its awareness of identity, seeking to establish precisely what kind of musical medium it actually is. Yet the guitar remains what it usually has been, a blend of the serious and the frivolous, the nationalist and the cosmopolitan, the reactionary and the avant-garde.

Most other European instruments such as the pianoforte or the violin offer a clear definition of their aesthetic triumphs. The peaks of their repertoire are too prominent to miss and one can point out the salient masterpieces without fear of contradiction. The guitar's inheritance has hitherto lacked the secure patronage of great composers. This means that a tradition of analytic evaluation is missing also. So discussion concerning the music of the guitar is energetic, urgent and passionately argued, but with little scholarly depth and few conclusions. One advantage of this palpable confusion in the ranks of aficionados is that the guitar continually elicits a clarification of one's attitudes towards music and art. A bland conservatism has not yet overtaken the guitar's ability to provoke controversy. The disadvantage, however, is that despite the heat generated, the true nature of the instrument's contribution to European musical culture remains indistinct and ill-defined.

The central battleground of critical dissent confronts the protagonists with a simple dichotomy. This is the area where the northern offerings to the shrine of the guitar by composers such as Britten, Henze or Berkeley are compared with the less intellectual Iberian and Latin-American stock repertoire. The exuberant Spanishry beloved by audiences is frequently dismissed by sterner critics as being inferior to the cooler inspiration of temperate climes.

The contemporary guitarist must resolve the question of a hierarchy of 'seriousness' within the structure of his recital programmes. Whether in essence Britten is a more 'profound' composer than Albéniz or the works of Henze more 'significant' than those of Turina and Lauro is a discriminative judgement that it is inadvisable to make in terms of the guitar's repertoire. Each composer must be faced and absorbed by a recitalist, and to do justice to the works of such diverse personalities within the space of a single concert is the guitar's supreme destiny.

The instrument's immense versatility in this respect brings together many strands of historical and contemporary developments within the organised dramatic involvement of a concert. The integration of the old and the new can be mutually illuminating and the guitarist has the remarkable opportunity of engaging his audiences in a surrender to many varieties of musical experience. It is the reconciliation of so many diverse elements which makes the recitalist's task exciting and sometimes controversial.

There is certainly no shortage nowadays of talented guitarists eager to take up the challenges posed by the instrument's repertoire and techniques. Inspired by the triumphant progress of Segovia, Bream, Williams, Diaz and Yepes (and often claiming discipleship to one or another of them), gifted musicians from many countries have undertaken the adventurous journey to fame. Though following in their masters' footsteps at first, their own creative identity soon asserts itself in recitals and recordings, enriching the guitar with the influx of new aspirations.

Indeed their task is arduous and the standards established by the acknowledged great players are formidable. Between 1950 and 1980 well over three hundred long-playing records have been issued. Of these, Segovia, Bream, Williams and Yepes have produced upwards of thirty albums each. The commanding heights of the repertoire have been securely possessed by such players. However, superlative musicianship is always in demand and the younger generation of players can anticipate a favourable response from the public as they struggle towards fulfilment of their artistic ambitions. The great players themselves have frequently provided encouragement and practical help in the founding of the careers of up and coming guitarists.

Some of the most impressive international recitalists (each of whom has recorded at least three albums) include players such as Turibio Santos (b. 1943) Sergio and Eduardo Abreu (b. 1948 and 1949 respectively), and Carlos Barbosa-Lima (b. 1944), of Brazil, Konrad Ragossnig (b. 1932) and Leo Witoszynskyj (b. 1941) of Austria, Siegfried Behrend of Germany, Evangelos and Liza, the Greek duo, Pepe and Angel Romero, and Diego Blanco (b. 1950) of Spain, Alice Artzt (b. 1943) and Christopher Parkening (b. 1949) of the U.S.A., Eric Hill (b. 1942), Timothy Walker (b. 1943), John Mills (b. 1947) and Carlos Bonell (b. 1949) of England, and Ricardo Fernandez Iznaola (b. 1949) of Venezuela.

Other fine players such as Akinobu Matsuda (b. 1933) of Japan, Leo Brouwer (b. 1939) of Cuba, also an outstanding composer, Michael Lorrimer of the U.S.A., Oscar Ghiglia and Angelo Gilardino of Italy, and younger guitarists such as Sharon Isbin (b. 1957) of the U.S.A., and Manuel Barrueco (b. 1952) of Cuba, though less well known through recordings, have already established considerable reputations for themselves. There are many others throughout the world who will sooner or later enrich the guitar's history. Such an array of virtuosity and enthusiasm was at one time devoutly to be wished, but has now become a permanent indication of the guitar's vitality.

Equally significant is the ceaseless activity of contemporary composers to create worthwhile music dedicated to the younger players. In Britain alone a remarkable number of composers have written for the instrument including (apart from those mentioned in previous chapters) Denis Apivor, David Bedford, Gilbert Biberian, M. Blake Watkins, Carey Blyton, David Cain, Colin Downs, Tom Eastwood, David Farquher, Sebastian Forbes, Colin Hand, Joseph Horovitz, Oliver Hunt, Michael Jacques, Wilfred Josephs, Bryan Kelly, William Kinghorn, Elisabeth Lutyens, Nicholas Marshall, John McCabe, Wilfred Mellers, Thea Musgrave, Humphrey Searle, Philip Selby, Bernard Stevens, Ronald Stevenson, Richard Stoker, Phyllis Tate, Gareth Walters, Roger Williams, Arthur Wills, Thomas Wilson and Brian Wright.

The most prolific and devoted British composer in the cause of the guitar is undoubtedly John W. Duarte. His original work and arrangements have been performed internationally by nearly all the leading guitarists and the scope and range of his output have exceeded that of all other writers for the instrument. As well as his remarkable creativity, his role as critic and writer, teacher and scholar, has provided a background of probing analysis which the guitar has desperately needed.

Out of so much creative effort, to be found in similar intensity throughout the world, the guitar's future will be nurtured. The fusion of excellent players and sensitive composers must ultimately produce a rich musical harvest.

So through a unique blend of contemporary fascination and centuries of devoted guitarists, the destiny of the instrument is steadily advanced. The artistic struggles of its practitioners will decide whether it is moving towards new glories or merely consolidating its present golden age.

Andrés Segovia has said many times that the guitar neither began nor will end with him. Yet without his massive presence in the twentieth century, the guitar would not exist in the splendour that it now enjoys. It cannot rest on its laurels or stagnate in the nostalgia of Segovia's achievement. Its history must move forward, to new adventures, new personalities and new horizons. But Segovia, above all in the guitar's long tale, enabled it to come to terms with its past and to contemplate the depths of its potential expressiveness. Four lines by Heine, originally a tribute to another great man of Granada, can be applied with equal appropriateness to Andrés Segovia:

Nimmer wird sein Ruhm verhallen,
Ehe nicht die letzte Saite,
Schnarrend losspringt von der letzten
Andalusischen Gitarre.

(Never will his fame diminish, not before the last string breaks harshly from the last Andalucian guitar.)

Appendices

Recital Programmes, 1888-1978

The changing character and structure of guitar recitals is a fascinating study, illustrating the development of the repertoire and expectations about the instrument's musical capabilities. It is to be expected that soloists will continue to experiment, innovate, and modify the traditional patterns of presentation. Guitar history has witnessed many evolutionary progressions and the instrument's survival as a creative medium will depend on its achievement of a balance between traditional and unprecedented aspects in the future.

(The idiosyncratic spelling of the early recital programmes has been maintained.)

10th May, 1888
Royal Academy of Saint Cecilia, Cadiz
FRANCISCO TÁRREGA

I.

Melody from Sicilian Vespers	Verdi
Fantasia de Marina	Arrieta
Gran Tremolo	Gottschalk
Fantasia Espanola	Tárrega

II.

Celebre Gavota	Arditi
Polonesa de Concierto	Arcas
Carnaval de Venecia	Tárrega

III.

Motivos Heterogeneos	Tárrega
Scherzo y Minuetto	Prudent

| Gran Marcha Funebre | Thalberg |
| Aires Nacionales | Tárrega |

8th June, 1918
Barcelona
EMILIO PUJOL

I.

Minuet	Sor
Canco de Bressol	Pujol
Vals intim	Pujol
Recuerdos de l'Alhambra	Tárrega
Dansa Moresca	Tárrega

II.

Adagio	Haydn
Loure	Bach
Moment musical	Schubert
Minuet	Schubert

III.

El Mestre	Llobet
El Testament d'Amelia	Llobet
Serenada Espanola	Malats
Granada	Albéniz
Danza	Granados

26th January, 1931
Institute of Music, Adria, Italy
MIGUEL LLOBET

I.

Minuet; Study	Sor
Andante (Don Giovanni)	Mozart
Prelude	Bach

Sueño	Tárrega

II.

Echos du paisage	Broque
Chanson de Leon	R. Villar
Nocturno	Torroba
Torre Bermeja	Albéniz
Danza	Granados

III.

Barcarolle	Mendelssohn
Chanson Gitane (de Amor Brujo)	M. de Falla
Trois melodies; Populaires catalans; Jota	Llobet

4th November, 1953
King's Hall, Ilkley
ANDRÉS SEGOVIA

I.

Aria con variazioni	G. Frescobaldi
Suite in A (for lute) Prelude-Ballet-Sarabande-Gigue	S.L. Weiss
Andante and Allegretto	F. Sor

II.

Prelude and Loure	J.S. Bach
Sonata	D. Scarlatti
Allegretto and Menuet	J. Ph. Rameau
Canzonetta	F. Mendelssohn

III.

Capriccio (Homage to Paganini) (dedicated to Segovia)	M. Castelnuovo-Tedesco
La Maja de Goya	E. Granados
Mallorca Torre Bermeja	I. Albéniz

10th November, 1957
Cambridge Arts Theatre
JULIAN BREAM

I.

Air — Rondeau — Hornpipe	Purcell
Overture	Weiss

Partita in A minor
  Prelude
  Fugue
  Sarabande
  Gigue
	Bach

Two Sonatas	Cimarosa
Variations Op. 9	Sor

II.

Garrotin Soleares	Turina

Sonatina
  Allegretto
  Lento
  Rondo
	Lennox Berkeley

Cancion Campo	Ponce
Leyenda	Albéniz

17th February, 1961
Wigmore Hall, London
NARCISO YEPES

I.

| Fantasia que contrahaze la Harpa
  de Ludovico | A. Mudarra |
| Spanish Suite
  Españoletas
  Gallarda y Villano
  Danza de las Hachas
  Rujero y Paradetas
  Zarabanda al ayre español
  Pasacelle | Gaspar Sanz |

La minoña de Cataluña
Canarios

Sonata	D. Scarlatti
Sonata (Zapateado)	Mateo Albéniz
Theme and Variations	F. Sor

II.

Chaconne in D minor	J.S. Bach

III.

Prelude No. 1 in E minor	Villa-Lobos
Sonatina Meridional	M. Ponce

　　Campo
　　Copla
　　Fiesta

Rumores de la Caleta (Malagueña)	I. Albéniz
Hommage au Tombeau de Debussy	M. de Falla
In the Wheat-fields	Joaquin Rodrigo
Song and Dance No. 1	Ruiz Pipo

1st November, 1961
Wigmore Hall, London
JOHN WILLIAMS

I.

Fantasia and Pavana	Luys Milán
Diferencias on "Guárdame las Vacas"	Luys de Narváez
Fantasia	Alonso Mudarra
Prelude; Sarabande; Bourrée	J.S. Bach
Sonatina (in three movements) (first performance)	John W. Duarte
Nocturno Burgalesa Los Mayos	F. Moreno Torroba
Fandanguillo	Turina

II.

Variations and Fugue on "Folia de España"	Manuel Ponce

4th December, 1967
Guildhall, Cambridge
ALIRIO DIAZ

I.

La Frescobalda; Galliard and Courante	G. Frescobaldi
Fugue in A minor	J.S. Bach
Third Cello Suite Prelude, Allemande, Courante, Sarabande, Bourrée I and II, Gigue	J.S. Bach (transcribed J. Duarte)

II.

Prelude No. 1 Etude No. 7 Choro No. 1	H. Villa-Lobos
Miller's Dance (Farruca)	M. de Falla
Fandanguillo	J. Turina
Leyenda (Asturias) Torre Bermeja Sevilla	I. Albéniz

13th and 15th January, 1978
Wigmore Hall, London
JULIAN BREAM

I.

Aria con Variazioni detta "La Frescobalda"	Frescobaldi
Prelude, Fugue, and Finale (Allegro) in E flat, BWV998	Bach
Sonata in A	Paganini

II.

Song Without Words, Op. 19, No. 6	Mendelssohn
Elegy (1971)	Rawsthorne
Impromptus (1968)	Bennett
Three Pieces from Suite Española no. 1 Granada no. 4 Cadiz no. 3 Sevilla	Albéniz

25th October, 1978
Free Trade Hall, Manchester
ANDRÉS SEGOVIA

I.

Song of the Emperor and Variations on a Spanish popular tune	L. de Narváez
Andante, Menuet, Rondo	F. Sor
Five Pieces from "Platero and I" Prelude-Tempo de habanera- Ronsard-Melancolia-Primavera	M. Castelnuovo-Tedesco

II.

Prelude-Siciliana-Corrente	J.S. Bach
Sonata	D. Scarlatti
Andante and Allegretto in D	J. Haydn

III.

Sonatina Meridional Campo-Copla-Fiesta	M. Ponce
La Maja de Goya	E. Granados
Sevilla	I. Albéniz

Discography

No discography of the classical guitar could ever be totally inclusive and it should be remembered that a discography does not include compositions that have not yet been recorded, though they may be performed at concerts and published as sheet music! Many fine recordings of the past are sure to slip though the net without acknowledgement, and every year brings more and more high quality albums to the list. The purpose of this compilation is primarily to bear witness to the efforts of so many players to do justice to the long and great traditions of the guitar.

By intelligent scrutiny of such a discography, the contours of the repertoire (with its strengths and limitations) as they have appealed to guitarists, can be adequately delineated. Moreover, the various versions of the most popular pieces provide an essential context for the development of discriminative awareness.

Nearly a hundred players are listed here, performing between them the works of over a hundred composers from the Renaissance to the 1970's. For obvious reasons, with a recording career of over fifty years to his credit, Segovia's discography, where applicable, is catalogued first in each list. Bream, Diaz, Williams and Yepes, then appear (in alphabetical order), followed in each instance by other artists, also in alphabetical order.

The recordings of even the most distinguished guitarists tend to be deleted from time to time, though certain tracks or entire albums may be re-issued thereafter. Availability of any items is often a matter of luck. The finest renderings of masterpieces are certainly not guaranteed an eternal niche on the shelves of the nearest record shop. This discography is also intended to give some indication of the number of re-issues of particular recordings, but can never unfortunately, be taken as an assurance that any of the versions are conveniently accessible to the prospective buyer.

List of Recording Artists

ABREU, Eduardo
ABREU, Sergio
ALMEIDA, Laurindo
ANIDO, Maria Luisa
ARTZT, Alice
AUBIN, Christian
BARBOSA-LIMA, Antonio Carlos
BARRIOS, Agustin
BARRUECO, Manuel
BARTOLI, René
BEHREND, Siegfried
BENITEZ, Baltazar
BITETTI, Ernesto
BLANCO, Diego
BLOCH, Suzanne
BONELL, Carlos
BOYD, Liona
BREAM, Julian
BROUWER, Leo
BYZANTINE, Julian
CACERES, Oscar
CANO, Manuel
COSTANZO, Irma
CUBEDO, Manuel
DIAZ, Alirio
DOMBOIS, Eugen
DORIGNY, Henri
ESTARELLAS, Gabriel
EVANGELOS, (Assimakopoulos)
FAMPAS, Dimitri
GERWIG, Walter
GHIGLIA, Oscar
GILARDINO, Angelino
GOMEZ, William
GONNISSEN, Olaf van

GONZALEZ, José Luis
HARKER, Roland
HENDERSON, Forbes
HILL, Eric
HOPE, Harvey
ITO, Aku
IVANOV-KRAMSKOI, Alexander
JOHNSON, Lawrence
LAGOYA, Alexandre
LEEB, Hermann
LIZA, (Zoi)
LOPATEGUI, José-Luis
LUCIA, Paco de
MARCOS, Maria Livia Sao
MAROTO, Sebastian
MATSUDA, Akinobu
MATTHEWS, William
MAVRUDIS, Notis
MERCADEL, Juan
MIKULKA, Vladimir
MILLS, John
MUNTING, Simon
NORTH, Nigel
OMEGA Quartet (Gilbert Biberian; Colin Downs; Gregory Pikler; Bernard Watson)
PARKENING, Christopher
POLASEK, Barbara
POMPONIO, Graciela
PONCE, Alberto
PRESTI, Ida
PROVOST, Richard
RAGOSSNIG, Konrad

RAMOS, Manuel Lopez
RIERA, Rodrigo
ROBERT, Guy
ROMERO, Angel
ROMERO, Celedonio
ROMERO, Celin
ROMERO, Pepe
SABICAS
SANTOS, Turibio
SAINZ DE LA MAZA, Regino
SCHAEFFER, Michael
SCHEIT, Karl
SCOTT, Ivan
SEGOVIA, Andrés
SIIRALA, Seppo
SILVA, Jesús
SZENDREY-KARPER, László
TARRAGO, Renata
TEUCHERT, Michael
TOMÁS, José
TORRE, Rey de la
TYLER, James
WALKER, Luise
WALKER, Timothy
WILLIAMS, John
WITOSZYNSKYJ, Leo
YBARRA, Ramón
YEPES, Narciso
ZALDUA, Edgard
ZARADIN, John
ZARATE, Jorge Martinez
ZAYAS, Rodrigo de
ZELENKA, Milan

Music for the Vihuela

Luys Milán (c.1500-c.1561)

Pavanas
Segovia *Three Pavanas* (78/10″) 710/
    40.075 (1949)
    Three Pavanas Decca DL 8022
    Pavana Decca DL 9647
    Pavanas Nos. 5, 6 Decca DL 710039
    Six Pavanas Decca DL 710167
    Pavanas Nos. 6, 5 MUCS 105
    Three Pavanas M 24018
Yepes *Six Pavanas* DG 2539087
    Two Pavanas Decca LXT 2974
Bitetti *Pavanas Nos. 1, 5* Hispavox
    Spain HH(S) 10.365
Ghiglia *Six Pavanas* Angel S-36508
Maroto *Pavana* Harmonia Mundi
    Opus 13
Matsuda *Three Pavanas* Argo ZDA 205
Ragossnig *Six Pavanas* Archiv 2533 183
    (Lute)
C. Romero *Pavanas Nos. 6, 4, 3* Philips
    6582001
Silva *Pavana* RCA MKL 1642
T. Walker *Two Pavanas* Saga 5426
Ybarra *Six Pavanas* Westminster Gold
    8142

Fantasias
Segovia *Fantasia XVI* Decca DL 9638
Bloch *Fantasia* Vox DL 1240 (Lute)
Ragossnig *Fantasias X, XVI, XII, XI*
    Archiv 2533 183 (Lute)
Riera *Two Fantasias* MHS 565

Luys de Narváez (c.1500-1555)

*Diferencias sobre 'Guárdame las
    Vacas'*
Segovia Decca DL 9931; DL 79931
    (stereo)
Diaz HM 32 SD; VPD 20002
Yepes DG 2726018
Bitetti Hispavox Spain HH(S) 10.365
Blanco Swedish Society SLT 33189
Ghiglia Angel S-36508
Lopategui HM 10/003
Ragossnig Archiv 2533 183 (Lute)
C. Romero Philips 6582001
Ybarra Westminster WVS 8142

Canción del Emperador
Segovia Decca DL 9931; DL 79931
    (stereo)
Yepes DG 2726018
Bitetti Hispavox Spain HH(S) 10.365
Fampas Odeon EMI OMGC 67
Ragossnig Archiv 2533 183 (Lute)
Riera MHS 565

Miscellaneous Pieces
Brouwer *Two Fantasias* DG 2555001
Ragossnig *Baxo de Contrapunto* Archiv
    2533 183 (Lute)
Riera *Baxo de Contrapunto* MHS 565

Alonso Mudarra (c.1510-1570)

Fantasia X
Bream RCA SB 6698 (Lute)
Diaz Vanguard VSD 71135; VPD
    20002; HM 32SD
Williams CBS 72526
Yepes DG 2539087
Bitetti Hispavox Spain HH(S) 10.365
Ghiglia Angel S-36508
Lopategui HM 10/003
Ragossnig Archiv 2533 183 (Lute);
    Oiseau Lyre SOL 349

Miscellaneous Pieces
Segovia *Romanesca* Decca DL 9633
Williams *Conde Claros* 72526
Ragossnig *Pavana, Gallarda,
    Romanesca, Conde Claros* Archiv
    2533 183 (Lute)
Ybarra *Gallarda* Mercury WST 17117

Vihuela Songs
Yepes/Berganza 2530 504
Tarrago/Barbany Everest 3197
Zayas/Perret Hispavox HHS 15 (Vihela)

Music for the Renaissance Lute

Vincenzo Galilei (1520-1591)

Miscellaneous Pieces
Segovia Decca DL 8022; Decca Album
    710/40.075 (1949); Decca DL 9795
Diaz BAM LD 032

Almeida   **Ember GUC 31**
Artzt   **GME 1018**
Bartoli   **RCA LSB 4032**
C. Romero   **Philips 6582001**
Silva   **RCA Victor Mexico MKL 1642**
Tyler   **Saga 5420**
T. Walker   **SOL 349**

John Dowland (1563-1626)

Melancholy Galliard
Segovia   **MCA S/26.073; Decca DL-
   710171**
Bream   **WG 1012** (Lute); **SER 5687-8;
   Westminster XWN 18429; RL
   42760**
Williams   **CBS 61126**
Behrend   **DG 2530 079**
Ragossnig   **Archiv 2533 157** (Lute)
Riera   **MHS 565**
T. Walker   **Saga 5426**

My Lady Hunsdon's Puffe
Segovia   **MCA S/26.073; Decca DL-
   710171**
Bream   **Westminster XWN 18429** (Lute);
   SER 5638; RL 42670
Williams   **CBS 61126**
Ragossnig   **Archiv 2533 157** (Lute)
T. Walker   **Saga 5426**

Fantasia No. 7
Segovia   **MCA S/26.073; Decca DL-
   710171**
Bream   **Westminster XWN 18429** (Lute);
   SER 5638
Williams   **CBS 61126**
Ragossnig   **Archiv 2533 157** (Lute)

Queen Elizabeth's Galliard
Bream   **Westminster XWN 18429** (Lute);
   SER 5687-8; SB 6698; SB 6646
Williams   **CBS 72728**
Behrend   **DG 2530 079**
Ragossnig   **Archiv 2533 150** (Lute); **2723
   051**

King of Denmark's Galliard
Bream   **Westminster XWN 18429** (Lute)
Behrend   **DG 2530 079**
Mills   **Discourses ABK 10**
Ragossnig   **Archiv 2533 157** (Lute)

C. Romero   **Philips 6582001**

Captain Digorie Piper's Galliard
Segovia   **MCA S/26.073; Decca DL-
   710171**
Bream   **RL 11491**
Behrend   **DG 2530 079**

The Four-Course Guitar

Adrien Le Roy (c.1520-1598)

Miscellaneous Pieces
Yepes   **DG 2726 018**
Ragossnig   **Archiv 2533 304** (Lute); **2723
   051**
T. Walker   **Saga 5426**

The Five-Course Guitar

Francesco Corbetta (c.1615-1681)

Miscellaneous Pieces
Hope   **Response Records RES 800**
Ragossnig   **Archiv ST-2533-365**
Tyler   **Saga 5438**

Ludovico Roncalli

Segovia   *Gigue & Gavotte* **MCA MACS
   6123; AXTL 1090**
   Passacaglia **AXTL 1090**
Behrend   *Suite in G* **2530 561**
Fampas   *Passacaglia* **Odeon EMI Greece
   OMGC 67**
Mills   *Gavotte & Gigue* **ABK 10**
Ragossnig   **Archiv ST-2533-365**

Santiago de Murcia

Segovia   *Prelude y Allegro* **Decca DL
   710034**
Hope   *Four Dances* **RES 800**
Ragossnig   **Archiv ST-2533-365**
Tyler   *Preludio, Gavotta, La Burlesca*
   Saga 5455

Francisco Guerau (c.1655)

Almeida   *Canarios* **Capitol P8546**

Ghiglia   *Canarios* Angel S-36508
Tyler   *Marionas* Saga 5455

Gaspar Sanz (1640-1710)

Segovia   *Gallardas & Españoleta* Decca
DL 710039
Bream   *Pavanas y Canarios* SB · 6673;
SB 6886
Diaz   *Pavanas, Españoletas, Marizapolos,
Canarios,* EMI HQS 1175
Pavanas y Folias SDBR 3155
Williams   *Canarios* 72860
Yepes   *Folia* Decca LXT 2974
Suite Española Decca SPA 278
Almeida   *Passacalle* Capitol P8546
Bartoli   *Six Dances* RCA LSB 4032
Bitetti   *Suite Española* Hispavox Spain
HH(S) 112.805
Blanco   *Castilian Dances* SLT 33189
Bonell   *Españoleta y Canarios* Enigma
VAR 1015
Brouwer   *Quatro Piezas, Cinco Aires de
Corte* DG Debut 2555 001
Ghiglia   *Five Dances* Angel S-36508
Hope   *Villanos, Folias, Canarios* RES 800
Fampas   *Pavana* Odeon EMI OMGC 67
Ivanov-Kramskoi   *Pavanas* 33CMO
3111-12
Maroto   *Folias, Canarios* Harmonia
Mundi Opus 13
Mills   *Pavanas y Canarios* ABK 10
Ragossnig   *Spanish Dances* Archiv
ST-2533-365
Santos   *Danses Populaires* Erato STU
70844
Tyler   *Preludio y Pavanas*   Saga 5455
Witosynzkyj   *Danzas Cervantinas* EMI
CFP 122
Ybarra   *Six Spanish Dances* Westminster
WGS 8142

Robert de Visée (c.1660-1725)

Suites and Miscellaneous Pieces
Segovia   Decca 710/40. 078 (1949); DL
8022; DL 9638*
Brunswick AXTL 1010; MUCS 105;
MCA M/24.018
Decca DL 710039

Bream   SB 6673*; SB 6886*
Diaz   BAM LDO53
Almeida   Ember GVC 31*
Bonell   K53555
Hope   RES 800*
North   DSL 0542
Provost   Arts Nova/Ars Antiqua*
Ragossnig   Archiv ST-2533-365
C. Romero   Philips 6582001*
Schaeffer   Turnabout   TV 341376*
(Lute)
Ybarra   Westminster WVS 8142

Transcriptions from the Harpsichord

Girolamo Frescobaldi (1583-1643)

*Aria con Variazioni detta La
Frescobalda*
Segovia   Decca DL 9733
Bream   RCA RB 16239; SB 6891
Diaz   BAM LDO32
Estarellas   FONAL MMS 56
Ragossnig   STU 70647
Riera   MHS 565
Zaradin   CFP 40012

Miscellaneous Pieces
Segovia   *Passacaglia, Corrente* DL 710054
Diaz   *Gagliarda, Corrente* BAM LDO 32
Ragossnig   *Five Pieces* STU 70647

Henry Purcell (1658-1695)

Miscellaneous Pieces
Segovia   Decca DL 710140
Diaz   Amadeo AVRS 6296
Ragossnig   STU 70647
T. Walker   Saga 5426

François Couperin (1668-1733)

Segovia   *Passacaglia* DL 9734

Jean Philippe Rameau (1683-1764)

Segovia   *Minuet* Decca A596 (1947)
Minuet DL 9733

---

* *Suite in D minor*

Minuet AXTL 1070
Bartoli   *Minuet* RCA LSB 4032
Mercadel   *Two Minuets* Artrec CLP
   62/1001
Riera   *Minuet* MHS 565
C. Romero   *Gavotte* Philips 6582001

George Frederick Handel
(1685-1759)

Segovia   *Sarabande & Variations* DL 9647
   Aylesford Pieces DL 710140
   Various Pieces DL 9638
Artzt   *Minuet* Meridian E77026
Lagoya   *Sarabande & Variations* Philips
   6581017
Mercadel   *Sonata (Aylesford Suite)* Artrec
   CLP 62/1001
Ragossnig   *Aylesford Pieces* STU 70647
Ybarra   *Sarabande & Variations*
   Westminster WVS8142

Duets
Presti/Lagoya   *Chaconne* Philips 6504003
   Fugue & Allegro Philips 6504003

Domenico Scarlatti (1685-1757)

Sonatas
Segovia   *L.352(K.11)* Decca A596 (1947);
   Decca ED 3503
   L.79(K.391), *L.483(K.322)* RCA
   ARL1 0865; DL 710140
Bream   *L.352(K.11)*, *L.33(K.87)* RB
   16239
Diaz   *L.352(K.11)*, *L.79(K.391)*, *L.423
   (K.32)* VSD 71135; VPD20002;
   HM32SD
   L.352(K.11) SDBR 3155; SQN 101
Williams   *L.352(K.11)* ECB 3151 (1958)
   L.352(K.11) SDDR 329
   L.23(K.380) CBS 30051
   L.23(K.380), *L.238(K.208)*, *L.429
   (K.175)*, *L.485(K.448)*, *L.108
   (K.213)*, *L.104(K.159)* CBS 73545
Yepes   *L.352(K.11)* 2726018
Artzt   *L.483(K.322)*, *L.79(K.391)* GME
   1018
Barbosa-Lima   *L.352(K.11)*, *L.79(K.391)*,
   L.423(K.32), *L.438(K.462)*, *L.483
   (K.322)*, *L.187(K.481)*, *L.83(K.431)*,
   L.454(K.309), *L.23(K.380)* ABC/
   ATS-20005

Blanco   *L.23(K.380)* SLT 33189
Lagoya   *L.483(K.322)*, *L.79(K.391)*
   Philips 6581017
Ramos   *L.352(K.11)* VICS 1541
Abreu Duo   *L.104(K.159)* SDD 219
   L.413(K.9) (Pastorale) CBS 61262
Evangelos/Liza   *L.23(K.380)* Edici Ed
   21290
Presti/Lagoya   *L.33(K.87)*, *L.23(K.380)*
   H 71161
Santos/Caceres   *L.288(K.432)* STU 70794

Christian Friedrich Schale
(1713-1800)
Segovia   *Minuets I & II* DL 710171

Georg Benda (1722-1795)
Segovia   *Two Sonatas* RCA ARL1 0865

Antonio Soler (1729-1783)
Presti/Lagoya   *Two Sonatas* Philips
   6505020

Jan Vanhal (1739-1813)
Lagoya   *Cantabile* Philips 6581017

Domenico Cimarosa (1749-1801)
Bream   *Two Sonatas* RCA RB 16239
Barbosa-Lima   *Sonata in A* (arr. Prat)
   Chantecler CMG 1004
Boyd   *Sonata* London CS 0175

Bach Transcriptions for the Guitar

Johann Sebastian Bach (1685-1750)

Chaconne
Segovia   MGM E3015/M2306 (1953);
   RCA 1442A (1952); Heliodor HS
   25010; Everest EV 3251E; Saga
   5248; AXTL 1069
Bream   Westminster XWN 18428
Diaz   EMI HQS 1145
Williams   CBS 72728
Yepes   DGM 2530096; DGM 2535248;

DGM 2720074
Parkening   EMI HQS 1218
Ramos   VICS 1541

Prelude, Fugue & Allegro BWV 998
Bream   Westminster 18428
Diaz   BAM LDO32
Williams   CBS 72526; CBS 79203
Dombois   6575 005 (Lute)
Mikulka   111 1585
Parkening   *(Prelude & Allegro)* EMI
   HQS 1316
Santos *(Prelude & Fugue)* Erato STU
   70885

*Prelude in C minor (arr. in D minor
for guitar) BWV 999*
Segovia   Decca DL9751; Saga 5248
Bream   Westminster XWN 18428; SB
   6673; SB 6886; RL 42378; DPS 2003
Diaz . BAM LDO53
Williams   CBS 79203
Yepes   2533 351; 2530 462; 2535 248;
   2533 152/3 (Lute)
Gerwig   BACH 1202 (Lute)
Mikulka   111 1585
Parkening   HQS 1218
Santos   STU 70885

*Fugue in G minor (arr. in A minor for
guitar) BWV 1000/1001*
Segovia   Heliodor HS 25010; MGM
   E3015/M2306(1953); MGM E123;
   Saga 5248; Decca DL 9795
Bream   RL 42378; SB 6673; SB 6886;
   DPS 2003
Diaz *(arr. Duarte)* HQS 1145
Williams   CBS 79203
Yepes   2533 351; 2530 461; 2535 248;
   2533 152/3 (Lute)
Fampas   Odeon EMI OMGC 67
Gerwig   BACH 1202 (Lute)
Mikulka   111 1585
Parkening   HQS 1218
Santos   STU 70885

Complete Lute Suites
Bream   *Nos. 1 & 2* SB 6684
   No. 1   SER 5638
Williams   *Nos. 1, 2, 3, 4* CBS 79203
Yepes   *Nos. 1, 2, 3, 4* Archiv 2533 152/3
   (Lute)
   Nos. 1, 2, 3, 4 2530 461/2

S. Abreu   *No. 3* Decca SDD 219
Blanco   *No. 1* SLT 33189
Bonell   *No. 2* Enigma VAR 1050
Dombois   *No. 3* Philips 6575 018 (Lute)
Gerwig   *No. 4* Oryx BACH 1202 (Lute)
   No. 3 Heliodor 89 734 (Lute)
Polasek *No. 3* Victrola VICS 1038
Santos   *No. 1* STU 70885

'Cello Suites (arr. John W. Duarte)
Segovia   *No. 3* MUCS 125; MCA 410
   031
Diaz   *No. 3* HQS 1145
Williams   *No. 1* ECB 3151 (1958); SDD
   329
   No. 3 SDDR 328 (1958)
   Nos. 1 & 3 DPAR 579-80; KDPCR
   579-80
Bitetti   *No. 1* Hispavox HH 10-331
Matsuda *No. 3* Columbia JX 19
Mavrudis   *No. 3* Vedette VST 6022
Ramos   *No. 3* Angel SAM 35024

*Miscellaneous Pieces from Segovia's
Repertoire*
Segovia   *Allemande (1st Lute Suite)*
   HMV D 1536; DL 710167
   Sarabande, Bourrée (1st Lute Suite)
   Saga XID 5248; Heliodor HS 25010;
   SQN 101
   Sarabande, Gigue (2nd Lute Suite)
   DL 710167
   Gavotte (4th Lute Suite) HMV D
   1255 (1927); Victor Red Seal 6766;
   DL 9751; Everest EV 3251 E
   Prelude (1st 'Cello Suite) AXTL 1005
   Courante (3rd 'Cello Suite) HMV
   475; Victrola 1298; MGM E123;
   RCA 1442A (1952); MGM E3015/
   M2306 (1953); Everest EV 3251 E;
   SQN 101; AXTL 1010
   Bourrée (3rd 'Cello Suite) DL 9647;
   DL 9751
   Gavotte (6th 'Cello Suite) AXTL
   1005
   Gavottes 1 & 2 (6th 'Cello Suite)
   Everest EV 3251 E; SQN 101
   *Sarabande, Bourrée, Double (from
   Suite in B minor for Unaccompanied
   Violin)* DL 710140; MACS 1032
   *Bourrée (from Suite in B minor for
   Unaccompanied Violin)* AXTL 1010

Baroque Composers: transcriptions
for the Guitar

Ybarra   *Minuet* **WGS 8142**
Zelenka   *Quartet in D* **Royale ROY 2004**

Antonio Vivaldi (1678-1741)

Concerto in D
Bream   **SB 6635; RK 11673; ARL1 1180**
(Lute)
Williams   **72798**
Yepes   **London CM 9270**
Aubin   **Vogue MC 20.134**
Behrend   **DG 139417**
Zelenka   **Royale ROY 2004**

Concerto in A
Diaz   **HM 32 SD**
Leeb   **GGC 4041**

Concerto in C
Behrend   **DG 139417**
Zelenka   **Royale ROY 2004**

Miscellaneous Pieces
Abreu Duo   *Prelude & Courante (arr. L.*
Williams) **SDD 219**
Evangelos/Liza   *Prelude & Courante (arr.*
L. Williams) **ED 21290**
Andante **ED 21290**
Presti/Lagoya   *Concerto for 2 Guitars in*
C **Philips 6504018**
Concerto for 2 Guitars in G **Philips**
6504018

Josef Haydn (1732-1809)

Segovia   *Largo assai & Minuet* **DL 710039**
Minuet **DL 9734**
Bream/Cremona   *Quintet in E Op. 2*
No. 2 **SB 6772; RCA GL 42753**
Diaz   *Minuet* **SDBR 3155**
Williams   *Quintet in E Op.2 No. 2* **CBS**
72678
Artzt   *Andante and Minuet* **Meridian**
E77026
Pomponio/Zarate   *Concerto No. 3 in G*
RCA Victor LM 2772
Schaeffer   *Quartet in E, Cassation in C,*
Trio in F (Hob.iv F2) **TV 34227S**
(Lute)
Scheit   *Quartet in G Op. 4, No. 5* **MHS**
525
L. Walker   *Cassation in C* **TV 34171S**

Wolfgang Amadeus Mozart
(1756-1791)

Bream   *Larghetto & Allegro K.anh. 229*
SB6796; RCA RL 42761

Baroque Lute Music

Esaias Reusner (1636-1679)

Williams   *Paduana (from Suite No. 4)*
CBS 7252S
Gerwig   *Suite in C minor* **Heliodor 89734**
(Lute)
M.L.S. Marcos   *Three Pieces* **SDBR 3248**
Ragossnig   *Suite of German Dances* **2533**
172 (Lute); **2723 051** (Lute)

Johann Anton Logy (c.1643-1721)

Partita in A minor
Matthews   **TV 34538S**

Sylvius Leopold Weiss (1686-1750)

Passacaglia
Bream **SB 6673; SB 6886**

Fantasia
Segovia   **DL 710054**
Bream   **SB 6673; SB 6886**
Yepes   **DG 2530 096**
Bartoli   **LSB 4032**
Blanco   **SLT 33189**
Lagoya   **Philips 6581 017**
Robert   **GOO 3551** (Lute)

Tombeau sur la Mort de M. le
Comte de Logy
Segovia   **DL 710171**
Bream   **SB 6673; DBS 2003; SER 5638**
SB 6886
Bonell   **K53555**
Dombois   **Philips 6578 018** (Lute)

Tombeau sur la Mort de M. Cajetan
Baron d'Hartig
Matthews   **TV 34538S**

Suites
Yepes   *Suite in E* DGM 2530096
Dombois   *L'Infidèle* Philips 6575 005
   (Lute)

Ernst Theophil Baron (1696-1760)

Suite No. 2
Matthews   TV 34538S

The Early Nineteenth Century

Luigi Boccherini (1743-1805)

Segovia   *Concerto* (arr. Cassado) DL
   710043
Bream   *Quintet No. 3* SB 6772
Bream/Malcolm   *Introduction &
   Fandango* GL 42753; DPS 2003
Diaz   *Quintets Nos. 2 & 5* HM 43
Yepes   *Quintets Nos. 4, 7, & 9* 2530 069
Szendrey-Karper   *Quintets Nos. 1 & 2*
   SLPX 1134
Tarrago   *Quintets Nos. 1 & 3* MHS 575

Mateo Albéniz (1760-1831)

Sonata in D
Bream   RB 16239; SB 6891
Williams   CBS 72860; CBS 73784
Blanco   SLT 33205

Ferdinando Carulli (1770-1841)

Duets
Bream/Williams   *Serenade in A, Op. 96*
   ARLI 0456
Presti/Lagoya   *Serenade in G, Op. 96
   No. 3* Philips 65040 049

Miscellaneous Pieces
Yepes   *Divertimento per il Decacordo*
   2531 113
Behrend   *Concerto Allegro in A* DG
   139417
Mills   *Andante grazioso in G, Andantino
   in G* G102
Zelenka   *Concerto in A* Royale ROY 2004

Fernando Sor (1778-1839)

Variations on a Theme of Mozart Op.9
Segovia   HMV D 1255 (1927); DL 9638
Diaz   SDBR 3155; HQS 1175
Williams   ECB 3151 (1958); CBS 72728
Yepes   SPA 179; DG 139366
Behrend   DG 3318016
Bitetti   Hispavox Spain HH(S) 10.365
Fampas   Odeon EMI OMGC 67
Hill   Saga 5355
Munting   Oryx ORPS 50
P. Romero   9500 295
T. Walker   Sol 349

Introduction & Allegro Op. 14
Segovia   DL 9794
Bream   SB6796; RL 42761
Munting   ORPS 50

Sonatas
Segovia   *Allegro from Op. 25* DL 9633
Bream   *Sonata in C, Op. 25* ARL1 08711
Artzt   *Sonata Op. 15b* Meridian E77006
Hill   *Sonata Op. 22* Saga 5406
Provost   *Sonata Op. 15* Arts Nova/Ars
   Antiqua
P. Romero   *Op. 15* Philips 9500 295

Rondo from Op. 22
Segovia   DL 710039
Bream   Westminster XWN 18135;
   WGM 8106
Diaz   HQS 1175
Yepes   Decca LXT 2974

Variations
Segovia   *Folies d'Espagne Op. 15a* RCA
   ARL1 0485
   Variations on 'Malbroug' Op. 28
   ARL1 1323
Yepes   *Variations on 'Malbroug' Op. 28*
   2530 871
Artzt   *Fantasia on 'Ye Banks & Braes'
   Op. 40* E77006
Barbosa-Lima   *Folies d'Espagne Op. 15a*
   Chantecler CMG-1004
Santos   *Variations on 'Malbroug' Op. 28*
   Erato STU 70767
L. Walker   *Folies d'Espagne Op. 15a*
   Supraphon 1 11 1230

Largo from Fantasia Op. 7

Segovia   ARLI 0865
Bream   **Westminster XWN** 18135;
    WGM 8106; SB 6673; SB 6886
Artzt   (complete *Fantasia Op. 7*)
    Meridian E77006
Mills   **Discourses ABK** 10

Fantasia Élégiaca Op. 59
Artzt   **Meridian E77006**
Bonell   **K.** 53527
Hill   *(Marche funèbre)* Saga 5406

Studies (Nos. given from Segovia
edition of Twenty Studies)
Segovia   *Four Studies (14, 16, 5, 12)* DL
    9794
    Three Studies (1, 9, 20) DL 710034
    Two Studies (3, 17) DL 710054
    Four Studies (10, 15, 19, 6) DL 710063
    Six Studies (Op. 31 No. 1, Op. 32
    No. 2, Op. 35 Nos. 3, 9, 11, 22)
    DL 710179
Bream   *Five Studies* **Westminster XWN**
    18135
Diaz   *Nos. 5 & 12* VSD 71135; VPD
    20002
Williams   *Twenty Studies* CLP 1702
Yepes   *Twenty-four Studies* DG 139364
    No. 17 GLB 1024
Almeida   *No. 12* CTL 7089
Artzt   *No. 14* **Meridian E** 77006
Blanco   *No. 5* SLT 33205
Caceres   *Nos. 17, 14, 19, 15* **Erato STU**
    70614
Estarellas   *No. 5* **Fonal MMS 56**
Mills   *Nos. 5 & 6* G101
Munting   *Nos. 3, 6, 7, 13* ORPS 50
Silva   *No. 5* RCA MKL 1642
Tomás   *No. 5* DGS 174
Witoszynskyj *Nos. 22 & 23* EMI CFP 122
Ybarra   *Nos. 11 & 18* Mercury WST 17117

Minuets
Segovia   *Minuet in C* DL 9647
    Minuets in D, C DL 9751
    Minuets in A,E DL 9794
    Minuets in E, G, E, DL 710145
    Minuets in A, C, CRCA ARL1 0865
Bream   *Minuet in C Op. 22* SB 6673; SB
    6886
Yepes   *Two Minuets* Decca LXT 2974
Blanco   *Minuet in C Op. 22, Minuet in A*
    Op. 11 SLT 33205

Gomez   *Two Minuets* SDD 158
Mills   *Minuet in A* **Discourses ABK** 10
Munting   *Minuets Nos. 8, 7* ORPS 50
Silva   *Minuet in C* **RCA MKL** 1642
Tomás   *Minuet in C Op. 22* DGS 174

Miscellaneous Pieces

Segovia   *Andante Largo, Op. 5, No. 5*
    DL 710039
Yepes   *Fantasie Villageoise* DG 2531 113

Duets

L'Encouragement Op. 34
Bream/Williams   SB 6862
Abreu Duo   CBS 61262
Presti/Lagoya   **Philips** 6504 020

Fantasia Op. 54
Bream/Williams   **RCA RL** 03090

Anton Diabelli (1781-1858)

Bream   *Sonata in A* SB 6796; DPS 2003;
    RL 42761

Mauro Giuliani (1781-1829)

Allegro from Sonata Op. 15
Segovia   **AXTL** 1010
Bream   SB 6796; SER 5638
Williams   CBS 72526
Yepes   DGM 2530871

Grande Ouverture Op. 61
Bream   SB 6796
Behrend   2530 561
P. Romero   **Philips** 9500513

Le Rossiniane Op. 121 & Op. 119
Bream   ARL1 0711

Concerto Op. 30 in A
Bream   **RCA RB** 16252; RCA SB 6826;
    ARL3 0907
Diaz   ASD 2363
Williams   72798; 40-77249; 77334
Yepes   2530 975
Behrend   DG 139417
P. Romero   6500 918
Scheit   TV 34123S

Concerto No. 2 in A, Op. 36

P. Romero 9500 320

Concerto No. 3 in F, Op. 70
P. Romero 9500 320

Duets

Variazioni Concertanti Op. 130
Bream/Williams ARL1 0456

Miscellaneous Pieces

Variations on a theme of Handel
Williams CBS 72728; CBS 73745
Hill Saga 5355
P. Romero Philips 9500513

Sonata Eroica in A Op. 150
Hill Saga 5406
P. Romero Philips 9500513

Introduction, Theme and Variations, & Polonaise, Op. 65
P. Romero 9500 042

Sonata for Violin and Guitar, Op. 25
Williams/Perlman 76525

Sonatina in D, Op. 71
Yepes 2530 871

Study Op. 48, No. 5
Caceres Erato STU 70614

Eight little Pieces
Segovia DL 710182

Three Studies
Segovia DL 710179

Niccolo Paganini (1782-1840)

Grand Sonata in A
Segovia *Andante variato* (arr. Ponce) DL 9647
Bream RCA SB 6844
Williams CBS 72348
Fampas *Andante variato* Odeon EMI OMGC 67

Miscellaneous Pieces
Segovia *Romanza* Decca A-596 (1947)
Williams *Caprice No. 24* CBS 72728
Behrend *Sonata in C Op. 25* 2530 561
Scheit *Romanza* TV 34123S

Ensemble and Duets

Williams/Loveday/Fleming *Terzetta for Violin, 'Cello & Guitar* CBS 73745
Williams/Perlman *Six Sonatas for Violin & Guitar Op. 3.* 76525
Presti/Lagoya *Sonata Concertante* Philips 6504 049
L. Walker *Quartet No. 7 in E* TV 34322S

Dionisio Aguado (1784-1849)

Segovia *Eight Lessons* DL 710063
Caceres *Lesson No. 35, Studies Nos. 3 & 6* Erato STU 70614

Matteo Carcassi (1792-1853)

Caceres *Three Studies Op. 60, Nos. 3, 10, 13* STU 70614
Mills *Study in A: Minuet* G101
    Studies, Op. 60, Nos. 7, 16, 10 G102
Riera *Two Studies* MHS 565

Franz Schubert (1797-1828)

Minuet, Op. 78. (D894)
Segovia AXTL 1005
Bream SB 6844
Artz Meridian E77026

Quartet in G (Schubert-Matiegka)
Ragossnig RCA Victor LM 2772
L. Walker TV 34171S

Felix Mendelssohn (1809-1847)

Canzonetta (from *String Quartet No. 1 in Eb, Op. 12*)
Segovia AXTL 1069
Bream SB 6844
Artzt Meridian E77026
Blanco SLT 33189
Hill Saga 5355

Songs without Words
Segovia *Op. 19 No. 6* DL 9633
    Op. 30 No. 3 MUCS 105
Bream *Op. 19 No. 6* SB 6844
Artzt *Op. 19 No. 6* Chantecler
Barbosa-Lima *Op. 19 No. 6* Chantecler CMG 1004

Frederic Chopin (1810-1849)

Segovia   *Prelude in A* DL 9647

Robert Schumann (1810-1856)

Segovia   *Romanza* AXTL 1060
    Eight Pieces from Album for the
    Young, Op. 68, Träumerei, Romanza
    RCA RL 12602
Hill   *Träumerei* Saga 5355

Jean Alard (1815-1888)

Study in A (arr. Tárrega)
Segovia   DL 9794; MCA S26091
Blanco   SLT 33189
Parkening   HQS 1218
A. Romero   HQS 1041
Santos   STU 70767

The Late Nineteenth, Early
Twentieth Century

Francisco Tárrega (1852-1909)

Recuerdos de la Alhambra
Segovia   HMV D1305 (1927); DL 9794;
    MCAS 26091
Diaz   SDBR 3155
Williams   S2339; 61843
Yepes   Decca LXT 2974; DG 2726018;
    DG 139366; SPA 179; SQN 101
Almeida   CTL 7089
Artzt   Meridian E77026
Bitetti   Hispavox Spain 112.805
Blanco   SLT 33205
Cano   Decca DURIUM DC 16562
Costanzo   EMI J06321010
Matsuda   7DA205
Munting   Oryx ORPS 50
Parkening   HQS 1218
P. Romero   Philips 9500 295
L. Walker   Philips LC 3055

Capricho Arabe
Segovia   DL 9794; MCA S26091
Yepes   SPA 179; 2530871
Almeida   CTL 7089
Artzt   Meridian E77026
Bartoli   LSB 4032

Bonell   VAR 1015
Costanzo   EMI J06321010
Hill   Saga 5355
Maroto   Harmonia Mundi Opus 13
Munting   Oryx ORPS 50
P. Romero   Philips 2500 295

Adelita, Lagrima, Marieta & Maria
Segovia   *Adelita, Marieta, Maria* DL
    9794; MCA S26091
Bream   *Adelita, Lagrima, Marieta* SB
    6844
Artzt   *Maria* Meridian E77026
Mills   *Adelita, Lagrima* G101
A. Romero   *Adelita, Maria* HQS 1041
T. Walker   *Lagrima* SOL 349

Miscellaneous Pieces
Segovia   *Minuet* Decca 710/40 077; DL
    8022
    Preludes Nos. 2 & 5 DL 9794
    Mazurka in G DL 9794; MCA
    S26091
Yepes   *Prelude, Tango* GLB 1024
Artzt   *Mazurka, Tango* Meridian E77026
Barbosa-Lima   *La Mariposa* Chantecler
    CMG 1004
Bitetti   *Minuet* Hispavox Spain HH(S)
    10.365
Gonzalez   *Six Preludes* CBS 61654
Mills   *Study No. 1, Three Preludes* G102
    Study in E minor G101
Munting   *Eleven Preludes* Oryx ORPS 50
A. Romero   *Mazurka, Preludes 2 & 5*
    HQS 1041
Silva   *Prelude, Mazurka* RCA MKL 1642
Ybarra   *Preludes 1 & 2* Mercury WST
    17117

Alborada
Yepes   LXT 2974
Gomez   SDD 158
T. Walker   SOL 349

Sueño
Yepes   SQN 101
Anido   Odeon 66035
Bonell   K53527

Gran Jota (probably by Arcas, arr.
Tárrega)
Yepes   SPA 278
P. Romero   Var 1015

Danza Mora
Segovia   Decca 710/40 077 (1949); DL
   8022
Diaz   VSD 71135; VPD 20002
Artzt   Meridian E77026

Variations on 'The Carnival of Venice'
Artzt   Meridian E77026

Isaac Albéniz (1860-1909)

Torre Bermeja
Segovia   Decca 384/29.155 (U.S.A. 1945);
   A-384; DL 8022; DU 707 (1949);
   RCA ARL1 0485; MCA M-24.018
Diaz   VPD 20002
Williams   SDD R328
Yepes   GLB 1024; SPA 179; 2530 159
Bitetti   Hispavox-Spain 112.805
de la Torre   Nonesuch 2590 001

Sevilla
Segovia   384/29.156 (U.S.A. 1945); ED
   3503 Vol I; Decca A-384; DL 8022;
   DU 707 (1949); DL 710160; MCA
   M-24.018
Diaz   VPD 20002
Williams   CBS 72339
Almeida   CTL 7089
Fampas   Odeon EMI OMGC 67
Mercadel   Artrec CLP 62/1001
Ragossnig   TV 34494S
Santos   STU 70844

Asturias (Leyenda)
Segovia   DL 9633; AXTL 1005; DL
   710160
Bream   RB 6593; SER 5638; SB 6887
Diaz   VSD 71135; VPD 20002; SDBR
   3155
Williams   CBS 72860; CBS 30051; CBS
   73784
Yepes   SPA 179; DG 2530 159
Almeida   CTL 7089
Barbosa-Lima   Chantecler CMG 1004
Bitetti   Hispavox Spain 112.805
Costanzo   J 06321010
Hill   Saga 5355
Maroto   Harmonia Mundi Opus 13
Parkening   HQS 1218
Ragossnig   Supraphon 111 1040
P. Romero   9500 295

Santos   STU 70844
de la Torre   Nonesuch 2590 001

Granada
Segovia   Decca 3824/29. 154 (U.S.A.
   1945); ED 3510 Vol II; A-384; DL
   8022; DU 707 (1949); 710063;
   MACS 1968; MCA M-24.018
Bream   RB 6593; DPS 2003; SB 6887
Diaz   VPD 20002
Yepes   GLB 1024; SPA 179
Ragossnig   TV 34494S
Zaradin   CFP 40012

Zambra Granadina
Segovia   DL 710039; MUCS 105
Almeida   P8367
Ghiglia   Angel S-36508
Matsuda   ZDA 205
Tomás   DGS 174

Rumores de la Caleta
Yepes   2530 159; 2720074
Almeida   P8367
Costanzo   J 06321 010
Hill   Saga 5355
Presti   HMV X4924
Ybarra   Mercury WST 17117

Oriental
Almeida   CTL 7089

Serenata Andaluza
Almeida   EMI P8467

Cádiz
Almeida   P 8367
Barbosa-Lima   Chantecler CMG 1004

Córdoba
Williams   CBS 72860
A. Romero   HQS 1401

Tango
Williams   CBS 72860
Almeida   P8367
A. Romero   HQS 1401

Malagueña Op. 165
Yepes   139 366

Capricho Catalan
Segovia   ARL1 1323

Mallorca
Segovia   DL 710167
Bitetti   Hispavox Spain HH(S) 10.365

Ghiglia   **Angel S-36508**

Duets
Abreu Duo   *El Puerto* **SDD 219**
   Evocación **CBS 61262**
Bream/Williams   *Evocación; Bajo la*
   Palmera **RCA ARL1 0456**
Presti/Lagoya   *Tango* **Philips 6502 020**
Santos/Caceres   *Tango* **STU 71092**

Enrique Granados (1867-1916)

La Maja de Goya
Segovia   **Decca 384/29.154** (1945); **A-384;**
   Decca DL 710046; Decca DL 710160;
   Decca DL 8022; MCA M24018;
   AXTL 1089
Williams   **ECB 3151; CBS 72860; CBS**
   73784
Costanzo   **EMI J 06321010**
Ghiglia   **Angel S-36508**
Mercadel   **Artrec CLP 62/1001**
Ragossnig   **TV 34494S**
A. Romero   **HQS 1401**
de la Torre   **Nonesuch 2590 001; H 71233**

Spanish Dances, Op. 37
Segovia   *No. 5* **384/29.156** (1945); **ED**
   3503; DL 710063
   No. 10 **ED 3510; DL 7100 34; DL**
   710160
   Nos. 5, 10 **A — 384; DL 8022; MCA**
   24018
Diaz   *No. 5* **VSD 71135**
   Nos. 5, 10 **VPD 20002**
Williams   *No. 5* **CBS 72348; CBS 61843**
Yepes   *No. 4* **2530 159**
   No. 10 **LXT 2974**
Almeida   *Nos. 5, 10* **P 8467**
Anido   *No. 5* **BSOA/E 4503**
Bitetti   *Nos. 5, 11* **Hispavox Spain**
   112.805
Costanzo   *No. 5* **J 06321010**
Hill   *No. 5* **Saga 5355**
Mills   *No. 5* **ABK 10**
Ragossnig   *No. 5* **TV 34494S; 111 1040**
de la Torre   *No. 5* **Nonesuch 2590 001;**
   H 71233

Duets: Spanish Dances
Bream/Williams   *No. 2* **RL 03090**
   Nos. 6, 11 **ARLI 0456**
Presti/Lagoya   *No. 2* **H 71161**

Goyescas — Intermezzo
Bream/Williams   **SB 6862**
Abreu Duo   **CBS 61262**
Presti/Lagoya   **RB 6589; Philips 6504020**

Valses Poeticos
Williams   **CBS 72860**

The Twentieth Century: French Composers

Albert Roussel (1869-1937)

Segovia, Op. 29
Segovia   **DL 710046**
Bream   **RB 16239; SB 6891**
Santos   **STU 70767**

Darius Milhaud (1892-1974)

Segoviana
Santos   **STU 70767**

Francis Poulenc (1899-1963)

Sarabande
Yepes   **2530 802**
Mills   **G 102**
Santos   **STU 70767**

Henri Sauguet (b. 1901)

Soliloque
Santos   **STU 70767**

André Jolivet (1905-1974)

Comme un Prélude
Santos   **STU 70767**

The Twentieth Century: Spanish Composers

Joaquín Malats (1872-1912)

Serenata Española
Segovia   **Decca DL 9734**
Diaz   **VPD 20002**
Yepes   **SPA 278**
Costanzo   **J06321010**

Maroto   Harmonia Mundi Opus 13
Presti   HMV X4924
Zaradin   CFP 40012

Manuel de Falla (1876-1946)

*Homenaje — Pour le tombeau
de Debussy*
Segovia   DL 9638
Bream   RB 6593; DPS 2003; SB 6887
Diaz   VPD 20002
Williams   CBS 72348
Yepes   DG 139366
Artzt   GME 1019.340
Blanco   SLT 33205
Costanzo   EMI J063-20873
Ponce   Orion 30 A 064
Ragossnig   TV 344 943
de la Torre   Polydor 2590 001
T. Walker   Sol 349
Witoszynskyj   CFP 122

Miller's Dance
Diaz   VPD 20002; VSD 71135
Williams   CBS 30051; CBS 72860
Yepes   SPA 179; DG 2538106; DG
   2530159
Bitetti   Hispavox Spain 112.805
Lucia   Philips 9113 008
Ragossnig   TV 34494S

*El Círculo Mágico & Canción del
Fuego Fatuo (El Amor Brujo)*
Yepes   2530 159
Almeida   CTL 7089
Lucia   Philips 9113008

Songs
Yepes/Berganza   *Siete Canciones* 2530 875
Harker/Doyle   *Nana, El Pano Moruno*
   ECS 2108

Duets

La Vida Breve: Spanish Dance No. 1
(arr. Pujol)
Abreu Duo   CBS 61262
Bream/Williams   SB 6862
Presti/Lagoya   6504 020
Santos/Caceres   STU 71092

Ritual Fire Dance
Presti/Lagoya 6504 049

Miguel Llobet (1878-1938)

El Testament d'Amelia
Segovia   Decca 710/40.077 (1949); DL
   8022; MCA M 24.018
Bream   RB 6953; SB 6887
Diaz   HQS 1175
Williams   CBS 72339; CBS 30051
Lopategui   HME10/034.334
Mills   G 102
Silva   RCA MKL 1642
Zaldua   ACL501X.301

Cançó del lladre
Diaz   HQS 1175; SDBR 3155
Yepes   GLB 1024; DG 2530 273; DG
   2538 106
Costanzo   EMI J 063-21010
Lopategui   HME10/034. 334
Zaldua   ACL501X.301

El Noy de la Mare
Segovia   Decca 710/40.077 (1949); DL
   8022; MCA M24.018
Diaz   HQS 1175; SDBR 3155
Williams   CBS 72860; CBS 30051
Yepes   DG 2530 273
Harker   ECS 2108

El Mestre
Segovia   DL 9832
Yepes   DG 2530273
Lopategui HME10/034.334

La Nit de Nadal
Williams   CBS 72860
Yepes   DG 2530 273; DG 2538 106
Harker   ECS 2108

La Filla del Marxant
Yepes   DG 2530 273; DG 2538 106
Costanzo   EMI J063-210 10

Joaquin Turina (1882-1949)

Fandanguillo, Op. 36
Segovia   HMV D-1305; Victor Red Seal
   6767; CAX 10569; LX 1248; HLM
   7134
Bream   XWN 18135; RB 6593; SB 6887;
   SER 5638; DPS 2003
Diaz   AVRS 6296; VPD 6296
Williams   CBS 72339

Yepes   DG 2530 159
Almeida   EMI P8367
Bitetti   Hispavox Spain HH(S) 10.365
Costanzo   EMI J063-20873
Ragossnig   TV 34494S; Supraphon 1 11
    1040
A. Romero   HQS 1401

Sevillana (Fantasia), Op. 29
Segovia   DL 710145; DL 710160; MCA
    410 034
Almeida   EMI P8367
Costanzo   EMI J063-20873
Ragossnig   TV 34494S
Tomás   DGS 174

Ráfaga Op. 53
Williams   CBS 72339
Yepes   SPA 179; GLB 1024
Almeida   EMI P8367
Costanzo   J063-20873
Ragossnig   TV 34494S
A. Romero   HQS 1401
Witoszynskyj   CFP 122

Sacromonte Op. 55
Almeida   EMI P8367

Sonata Op. 61
Yepes   2530159
Almeida   Everest 3287
Costanzo   EMI J063-20873
Ponce   30S 150
Ragossnig   *(Andante)* TV 34494S
L. Walker   Supraphon 1 11 1230
Ybarra   Mercury WST 17117

*Hommage à Tárrega Op. 69
(Garrotin, Soleares)*
Bream   RB 6593; SB 6887
Williams   *(Soleares)* CBS 72339
Yepes   SPA 179
Almeida   CTL 7089
Bitetti   Hispavox Spain 112.805
Blanco   SLT 33205
Costanzo   EMI J063-20873
Ponce   Orion 30 A 064
Ragossnig   TV 34494S
A. Romero   HQS 1401
Santos   STV 70844
Witoszynskyj   CFP 122

Oscar Esplá (1886-1976)

Segovia   *Antaño* DL 710046
    Two Danzas Levantinas DL 9931
Yepes   *Three Danzas Levantinas* DG
    2530 273

Emilio Pujol (b. 1886)

El Abejorro
Yepes   GLB 1024; SPA 278; DG 2538 106
Blanco   SLT 33189

Miscellaneous Pieces
Bonell   *Guajira, Tango* VAR 1015
Caceres   *Study No. 38* STU 70614
Fampas   *Guajira* Odeon EMI OMGC 67
Mills   *Study No. 30* G102
Presti   *Guajira* HMV

Federico Moreno Torroba (b. 1891)

Sonatina in A
Segovia   HMV E 475; Victrola 1298; DL
    9633
    Allegro DL 710160
    Allegretto ARL1 0485
    Allegro MCA 410 034
Bream   XWN 18137; WGM 8106
Diaz   VPD 20002
Williams   WGS 8109
Bitetti   *Allegro* (1st Mvt.) Hispavox
    Spain 112.805
Hill   Saga 5462

Suite Castellana
Segovia   *Fandanguillo, Preludio* HMV E-
    526
    Fandanguillo, Preludio Victor Red
    Seal 1487
    Arada Decca 710-40.076 (U.S.A.
    1949)
    Fandanguillo Columbia LX 1248
    (1950)
    Arada, Danza Columbia LX 1248
    (1950)
    Arada, Fandanguillo CAX 10568
    Arada, Fandanguillo DL 8022
    Arada, Danza Columbia ML-4732
    Arada, Fandanguillo ARL1 0485
    Arada, Fandanguillo HLM 7134
    (1978)
Williams   (complete) WGS 8109

Ghiglia   *Arada; Fandanguillo* **Angel S-36508**
Gomez   *Fandanguillo* **SDD 158**
Hill   (complete) **Saga 5462**
Ivanov-Kramskoi   *Fandanguillo* **33CMO3111-12A**
Mercadel   *Fandanguillo* **Artrec CLP 62/1001**
Ragossnig   *Arada* **111 1040**

Pièces caractéristiques
Segovia   (complete **DL 710046; DXL 148; DL 9995/6/7**
   Albada **Decca 710-40.076** (U.S.A. 1949); **DL 8022; DL 710160; MCA 410 034**
Diaz   *Albada, Los Mayos* **AVRS 6296**
Ghiglia   *Albada* **Angel S-36508**
Hill   (complete) **Saga 5462**
Tomás   *Albada, Oliveras* **DGS 174**
Witoszynskyj   *Melodia* **CFP 122**

Nocturno
Segovia   **HMV E—569; DL 9733; ARLI 0485; AXTL 1070**
Bream   **XWN 18137**
Diaz   **VSD 71135**
Williams   **CBS 72860**
Blanco   **SLT 33205**
Hill   **Saga 5462**

Miscellaneous
Segovia   *Romance de los Pinos* **DL 710039**
   Castellana **RL 12602**
   Serenata Burlesca **DL 9734**
   Castillos de España **DL 710171; MCA S 26.073**
Bream   *Preludio in E* **XWN 18137**
Williams   *Aires de la Mancha* **CBS 72526**
Almeida   *Serenata Burlesca* **CTL 7089**
Harker   *Romance de los Pinos* **ECS 2108**
Hill   *Aires de la Mancha* **Saga 5462**
Mills   *Cancionella* **ABK 10**
Parkening   *Romance de los Pinos* **HQS 1218**
Sabicas   *Flamenco Concerto* **EFM 8080**
Tarrago   *Concierto de Castille* **EFM 8080**

Burgalesa
Segovia   **Decca 710-40.076** (U.S.A. 1949); **DL 8022; ARL1 0485**
Bream   **XWN 18137**
Blanco   **SLT 33205**
Bonell   **VAR 1015**

Mills   **ABK 10**
Tomás   **DGS 174**

Madroños
Segovia   **DL 9467**
Bream   **RB 6593; DPS 2003; SER 5638**
Williams   **CBS 72860**
Yepes   **SPA 179; GLB 1024; DG 139366**
E. Abreu   **SDD 219**
Costanzo   **J06321010**
Hill   **Saga 5462**
Ragossnig   **111 1040**
A. Romero   **HQS 1401**

Andrés Segovia (b. 1893)

Miscellaneous Pieces
Segovia   *Estudio sin Luz* **AXTL 1089**
Diaz   *Estudio remembranza* **VPD 20002**
Williams   *Oración, Estudio, Humorada* **ECB 3151**
E. Abreu   *Estudio sin Luz* **SDD 219**
Almeida   *Anecdote 2, Neblina* **CTL 7089**
Abreu Duo   *Divertimento* **SDD 219**

Federico Mompou (b. 1893)

Segovia   *Suite Compostellana* **DA 130**
Diaz   *Canción* **HQS 1175**
Yepes   *Canción y Danza No. 1* **2530 273**

Regino Sainz de la Maza (b. 1897)

Diaz   *3 Spanish Dances* **VPD 20002**
   Petenera **HQS 1175**
Boyd   *Bells of Dawn* **BMC-3002**
L. Walker   *Rondeña* **111 1230**

Eduardo Sainz de la Maza

Diaz   *Bolero* **VSD 71135**
Yepes   *Habanera* **SPA 278**
Byzantine   *Homage a la guitarra* **CFP 40209**
Gomez   *Habanera* **SDD 158**

Salvador Bacarisse (1898-1963)

Yepes   *Concertino in A minor Op. 72* **2530 326**
   Passapie **2538 106**

Cubedo *Concertino in A minor Op. 72*
  GSGC 15030

Joaquín Rodrigo (b. 1902)

Concierto de Aranjuez
Bream SB 6635; ARL1 1181
Diaz ASD 2363
Williams CBS 77334; CBS 76369; 2094/ 2003
Yepes MCC 30054; SXL 2091; SPA 233; DG 139440; DG 2720074; DG 2726018
Behrend DG 3318016
Bitetti Hispavox
Cubedo GSGC 15030
Lagoya 6500454.289
A. Romero SAL 3677; 6747 430; ASD 3415
P. Romero 9500 563
Santos STU 71128
R. Sainz de la Maza VICS 1322
Tarrago Hispavox
Zaradin CFP 40012

Fantasia para un Gentilhombre
Segovia DXL 148; DL 9995/6/7; MCA 410 034
Williams CBS 72661; CBS 77334
Yepes SPA 233; 2530 975; London CM 9356
Lagoya Philips 6500 454
Mikulka Panton 110608G
A. Romero ASD 3415
P. Romero 9500 042
Santos STU 71128
R. Sainz de la Maza VICS 1322

Concierto Andaluz
Los Romeros SAL 3677; 9500 563

Concierto Madrigal
P. & A. Romero 6500 918

En los Trigales
Bream RB 16239; SB 6891; DPS 2003
Diaz VPD 20002; VSD 71135
Yepes 139366
Almeida Everest 3287
Bitetti Hispavox Spain 112.805
Ponce Orion 30A 064

Duets: Tonadilla
Abreu Duo CBS 61262
Presti/Lagoya 6504020
Santos/Caceres STU 70794

Fandango
Segovia DL 710034
Williams CBS 72860
Bonell VAR 1015
A. Romero HQS 1401
Santos *(& Zapateado)* STU 70844

Miscellaneous
Segovia *Zarabanda Lejana* DL 9751
Diaz *Invocación y Danza* RCA
Bonell *Pequeñas Sevillanas* VAR 1015
  Ya se van los Pastores VAR 1015
A. Romero *Elogio de la Guitarra* Angel S-37312
de la Torre *Zarabanda Lejana* H 71233
L. Walker *Adagio & Bolero (Sonata a la Española)* 111 1230

Vicente Asencio (b. 1903)

Segovia *Mystic Suite* RL 12602 (1977)
Yepes *Five Pieces* 2530 273

Ernesto Halffter (b. 1905)

Yepes *Concerto* 2530 326
  Madrigal (arr. Yepes) 139 366

Xavier Montsalvatge (b. 1912)

Yepes *Habanera* (arr. Yepes) 139 366

Mauricio Ohana (b. 1914)

Yepes *Tiento* DG 139 366
  Tres Graficos (guitar & orchestra) 2530 585; London CM 9270
Ponce *Tiento* Orion 30 A 064
  Si le jour parâit 30 S 150

Bruno Maderna (b. 1920)

Yepes *Y Despúes* 2530 802

Leonardo Balada (b. 1933)

Yepes *Analogiás* 2530 802

Antonio Ruiz-Pipo (b. 1933)

Yepes   *Tablas for Guitar & Orchestra*
DG 2530 585
Danza No. 1 DG 2538 106
Estancias DG 2530 802
Blanco   *Canción y Danza No. 1* SLT
33205
Costanzo   *Canción y Danza No. 1*
J0621010
Gomez   *Danza No. 1* SDD 158
L. Walker   *Canción y Danza No. 1*
Supraphon 1 11 1230
T. Walker   *Canción y Danza No. 1* SOL
349

The Twentieth Century: Central and South American Composers

Manuel Ponce (1882-1948)

Sonatas
Segovia   *Allegro (Sonata Mexicana)*
HMV AB-656
Rondo (Sonata Clásica) Columbia
LB-130 (1951)
Sonata No. 3 DL 9795
Allegro (Sonata Mexicana) DL
710046
Sonata Mexicana DL 710145
Sonata Clásica DL 710145
Sonata Romántica DL 710093
Sonatina Meridional ML 4732;
Odeon 33QCX 127
Campo (Sonatina Meridional) DL
710063; MCA 410 034
Williams   *Sonatina Meridional* CBS 73205
Bitetti   *Sonatina Meridional* WGS 8149
Byzantine   *Campo (Sonatina Meridional)*
CFP 40209
Mills   *1st Movement Sonata Mexicana*
ABK 10
Ponce   *Sonatina Meridional* Orion 30 A
064
Witoszynskyj   *Sonata No. 3* CFP 122

Variations: Folia de España
Segovia   HMV DB 1567/8
Williams   CBS 76730
Blanco   BIS-LP-33
Szendrey-Karper   LPX 1162

Thème varié et Finale
Segovia   DL 9734
Williams   WGS 8109
Gonzalez   CBS 61654
Ponce   Orion 30 A 064

Concierto del Sur
Segovia   DL 710027; DXL 148; DL
9995/6/7; HOF 522; MCA 410 033
Williams   CBS 73060

Pastiches
Segovia   *Sarabande & Gavotte* (Weiss)
HMV DA 1225
Prelude, Allemande, Gigue (Weiss)
HMV DB-1565
Gavotte & Sarabande (A. Scarlatti)
Decca 596/24.147 (1949); ED 3510
Prelude, Ballet, Gigue (Weiss) DL
9633
Prelude, Allemande (Weiss) DL 9734
Prelude (Weiss) DL 710046
Williams   *Gavotte* (A. Scarlatti) ECB 3151
Preludio, Ballet (Weiss) CBS 76730

Matsuda   *Prelude & Gigue* (Weiss) ZDA
205
Hill   *Suite in A minor* (Weiss) Saga 5406

Scherzino Mexicano
Diaz   HQS 1175
Williams   CBS 72339
L. Walker   Supraphon 1 11 1230

Preludes
Segovia   *Six Preludes* AXTL 1070
Williams   *Twelve Preludes* WGS 8109
Almeida   *Six Preludes* Everest 3287
Gonzalez   *Six Preludes* CBS 61654
Mills   *Prelude No. 6* G 101
Six Preludes G 105
Parkening   *Four Preludes* HQS 1218

Tres Canciónes populares mexicanas
Segovia   *No. 2* DL 9734; 710063
Williams   *Nos. 1, 2, 3* SDD R328; CBS
76730
Mills   *No. 2* G105
Ponce   *Nos. 1, 2, 3* Orion 30 A 064
Ragossnig   *Nos. 1, 2, 3* Saga 5412
L. Walker   *No. 1* Supraphon 1 11 1230

Valse
Segovia   HMV DA 1552; DL 9795; DL
    710160; MCA 410 034
Williams   WGS 8109; CBS 76730
Almeida   P8321
Ragossnig   Saga 5412

Mazurka
Segovia   HMV DA 1552; DL 9795

Miscellaneous Pieces
Segovia   *Rondo on a Theme by Sor* ML
    4732
    Prelude in E ARL1 0865
Williams   *Three Pieces* (arr. Harker) CBS
    76730
Benitez   *Theme, Variations & Fughetta*
    on a theme by Cabezón H-71349
Ramos/Lacroix   *Sonata for guitar &*
    harpsichord VICS 1541
Silva   *Estrellita, El Hijo de la Madre* RCA
    MKL 1642
L. Walker   *Estrellita* Supraphon 1 11 1230

Agustín Barrios (1885-1944)

Las Abejas
Bitetti   WGS 8149; ABC MS-871
Blanco   LP33B BIS

Aconquija
Williams   76662

Aire de Zamba
Diaz   HQS 1175
Williams   76662

La Catedral
Williams   76662
Blanco   LP33B BIS
Caceres   STU 70614

Choro de Saudade
Williams   76662
Almeida   P 8321
Barbosa-Lima   Chantecler CMG 1004

Cueca
Diaz   HQS 1175
Williams   76662

Danza Paraguaya
Diaz   HQS 1175
Williams   CBS 73205

Blanco   LP33B BIS
Ragossnig   Saga 5412
T. Walker   SOL 349

Ultima Canción
Williams   76662
Benitez   H 71349

Valse No. 3
Williams   76662
Benitez   *(& No. 4)* H 71349

Miscellaneous
Williams   76662
Almeida   *Preludio para Guitarra Op. 5*
    No. 1 P 8321
Gonzalez   *Medallon antiguo* CBS 61654

Agustín Barrios himself recorded
the following pieces between 1915
and 1927.

1) Compositions by Barrios:
    Contemplación, Confesión, Danza
    Paraguaya, Aire de Zamba, Cueca,
    Sarita, Maxixe, Tarantella, Vals
    Op. 8 No. 3, Minuet, Romance en
    Imitacion al Violoncello, La
    Bananita, Aires Criolles, San
    Lorenzo March, Vidalita,
    Divagación en Imitación al Violin,
    Milonga, Oración, Vals Op. 8 No. 4,
    Oro y Plata Waltz, Divagaciones,
    Estilo Urugayo, Un Sueño en la
    Floresta, Madrigal Gavota,
    Caazapá — Aire Popular Paraguayo,
    Aconquija, Junto a tu Corazón, La
    Catedral, Armoniás de America,
    Pericón, Madrigal (Sosa Escalada),
    Tango No. 2, Matilde, A mi Madre,
    Pepita Waltz, Aires Andaluces, Jota
    Aragonesa, Divagaciones
    Chopiniana.

2) Compositions by various composers:
    Bourrée (Bach); *Minuet* (Beethoven);
    Minuet Op. 11, No. 6 (Sor);
    Träumerei (Schumann); *Capricho*
    Arabe (Tárrega); *La Paloma* (Yradier)

Vicente Emilio Sojo (1887-1974)

Diaz   *3 Pieces* SDBR 3155
    3 Pieces VSD 71135

Williams *5 Pieces* CBS 73205
Blanco *5 Pieces* LP33B BIS
Ponce *4 Pieces* 30S 150

Heitor Villa-Lobos (1887-1959)

Preludes
Segovia *No. 1* DL 9647; DL 710167
 No. 3 DL 9751
Bream *Nos. 1, 2, 3, 4, 5* XWN 18137;
 SB 6852
 No. 1 WGM 8106
 No. 4 SB 6887
Williams *Nos. 1, 2, 3, 4, 5* CBS 73350;
 CBS 73545
 No. 1 CBS 73784
 Nos. 2, 4 CBS 72526
Yepes *Nos. 1, 2, 3, 4, 5* 2530 140
 No. 1 2538 106
 No. 1 SPA 179
 No. 3 SPA 278
E. Abreu *No. 1* SDD 219
Almeida *Nos. 2, 4* P 8321
Bartoli *Nos. 3, 4* I.SB 4032
Byzantine *Nos. 1, 2, 3, 4, 5* CFP 40209
Costanzo *Nos. 1, 2, 3, 4, 5* Qualiton
 Q1 4.000
Harker *No. 3* ECS 2108
Hill *Nos. 1, 2, 3, 4, 5* Saga 5453
Mills *No. 4* ABK 10
Parkening *No. 2* HQS 1218
Ragossnig *Nos. 1, 2, 3, 4, 5* 111 1040
P. Romero *No. 1* 9500 295
Scott *Nos. 1, 2, 3, 4, 5* DCM 1217
Tomás *No. 3* DGS 174
T. Walker *Nos. 1, 2* SOL 349

Studies
Segovia *Nos. 1, 8* Columbia LX 1248
 (1949); HLM 7134; DL 9832
 No. 7 DL 7638
 No. 1 DL 710160; MCA 410034
Bream *12 Studies* RL 12499
 Nos. 5, 7 SB 6723
 No. 11 RB 6593; SB 6887
Diaz *No. 1* BAM LD032
 No. 7 AVRS 6296
 No. 11 VPD 20002; VSD 71135
Williams *No. 1* SDD R328 (1958)
 No. 8 CBS 72348
Yepes *12 Studies* 2530 140
 No. 1 SPA 278

E. Abreu *No. 1* SDD 219
Almeida *Nos. 5, 11* P8321
Barrueco *8 Studies* TV 34676S
Bitetti *Nos. 6, 11* WGS 8149
Caceres *No. 10* STU 70614
Hill *8 Studies* Saga 5453
Parkening *No. 1* HQS 1218
Ponce *No. 7* Orion 30A 064
P. Romero *No. 1* 9500 295
Santos *12 Studies* Erato ST 1007
L. Walker *No. 11* 111 1230
Witoszynskyj *Nos. 7, 11, 12* CFP 122

Choros No. 1
Bream RB 6593
Williams 73205
Yepes SPA 179
Byzantine CFP 40209
Gonzalez CBS 61654
Mills ABK 10
Ragossnig Saga 5412; TV 34605S
Riera MHS 565
Scott DCM 1217
Ybarra Mercury WST 17117

*Concerto for guitar and small
orchestra*
Bream SB 6852
Williams CBS 76369
Yepes 2530718

Suite populaire Brasilienne
Bream RL 12499; *(Schottisch-Choro)*
 SSB 6852
Barrueco TV 34676S
Hill Saga 5453
Marcos *Mazurka* SDBR 3248
Scott DCM 1217

Bachianas Brasileiras
Almeida *No. 5* P 8406
Harker *No. 5* ECS 2108

Duets
Ragossnig/Feybli *Therezina de Jesus
 (Ciranda No. 1)* Saga 5412
 A canoa virou (Cirandinha No. 10)
 Saga 5412

Carlos Chavez (1899-1978)

Barrueco *3 Pieces for Guitar* TV 34676S

Guido Santórsola (b. 1904)

L. Walker   *Prelude No. 1* (from *Suite antiqua*) **Supraphon 1 11 1230**

Jorge Gomez Crespo

Norteña

Segovia   **LB 130** (1949); **HLM 7134; Odeon 33QCX127; DL 9795**
Diaz   **HQS 1175**
Williams   **SDDR328** (1958)
Ragossnig   **Saga 5412**

Isaias Savio (1900-1977)

Yepes   *Escenas Brasilenas* **SPA 278**
Harker   *Escuta Coraçao* **ECS 2108**
Marcos   *Three Pieces* **SDBR 3248**
L. Walker   *Batucada* **1 11 1230**
T. Walker   *Batucada, Seroes* **SOL 349**

Carmargo Guarnieri (b. 1907)

Almeida   *Valse No. 4* **Capitol P8546**
Barrueco   *Estudo No. 1* **TV 34676S**

Antonio Lauro (b. 1917)

Diaz   *Six Venezuelan Waltzes* **HQS 1175**
Williams   *Valse Criollo* **ECB 3151** (1958); **CBS 73205**
Bartoli   *Waltzes, Nos. 2 & 3* **LSB 4032**
Blanco   *Four Waltzes* **Bis-LP-33B**
Byzantine   *Danza Negra, Waltz No. 3* **CFP 40209**
Ragossnig   *Waltz No. 3* **Saga 5412; TV 34605S**
de la Torre   *Waltzes Nos. 3 & 4* **LSD 3567**
Ybarra   *Waltz No. 3* **Mercury WST 17117**
T. Walker   *Waltz No. 3* **SOL 349**
Zaradin   *Waltz No. 3* **CFP40012**

Abel Carlevaro (b. 1918)

Benitez   *Preludios Americanos* **Nonesuch H 71349**
Costanzo   *Camp* **Qualiton Q1 4.000**

Julio Sagreras

El Colibri
Williams   **CBS 72339**
Boyd   **BMC 3002**
P. Romero   **9500 295**

Joao Pernambuco (Joao Guimaraes)

Sans da Carrilhoes (Sounds of Bells)
Bartoli   **LSB 4032**
Boyd   **BMC 3002**
Scott   **DCM 1217**
Ybarra   **WST 17164**
Zaldua   **ACL501X. 301**

*The Twentieth Century:
Italian Composers*

Mario Castelnuovo-Tedesco (1895-1968)

Concerto in D Op. 99
Segovia   **Columbia LX 1404/5/6** (1949); **Columbia ML 4732; Odeon 33QCX 127; HOF 522; HLM 7134**
Diaz   **TC ASD 2363**
Williams   **CBS 77334; CBS 76634**
Yepes   **2530 718**
Mikulka   **Panton 110608G**

Concerto for Two Guitars
Abreu Duo   **CBS 61469**

Sonata Op. 77 (Homage to Boccherini)
Segovia   **DL 710034; DXL 148; DL 9995-7**
    4th Movement **HMV DB 3243**
Williams   *4th Movement* **CBS 72348**

Tarantella
Segovia   **Columbia LX-1229** (1949); **HLM 7134**
Almeida   **Everest 3287**
Barbosa-Lima   **Chantecler CMG 1004**
Behrend   **2530 561**
Gonzalez   **61654**

Platero y Yo
Segovia   *5 Pieces* **DL 710054; MCA S-26.036; MCA S-26.087**
    Ronsard **RL 12602**

Matsuda *El loco, A Platero en el cielo de Moguer* **Argo ZDA 205**
Mills *A Platero en el cielo de Moguer*
ABK 10

Duets
Presti/Lagoya *Prelude & Fugue in E*
Philips 6504049
Santos/Caceres *Sonata Canonica Op. 196* **STU 70794**

Quintet Op. 143
Segovia **DL 9832**
Ramos **RCA VICS 1367**

Miscellaneous
Segovia *Capriccio diabolico* **DL 9733;
AXTL 1070**
Tonadilla on the name Andrés Segovia **DL 9795**
Almeida *La Guarda Cuydadosa* **Everest 3287**
Bitetti *Canción Argentina on the name Ernesto Bitetti* **WGS 8149**
Gonzalez *Tonadilla on the name Andrés Segovia* **CBS 61654**

Giuseppe Rosetta (b. 1901)
Gilardino *Sonatina* **RRCL 606616**

Goffredo Petrassi (b. 1904)
Szendrey-Karper *Suoni Notturni* **LPX 11 629**

Bruno Bettinelli (b. 1913)
Gilardino *Quatro Pezzi* **RRCL 606616**

Luciano Chailly (b. 1920)
Gilardino *Invenzione su Quattro Note* **RRCL 606616**

Carlo Mosso (b. 1931)
Gilardino *Tre Canzoni Piemontesi* **RRCL 606616**

Ruggero Maghini
Gilardino *Umbra* **RRCL 606616**

The Twentieth Century:
British Composers

William Walton (b. 1902)
Bream *Bagatelles* **SB 6876**
Mills *Bagatelle No. 2* **G 105**

Lennox Berkeley (b. 1903)
Bream *Concerto* **ARL1 1181**
Sonatina, Op. 51 **RB 16239** (1960);
SB 6891
Theme & Variations **SB 6876**
Estarellas *Theme & Variations* **Fonal MM-S 56**
Gilardino *Theme & Variations* **B 343**
Provost *Sonatina, Op. 51* **Ars Nova/Ars Antiqua**

Alan Rawsthorne (1905-1971)
Bream *Elegy* **SB 6876**

Benjamin Britten (1913-1976)
Nocturnal Op. 70
Bream **RB 6723; SB 6723**
Artzt **GME 1018**
T. Walker **DSL03**

Miscellaneous
Bream *Courtly Dances from 'Gloriana'* **SB 6635**
Courtly Dances **ARL3 0997**

Songs
Bream/Pears *Folk Songs* (arr. Britten) **RCA GL 42752**
Songs from the Chinese Op. 58 **RCA GL 42752; RCA Victor LM 2718**
Williams/Brown *Songs from the Cinese Op. 58* **CBS 61126**
T. Walker/Tear *Folk Songs* (arr. Britten) **ZK 39**

Reginald Smith Brindle (b. 1917)
Bream *El Polifemo de Oro* **SB 6723; RB 6723**
Henderson *Sonata 'El Verbo'* **G 121**

John W. Duarte (b. 1919)

English Suite Op. 31
Segovia   **MACS 1032**
Behrend   **2530 079**
van Gonnissen   **Solist 1177**
Mavrudis   **Vedette VST 6022**
Ramos   **Angel SAM 35024**

Variations on a Catalan
Folk Song Op. 25
Williams   **SDD R328** (1958)
Artzt   **GME 1019.340**

Miscellaneous
Almeida   *Miniature Suite Op. 6* **Everest 3287**
Artzt   *Sonatinette* **GME 1018**
Bitetti   *Sua Cosa Op. 52* **Hispavox HHS 10-450**
Gilardino   *Suite Piedmontese Op. 46* **B 343**
Henderson   *Night-Music* **G 121**
Johnson   *Prelude Op. 13* **CRG 1**

Duets
Dorigny/Ito   *Six Friendships* **RCA FY 008**
   Sans Cesse **FY 008**
Teuchert/van Gornissen (Frankfurt Duo)
   Variations on a French Nursery Song
   Op. 32 **Solist 1177**

Ensemble
Cuarteto Martínez Zarate   *Going Dutch Op. 36* **Discos Fauta 080A**
Siirala/Lehtinen   *Danse Joyeuse Op. 42* (for guitar & flute) **Love LRLP 140**

Malcolm Arnold (b. 1921)

Concerto Op. 67
Bream   **RB 16252; SB6826; ARL3 0997**
Williams   **CBS 76715**

Stephen Dodgson (b. 1924)

Partita
Williams   **CBS 72348**
Ponce   **30 S 150**

Miscellaneous Pieces
Williams   *Concerto No. 1* **CBS 77334**
   Concerto No. 2 **CBS 76634**
   Fantasy Divisions **CBS 73205**
Caceres   *Studies Nos. 8 & 13* **STU 70614**

Henderson   *Legend* **G121**
Mills   *Study & Serenade* **G105**

Richard Rodney Bennett (b. 1936)

Bream   *Concerto* **SB 6876; ARL3 0997**

Patrick Gowers

Williams   *Chamber Concerto for Guitar & Ensemble* **61790**
   Rhapsody for Guitar and Electric Guitars **73350; 61790**

Twentieth Century:
Other Countries

Frank Martin (1890-1974, Switzerland)

Quatre Pièces brèves
Bream   **RB 6723**
Mills   *(Air)* **G105**
Ponce   **30 S 150**

Aleksander Tansman (b. 1897, Poland)

In Modo Polonico
Segovia   **DA 130; DL 710112**
Mills   *3 Pieces* **G 105**

Miscellaneous
Segovia   *Cavatina (Suite)* **DL 9733**
   Mazurka **DL 710063**
   Prelude **DL 710167**
   3 Pieces **DL 710046; DXL 148**
Williams   *Barcarolle* **ECB 3151** (1958)
Artzt   *Cavatina, Berceuse d'Orient* **GME 1019 340**
Bitetti   *Cavatina* **WGS 8149**
Gilardino   *Pezzo in modo antico* **B 343**
Gomez   *Danza Pomposa* **SDD 158**
Gonzalez   *Mazurka* **CBS 61654**
Matsuda   *2 Pieces* **ZDA 205**

Hans Haug (1900-1967, Switzerland)

Segovia   *Alba & Postlude* **DL 9832**
Gilardino   *Alba* **B. 343**
Mills   *Alba* **G105**

Albert Harris (1916, U.S.A.)
Segovia   *Variations & Fugue on a Theme of Handel* DL 710167
Almeida   *Sonatina* Everest 3287

Hans Werner Henze (b. 1926, W. Germany)
Bream   *Drei Tentos* RB 6723
Artzt   *Drei Tentos* GME 1019.340
Brouwer   *Memories from 'El Cimarron'* Debut 255001

Leo Brouwer (b. 1939, Cuba)

Miscellaneous Pieces
Williams   *Concerto for Guitar & small orchestra* CBS 76715
Yepes   *Parábola* DG 2530 802
Tarantos DG 2531 113
Brouwer   *Exaedros I* DG 2555 001

Caceres   *Five Studies* STU 70614
Pieza sin Titulo, Danza Caracteristica, Tres Danzas Concertantes, Per Sonare a tre, Canticum, La Espiral Eterna, Elogio de la Danza STU 70734
Caceres/Brouwer   *Cuatro Micropiezas* STU 70734
Caceres/Santos   *Cuatro Micropiezas* STU 71092
Mercadel   *Prelude* Artrec CLP 62/1001
Mills   *Twelve Studies* G105
Ponce   *Elogio de la Danza* 30 S 150
Ybarra   *Danza Caracteristica* Mercury WST 17117

Gilbert Biberian (b. 1944, Turkey)
Omega Quartet   *Greek Serenade* PTLS 1066
Five Waltzes PTLS 1066
Henderson   *Sonata No. 3* G121

Select Bibliography

General

BELLOW, Alexander: *The Illustrated History of the Guitar*, New York, 1970
BONE, Philip J: *The Guitar and Mandolin*, reprint of 2nd ed. London 1972
CARFAGNO, Carlo and CAPRANI, Alberto: *Profilo Storico della Chitarra*, Ancona, Milan, 1966
EVANS, Tom and Mary: *Guitars from the Renaissance to Rock*, London, 1977
GRUNFELD, Frederic V: *The Art and Times of the Guitar*, New York, 1969
GUITAR PLAYER MAGAZINE: *The Guitar Player Book*, New York, 1978
SHARPE, A.P: *The Story of the Spanish Guitar*, 4th ed. London, 1968
TURNBULL, Harvey: *The Guitar from the Renaissance to the Present Day*, London, 1974

Periodicals

EARLY MUSIC: ed. J.M. Thomson, Oxford University Press, Oxford
GUITAR: ed. George Clinton, Musical New Services Ltd., London
THE GUITAR REVIEW: ed. Vladimir Bobri, The Society of the Classic Guitar, New York
GUITAR & LUTE: ed. Henry Adams, Galliard Press Ltd, Honolulu, Hawaii
IL FRONIMO: ed. Ruggero Chiesa, Presso le Edizioni Suvini Zerboni, Milan

Autobiographies and Biographies

GIULIANI, Mauro   Thomas F. Heck: *The Birth of the Classic Guitar and its Cultivation in Vienna, reflected in the Career and Compositions of Mauro Giuliani*, Vols. I and II, Ph D. Dissertation, Yale University, 1970

LLOBET, Miguel   Bruno Tonazzi: *Miguel Llobet, Chitarrista dell' Impressionismo*, Ancona, Milan, 1966

PUJOL, Emilio   Emilio Pujol: *El Dilema del Sonido en la Guitarra*, Buenos Aires, 1960

PUJOL, Emilio   Juan Riera: *Emilio Pujol*, Lerida, 1974

RODRIGO, Joaquín   Vicente Vayá Pla: *Joaquín Rodrigo, Su Vida y Su Obra*, Madrid, 1977

SEGOVIA, Andrés   Vladimir Bobri: *The Segovia Technique*, New York, 1972
George Clinton: *Andrés Segovia, An Appreciation*, London 1978
Bernard Gavoty: *Andrés Segovia*, Geneva, 1955
Ronald C. Purcell: *Andrés Segovia, Contributions to the World of Guitar*, New York, 1975
Andrés Segovia: An Autobiography of the Years 1893-1920, New York, 1976 and London, 1978.

SOR, Fernando   Brian Jeffery: *Fernando Sor, Composer and Guitarist*, London, 1977

TÁRREGA, Francisco Emilio Pujol: *Tárrega, Ensayo Biográfico*, Lisbon, 1960

VILLA-LOBOS, Heitor Andrade Muricy: *Villa-Lobos — Uma Interpretação*, Brazil

Guitar Construction

McLEOD, Donald and WELFORD, Robert: *The Classical Guitar, Design and Construction*, Leicester, 1971

SHARPE, A.P.: *Make Your Own Spanish Guitar*, revised ed. London, 1971

SLOANE, Irving: *Classic Guitar Construction*, New York, 1966

SLOANE, Irving: *Guitar Repair*, London, 1973

The Lute and Vihuela

BARON, Ernst Theophil: *Study of the Lute*, Translated by Douglas Alton Smith, California, 1976

POHLMANN, Ernst: *Laute Theorbe Chitarrone; Die Lauten-Instrumente ihre Musik und Literatur von 1500 bis zur Gegenwart*, Bremen, 1972

POULTON, Diana: *John Dowland*, London, 1972

TONAZZI, Bruno: *Liuto, Vihuela, Chitarra e Strumenti Similari Nelle Loro Intavolature. Con Cenni Sulle Loro Letterature*, Ancona, 1974

TREND, J.B.: *Luys Milán and the Vihuelistas*, Oxford, 1925

WARLOCK, Peter: *The English Ayre*, London, 1926

Flamenco

HOWSON, Gerald: *The Flamencos of Cádiz Bay*, London, 1965

POHREN, D.E.: *The Art of Flamenco*, 2nd ed. Seville, 1967

POHREN, D.E.: *Lives and Legends of Flamenco*, Seville, 1964

Index